Hitler: The Man and the Military Leader

Hitler: The Man and the Military Leader

by
Percy Ernst
Schramm

Translated, Edited, and with an Introduction
by Donald S. Detwiler

Chicago: **Quadrangle Books,** 1971

To the memory of the late Martin Göhring

Editor's Acknowledgment

The publication in English of these two studies and the appendices was undertaken upon
my initiative with the encouragement of the
author. He gave me a free hand in translating
and editing, but also gave freely of his time
and energy when I consulted him with regard
to different shades of meaning, minor revi-
sions reflecting recent scholarship, and the
like. Professor Schramm unexpectedly died
on November 12, a few days after the manu-
script had gone to press.

Very few changes or deletions were necessary to avoid undue overlapping of the two
essays, even though they have not previously
been published in a single volume. I did,
however, omit a number of footnotes, particularly those which cited specialized foreign-
language publications useful only to those
who, in any case, would probably wish to
refer to the meticulously documented volumes containing Schramm's original scholarly
German version. In addition to retaining virtually all his explanatory notes, I contributed

a number of additional ones providing information that could be presupposed on the part of most German readers, but hardly those of the English-speaking world. The abbreviation ED. identifies footnotes I supplied as editor.

This book is dedicated to the late Dr. Martin Göhring, Professor of History at Giessen University and Director of the Institute of European History in Mainz. For many years he was a friend and colleague of the author. I am indebted to him for the counsel and support he afforded me while I held a research fellowship at his institute ten years ago.

D.S.D.

Carbondale, Illinois
November 1970

Contents

Hitler: The Man and the Military Leader

Introduction

by Donald S. Detwiler

The two essays that follow were written as introductions to critical editions of two of the most important documents of the history of the Third Reich: the record of Hitler's informal *Table Conversations* in 1941 and 1942, and the official *War Diary of the High Command of the Wehrmacht (Operations Staff)*.[1] Although their author, the Göttingen historian Percy Ernst Schramm, is well known in Germany for more than twenty major works, plus innumerable popular and scholarly articles and reviews, he is virtually a stranger to the English-speaking audience. Only his book on the English monarchy as reflected in the history of the coronation has previously been published in English translation, and that more than thirty years ago.[2] But readers familiar with William Sheridan Allen's model

[1]"The Anatomy of a Dictator" was originally published as part of the introduction to Dr. Henry Picker, *Hitlers Tischgespräche im Führerhauptquartier 1941–1942*, edited by Percy E. Schramm, *et al.* (Stuttgart, 1963; 2nd ed., 1965), pp. 29–119. "The Military Leader" first appeared in the introduction to the *Kriegstagebuch des Oberkommandos der Wehrmacht (Wehrmachtführungsstab)*, edited by Percy E. Schramm, IV, Pt. 1: 37–74 (Frankfurt am Main, 1961). The two appendices are from pp. 1705–1722 of Part 2 of the same volume.

[2]*A History of the English Coronation* (Oxford, 1937), translated by Leopold G. Wickham Legg from *Geschichte des englischen Königtums im Lichte der Krönung,* 2 vols. (1937; 2nd ed., 1970). Among Schramm's other books are a

3

study of the Nazi seizure of power at the grass-roots level may recall Dr. Schramm as the history professor who, during the spring of 1932 in the town of Thalburg, spoke in behalf of old Marshal Hindenburg in his successful campaign for re-election as president of Germany. Hindenburg had been challenged by an Austrian immigrant named Adolf Hitler.[3]

---

parallel study of the French monarchy (*Der König von Frankreich*, 2 vols., 1939; 2nd rev. ed., 1960), three volumes on medieval Europe as a whole (*Herrschaftszeichen und Staatssymbolik*, 1954–1956), a history of the medieval concept of the Roman Empire and its restoration (*Kaiser, Rom und Renovatio*, 2 vols., 1929; 2nd ed., 1957), and two magnificently illustrated quarto volumes, *Sphaira—Globus—Reichsapfel*, a history of the orb from antiquity to the present (1958) and, with Florentine Mütherich, *Denkmale der deutschen Könige und Kaiser*, a compilation of all surviving monuments —thrones, crowns, vestments, medallions, and so forth—of the medieval German kings and emperors from Charlemagne to Frederick II (1962). Although these books, and his steady flow of shorter monographs, articles, and reviews (collected and reprinted as *Kaiser, Könige und Päpste: Gesammelte Aufsätze zur Geschichte des Mittelalters*, 4 vols., 1968–1970) established him as one of the world's leading medievalists, Schramm turned, particularly since the Second World War, to other fields as well, writing a history of German overseas trade from the end of the Middle Ages to the beginning of the twentieth century (*Deutschland und Übersee*, 1950), a social and economic history of his native Hamburg during the nineteenth century (*Hamburg, Deutschland und die Welt*, 1943; 2nd rev. ed., 1952), and a cultural history of Hamburg in the form of an account of his own family during the past three centuries (*Neun Generationen*, 2 vols., 1963–64). His three most important publications on the Second World War, each in collaboration with former students, have been the *War Diary of the High Command of the Wehrmacht* (4 vols., 1961–1965), the critical edition of Hitler's conversations, and the first detailed chronological outline history of the war (*Geschichte des Zweiten Weltkriegs*, 1960). His introduction to the *War Diary*, as translated here, was also published in booklet form for a wider public under the title *Hitler als militärischer Diktator* (1961) and, with excerpts from the *War Diary*, as a paperback entitled *Hitler als militärischer Führer* (1962; 2nd rev. ed., 1965). The two-volume collection of essays published in Schramm's honor on his seventieth birthday contains a thirty-page bibliography of his writings through 1963, showing over 350 items, including reviews, plus some sixty doctoral dissertations, including the editor's, which he supervised (Peter Classen and Peter Scheibert, eds., *Festschrift Percy Ernst Schramm zu seinem siebzigsten Geburtstag*, Wiesbaden, 1964, II, 290–321).

[3]William Sheridan Allen, *The Nazi Seizure of Power: The Experience of a Single German Town, 1930–1935* (Chicago, 1965), p. 93. "Thalburg," as the town was called in this excellent community study, is actually Northeim, several miles north of Göttingen.

Professor Schramm was not in Germany to witness Hindenburg's betrayal of his supporters when he appointed none other than his defeated Nazi opponent to the chancellorship. At the beginning of 1933 Schramm had gone to Princeton University on a fellowship, returning to Göttingen later the same year. He continued his teaching and medieval studies undisturbed until the war, when, as a reserve officer, he was called to active service. Given staff assignments in which he invariably was charged with the additional duty of keeping the unit war diary, Schramm was ordered to Hitler's headquarters in 1943 to keep the official diary of the High Command of the Wehrmacht. Understandably the professional soldiers of the German General Staff wished to entrust this responsibility to a professional historian.

Until replaced by Schramm in 1943, Helmuth Greiner, originally from the Reich Archives, had kept the diary. But he was neither a party man nor a regular officer, so he was vulnerable. Using a petty conflict with a minor Nazi official as a pretext, the head of the Party Chancellery, Martin Bormann, was able to prevail upon Hitler to transfer Greiner into the field. The generals had every reason to be disturbed by this action, surmising that Bormann had moved against Greiner so as to free his position for a militant Nazi.

The generals had a vested interest in the scrupulous objectivity of the historical record. Few, if any, could foresee in any detail what was to come. But they had already experienced serious conflicts with Hitler, whom they did *not* venerate as "the greatest warlord of all times." As hardheaded professionals, they knew the record would bear them out if it were kept by a professional rather than a party hack. So when Greiner, a reputable military historian tailored to their tastes, was forced out, they were desperate to find the right sort of replacement quickly. Fortunately, a colonel on the Operations Staff remembered Schramm, at whose home he had been a guest while on garrison duty in Göttingen before the war. With an alacrity unusual even in German military practice, the assignment was made, effective January 1, 1943.

Things went smoothly enough for Schramm until 1944, when his sister-in-law was executed for opposition to the Nazi regime. At about the same time, formal allegations of his own unreliability were transmitted to the Führer Headquarters from Göttingen by Himmler's security service. Fortunately Schramm's superior officer, General Alfred Jodl, disregarded these charges, so that he was allowed to retain his position to the very end. This meant that he was able, in defiance of Hitler's destruction order, to save copies or drafts of the greater part of the official diary covering the years 1943–1945. His predecessor, Greiner, meanwhile had secretly hidden copies of his drafts covering the first years of the war. Thus it was possible for Schramm, in association with Professors Hans-Adolf Jacobsen (Bonn), Andreas Hillgruber (Freiburg), and Walther Hubatsch (Bonn), three of his former students, to reconstruct and publish this extraordinary document as a whole. Comprising well over six thousand printed pages, the *War Diary of the High Command* is an absolutely unique historical record. No such compilation from the highest echelon is available on the history of the war as waged by the United States, the United Kingdom, or, for that matter, any other major power.

The first of the two essays in this volume, "The Anatomy of a Dictator," is based primarily on the record of Hitler's own self-revealing statements made during and after meals at his headquarters on the Russian Front from July 1941 through July 1942. This information is frequently supplemented by insights Schramm gained while in the Führer Headquarters from the beginning of 1943 until the end of the war, as well as by what he was able to learn during postwar internment from persons who had been very close to Hitler. Schramm himself never conversed with Hitler and on only a few occasions was he in a position to observe him for an extended time. He was, however, in daily contact with officers directly under Hitler's influence, and immediately after the war he was able to confer at length with two of Hitler's personal physicians as well as his dentist.

The picture of Hitler which flows from Schramm's skillful pen is worlds removed from the widely known caricature of a petty little street-corner agitator with a Charlie Chaplin moustache. A certain sinister pettiness is there, to be sure, and it is more specifically documented than ever before. But this is not the point. In "The Anatomy of a Dictator," the awkwardly woven veil of uneasy familiarity, insecure contempt, and feigned amusement, which for so long has

instinct for the significance of apparently trivial gestures and observations most certainly are.

In constructing his portrait of Hitler, Schramm has not hesitated, particularly in "The Anatomy of a Dictator," to describe the positive as well as the negative side, the areas of light as well as darkness, thereby bringing out the shadows and contrasts of Hitler's extraordinary personality. When this portrait was serialized early in 1964 in the leading German newsweekly *Der Spiegel*, it provoked a heavy and varied response. While many of the more than one hundred published letters to the editor reflected appreciation of the candor and insight of Schramm's portrait, others expressed misgivings and even hostility. One recurring objection was the apprehension that many Germans would read Schramm's description of Hitler's "nice characteristics" with a nostalgic yearning for the "good old days" of the Third Reich, never grasping the study's wider import. This is one reason why some Germans are, in fact, opposed to the publication of anything which might conceivably be construed as favorable to National Socialism or to Adolf Hitler, lest it lead to a sort of socio-psychological relapse. Schramm has consistently maintained the opposite position, insisting that the German people, and particularly the youth in the schools and universities, be told the whole truth about the Third Reich. That Adolf Hitler may prove posthumously beguiling to certain elements in the population is a risk that must be taken. To the many who protest that this is also dangerous because of the German susceptibility to authoritarianism, Schramm answers that it is precisely this which makes it so urgent to immunize the people intellectually with as much knowledge as possible of the most terrible regime ever to tyrannize Germany.

We already know the contours of Hitler's life. We know that he was an extraordinary demagogue able to play on the sensitivities of the masses with breathtaking virtuosity, mesmerizing listeners with his infectious conviction that he could not fail. We know, too, of his appeal to many intellectuals and his acceptability, to say the least, to important leaders of the Church.[4] We know of his ele-

---

[4]Long before Hitler came to power in Germany, National Socialism was strong in the universities, with support not only among a large number of

mentary instinct for power and his utter ruthlessness in exercising it. We know of his unspeakable crimes against minorities, the German people, and mankind. Now, in these essays, Schramm has brought us a long step closer to an understanding of Hitler the man. Schramm clearly has no intention of changing, let alone basically revising, the general conception of Hitler that has come to be accepted by most German and American historians, but he has suggested that it may not do full justice to that uncanny and inscrutable dictator's personality. In a number of important respects, certainly, Schramm gives us a far more sophisticated picture of Hitler than we have had.

At the same time, however, Schramm's interpretation of Hitler is disturbing. It is disturbing to see in that consummately evil man so many commonly and legitimately admired virtues so clearly mirrored. They are not even parodied; they are genuine. Hitler was, beyond any doubt, a man of uncommon self-discipline who led what can be fairly described as a relatively austere personal life. It is not congenial to think of him in this way. It is not congenial to see him portrayed as a charming gentleman with a quick wit and a wholesome sense of humor. Certainly he was also a personally brave man with an excellent combat record. He had been a common soldier during the First World War, serving as a regimental courier. Before the end of 1914 he had received the coveted Iron Cross Second Class, and before the end of the war one of Germany's highest decorations, the Iron Cross First Class.[5] On the basis of a close reading of his conversations, there is, furthermore, little doubt that Hitler took friendship seriously and in many cases was a sensitive and loyal friend, not to mention being a tirelessly hard worker.

Thus by conventional standards Hitler could *and did* command

the students but also prestigious faculty members. It was the Catholic Center party which provided Hitler the votes in the Reichstag that were essential for passage of the "Enabling Act" granting him dictatorial powers in March 1933. The Vatican, with the Concordat later that year, was the first foreign power to conclude a major treaty with the new and still rather widely distrusted Nazi regime. Because of the papacy's great moral prestige both in Germany and abroad, the Concordat was, of course, exceedingly valuable to Hitler.

[5] On Hitler's war record and his experience of World War I, see Chapter IV, "Hitler Finds His Home" in Konrad Heiden's dated but still valuable *Der Fuehrer: Hitler's Rise to Power* (Boston, 1944), pp. 77–86.

respect, aside from the particular admiration inspired by his extraordinary mind and exceptional abilities.[6] Today, of course, we know that in Hitler's case these conventional standards were not adequate and perhaps not even relevant. We know that everyone who attempted to deal with him as though he were just another cunning politician or even a gifted statesman was gravely underestimating him. It is now clear that during the years before the Second World War, for example, the reasonably sensible leaders of France and Britain were mistaken in trying to find an honest and practical accommodation with him.

More than any other characteristic, it is Hitler's ambivalence which Schramm singles out as the key to understanding him. It was not merely the superficial duplicity of a crude liar or even a shrewd dissimulator. It was a Janus-like ambivalence reaching to the very ground of Hitler's being. German politicians and foreign statesmen who dealt seriously with Hitler could not have known that he would betray them as he did. Many ambitious politicians may exhibit a ruthless opportunism; but who, except a fool or fanatic, will insist that his antagonist is intrinsically evil and therefore can be dealt with only by force of arms? Even as late as the Munich Conference of 1938, who could have predicted that the German Führer and Reich Chancellor was an historical phenomenon no less radical than the type suggested in literature by *The Picture of Dorian Gray* or *Dr. Jekyll and Mr. Hyde*?

Hitler's success, despite his compulsive candor and the relentless directness with which he pursued his goals, was not due merely to the inefficiency or ineptitude of European politicians and statesmen during the thirties. Hitler did not get as far as he did because other

---

[6]One aspect of the all too common trivialization of Hitler has been the tendency to regard him as a man of limited intelligence. Ten years before the initial publication of Schramm's detailed evaluation now translated as the first essay in this volume, the distinguished British historian H. R. Trevor-Roper, author of *The Last Days of Hitler* (London, 1947), wrote a brilliant essay which did much to correct this, "The Mind of Adolf Hitler," published as the introduction to an English translation of Hitler's table conversations, *Hitler's Secret Conversations, 1941–1944* (New York, 1953). The Oxford professor writes of Hitler's mind as being "like some huge barbarian monolith, the expression of giant strength and savage genius, surrounded by a festering heap of refuse. . . ."

leaders failed to do their homework. It was a problem of an entirely different quality and dimension. This is dramatized by Schramm in "The Anatomy of a Dictator" in a powerful allusion to the myth of Medusa, whose face was supposed to have petrified those who beheld it. Schramm explains in detail how Hitler in a sense actually had two faces, both of which were real. The mealtime companions with whom he held conversations saw only one of his faces. Had they been able to see the other, writes Schramm, "even the most loyal and devoted of them would have turned to stone."

This phenomenal ambivalence accounts in part for Hitler's extraordinary historical stature. In terms of the sheer magnitude of what he wrought during his twelve years and three months in power, he was one of the "great" men of history. But his perverse greatness was informed less by creative energy than by some malevolent genius, so that even his most positive intentions and deeds acquired a dubious and ultimately sinister character. His ambivalence contributed to his great impact upon history; had he been anchored by that integrity and respect for law, human dignity, and the tradition of civility which has generally inhibited even the most cynical of tyrants, he would never have been able to achieve all he did through brutal threats. But Hitler was not inhibited. As Schramm shows, there was something frigid about him; in Hitler's own words, he was "ice-cold." Others also sensed this—when he wanted them to. Realizing that he was indeed not bluffing when he threatened drastic retaliation for any resistance, and unwilling to risk the consequences of denying him whatever momentary object he sought, most of his antagonists backed down again and again, permitting him to reach that pinnacle of power from which he was torn only at enormous cost.

Unfettered by the discipline of custom and law, drawing on unholy drives within himself and others, Hitler built within Germany the power base for his foreign expansion by the same unrestrained methods, achieving far more than he conceivably could have if he had not moved with such complete disregard for any authority that challenged his imperious will. By comparison, the autocracy of previous despots seems almost timorous and halting.

Hitler's unique tyranny was rooted in his undisputed control of the masses. Though at times the administered terror of Himmler and the cunning propaganda of Goebbels were all but indispensable, the foundation always remained Hitler's own incomparable hold on the people. As his biographer Alan Bullock writes, "Hitler was the greatest demagogue in history."[7] Just as his effective diplomacy can in part be attributed to his cynical opportunism, his demagogic success was so great in large measure because he had no scruples. He was utterly ruthless in his exploitation of the sentiments, fears, prejudices, and animosities of his listeners. He was able to play on the dark forces within their souls with diabolical mastery. Insofar as he could sweep the masses into his camp by appealing to their baser natures, bringing out the worst in them, he did so with evil genius. As he had written in *Mein Kampf,* "To lead means to be able to move the masses."

Hitler had extraordinary gifts, then, but turned them to hideous ends. If ever there was a man in history who illustrated the validity of the traditional teaching of the Church concerning the demonic in human nature, it was Hitler. And this perspective raises questions which can ultimately be dealt with only on the metaphysical or theological level. Here it must be sufficient to say that Hitler wrought untold evil; that if he had not embraced such evil means, he would have achieved much more modest but probably more lasting results; and, finally, that the German people, in accepting him as their Führer, did not know and could hardly have been expected to know what he would do with them and make of them. To say this is not to excuse the Germans for following Hitler. The point is neither to condemn nor to exculpate them, but rather to understand the motives and consequences of their actions. It is clear that, however innocent their intentions, the German people, first indirectly through their representatives in the Reichstag and then directly through plebiscites, resoundingly endorsed Hitler's Third Reich—a totalitarian regime without effective provision for separation of powers or even for registering the dissent of the governed. In terms of the final outcome, therefore, it was tragically irrelevant that the German

[7]Alan Bullock, *Hitler, A Study in Tyranny* (rev. ed.; New York, 1964), p. 68.

people had not intended to embrace a criminal regime under one of the most baleful tyrants since the beginning of recorded time. If there be lessons in history, surely this is one: abdication of political responsibility frees a people neither from the consequences of its abuse nor—insofar as they take count of such values—from the burden of guilt that is sure to follow.

Because his point of departure is the *Table Conversations*, Schramm in the first of the two essays in this book does not go deeply into one of the most important aspects of Hitler's career— his role as military leader. In his table talk Hitler made a number of references to famous generals in history, to the art of war, and even to events since 1939, but generally he was not interested in sustained or serious discussion of the Second World War, its course, or the current operations which preoccupied him. These mealtime conversations were virtually his sole form of relaxation, if only an hour or two during and after lunch or supper. Yet no analysis of Hitler's personality could exclude military questions altogether. Schramm shows, in fact, that political and military considerations were so intimately connected in Hitler's mind that he made crucial command decisions on the basis of strategically irrelevant political or even propagandistic considerations—with catastrophic results.

Military questions are evident, then, in the first essay, as an important aspect of Hitler's total personality, but in the second essay his military leadership is the central theme. The two studies therefore overlap, but in a complementary manner.

Like the work on Hitler's personality, Schramm's study of Hitler the warlord is based on one of the central primary sources for the history of the Third Reich, the *War Diary of the High Command of the Wehrmacht,* which Schramm himself kept for the last two and a half years of the war.[8] His observations in "The Military Leader" are drawn primarily from that period. As in his study of Hitler's personality, Schramm stays relatively close to the material, generally refraining from posing broader questions which might lead him

---

[8]Schramm began keeping the *War Diary* as of January 1, 1943, but did so at first under the supervision of and then in association with Greiner, who did not actually leave the Führer Headquarters until the beginning of March.

to conclusions beyond the self-imposed limitations appropriate to the *War Diary*. The *War Diary,* he emphasizes, is not yet military history but rather the source material from which military history will be written. Schramm's purpose is not to indulge in extensive interpretation but rather to underscore the basic points that emerge from the material. The most important of these pertain to Hitler's conduct of the last phase of the war, the extent to which he assumed personal control of operations, and the principles that guided him in the exercise of that control. Schramm shows that in 1943, at the very latest, Hitler knew that the war was irretrievably lost, yet deliberately continued it with no prospect of victory or even of bettering Germany's condition in defeat. Thereby he wantonly assured not only that the empire of Bismarck would be dismembered and the very name of Prussia erased from the map, but that hundreds of thousands, if not indeed millions more would fall and their survivors be stripped of even the most primitive means of existence.

Schramm's essay on Hitler's personality, based primarily on conversations held during the middle years of the war, reflects Hitler as the conqueror of an empire stretching from the Pyrenees to the Crimea, from the Arctic Circle to the Sahara. But the study of him as a military dictator, based on the last two and a half years of the *War Diary,* shows us how Hitler reacted to the gradual but relentless reduction of that empire until its final destruction in the rubble of Berlin. Under the constraint of circumstances over which he had lost control, Hitler came to devote all his time and energy to the military struggle for survival. Toward the end, the elementary character of this *Existenzkampf* was the only rationale of Hitler's military dictatorship, a regime of terror ultimately resting on brute force. All else—the social, economic, and political structure of Germany, and even the lifeblood of the youth and the aged—was grimly squandered in order to keep the military machine going, if only a short while longer. The sheer madness of it was enough to rouse conservative militarists as well as Christian liberals to an unsuccessful attempt on Hitler's life nine months before the end. The savage vengeance he wreaked not only upon them but also on their kin further vindicated their cause. In his Berlin bunker, the megalomaniacal tyrant continued to direct his war as the world closed in upon him. He was by no means oblivious to the fantastic cost of his sordid *Götterdämmerung,* but grimly indifferent to it, proclaiming as a final monstrosity that the German people, the vast majority of whom had kept faith with him to the last, had proven themselves unworthy of him and inferior to the enemy, and consequently deserved the terrible fate he was bringing down on them.

I

The Anatomy
of a Dictator

1. Hitler the Man

He fascinated people with his deep blue, slightly protruding, almost radiant eyes. Many who met him were unable to stand up to his gaze; knowing this, Hitler looked people straight in the eye without blinking. Although he had always had good vision, he became increasingly farsighted during the war and was forced to use glasses, particularly while working over situation maps. Care was taken to conceal this fact, but some pictures show Hitler wearing glasses. To facilitate his reading written material that demanded his personal attention, it was transcribed on special typewriters in so-called "Führer script," which had letters about twice normal size.

Hitler had his eyes so well under control that in jest he was able to cross them. He also had keen hearing, and could recognize people by the sound of their footsteps. His nose was ugly, having something of the shape of a pyramid. The unpleasant impression of the large, broad nostrils was minimized, however, by his closely trimmed moustache. His mouth was relatively small, his chin not well developed. His lips were thin and pinched. He had a high forehead but it did not stand out because it was covered by his forelock. He had few lashes on his eyelids, but his eyebrows were thick, and above them slight bulges appeared in his forehead. His cheeks were rela-

17

tively broad, his ears well formed. Hitler's complexion and coloring could be described as almost girl-like. He was sensitive to light and to the sun and would probably have found sunglasses a help, though he chose not to wear them. When a bright light bothered him, he would shade his eyes with his hand. Heat also disturbed him, as did the *Föhn,* that warm, dry Alpine wind often felt in parts of southern Germany.

Toward the end of his life Hitler was evenly grey-haired, though he showed no tendency toward baldness. His beard was not heavy. He did his own shaving, cutting himself only rarely. He cared for his teeth meticulously, but they were poor and a number of them had been replaced by permanent bridges.[1] Hitler must have been instinctively self-conscious about this; when he laughed he held his hand in front of his mouth.

The man's head seemed to dominate his entire body; torso, arms, legs—all seemed to hang down from it. Hitler generally let his arms dangle carelessly, putting his hands in his pockets only when he was in the most intimate circles. His legs were not strong. He strode on his heels and, keeping his knees straight, walked quickly. His other movements were quite deliberate. If something caught his attention, he would stop to investigate whatever it was. When he discovered that he had a tendency toward obesity, he found it sufficiently embarrassing to cut down his eating.

[1]In postwar internment I shared a room for a time with Hitler's dentist, a competent man who had gotten the job by accident and had received the SS rank corresponding to major general (anyone without a uniform and a rank around Hitler's headquarters was out of place and would have found himself in an awkward position). The dentist was given plaster and tools by our American captors and reconstructed from memory models of Hitler's upper and lower jaws. They lay for days on our table; thus I know that there were more gaps than teeth. The models were probably turned over by the Americans to the Russians, in order to determine whether the remains discovered near the Reich Chancellery were really those of Hitler; if his jaws were found, positive identification would be possible. (The American writer Cornelius Ryan received, according to *Der Stern,* June 2, 1963, the information from Marshal Sokolovsky "that Hitler's burned body was identified by means of his dental bridges"; for the official Soviet autopsy report, see Lev Bezymenski, *The Death of Adolf Hitler* [New York, 1968].) The dentist reported to me that Hitler maintained his composure while dental work was being performed on him, whereas Himmler had been frightened.

Hitler kept himself very clean. He washed his hands often. He changed underclothes frequently and made sarcastic remarks about visitors with dirty underwear. He bathed daily, sometimes more than once. After eating, he rinsed out his mouth. Having a good haircut was an important matter to him. He took care to wear gloves outdoors. Yet he never achieved elegance. His jacket hung about him like a sack; his trousers did not sit well; and his coat, which he could not bear to have constrict him in any way, was completely shapeless. He wore his cap pulled down over his eyes. In the matter of caps, he preferred the older fashions, but his entourage discreetly provided him with caps in the new "sharper" style.

In civilian clothes, Hitler always chose double-breasted suits of the same cut. His neckties were selected by Eva Braun, but they had to be inconspicuous, so they were invariably of a subdued, rather dull color. Whenever Hitler wore the National Socialist uniform, he dispensed with the belt. His high double-soled boots, which were made of thick though soft leather, were inelegantly buckled at the top. His riding breeches were cut quite loose at the knees. As far as his uniform was concerned, even his admirers must have felt that their "Leader"—the literal meaning of the word *Führer*—suffered by comparison with many of them.

Hitler required only a minimum of sleep. He attributed this to the fact that when he was a courier in the First World War, the difference between day and night had been gradually lost for him. During the years of his rise to power, he would eat only after making his speeches in the evening and would then go to bed quite late. During the Second World War he would stay up to look at the first reports coming in after midnight and finally retire. Actually this was of no great consequence, for the situation usually was not clarified before noon. Since there would normally be no decisions for him to make until then, he would sleep late in the morning. A midday nap was out of the question.

With his excellent memory, Hitler had an uncommon ability to recognize people. He could react quickly under all sorts of circumstances, and thus adjusted himself fairly easily to unexpected situations. He considered himself to be rational, yet able to rely upon his instincts.

Hitler generally weighed important decisions at length, consciously turning them over and over in his mind in rational terms. In the last analysis, however, he invariably depended upon what he called "instinct"—a word synonymous in his mind with political shrewdness. In unimportant matters, when his reason led him to no clear decision, he fell back on the old device of flipping a coin. Yet he was not at all superstitious.

Hitler saw his particular strength in an ability to simplify complex problems and to think consistently. Once he had made a decision, it was difficult to bring him to change it, as he feared that his authority might thereby be compromised. Yet occasionally he could change his course with startling swiftness, without showing the slightest concern about doing something that directly contradicted his previous position.

In conversation, Hitler, especially when talking in private, retained a surprisingly large number of words from his youth. This comes through clearly in the transcripts of the *Table Conversations,* where he speaks of lads and lasses, of fops and churls, and uses any number of similarly old-fashioned expressions. In military situations, however, as we know from the stenographic transcripts of his secret conferences,[2] this style of diction was replaced by a more casual military and party jargon. Hitler did not hesitate to use foreign words to lend a certain coloring to his speech, and he used them correctly. Contrived Germanizations he ridiculed, having no sympathy for this sort of linguistic chauvinism. "Just imagine," he remarked early in July 1942, "what would happen if we tried to eliminate foreign words! Where would we stop?"

Hitler regarded Schopenhauer as a linguistic model; he mentions him in the *Table Conversations* as the only German capable of making changes in the language. Yet Hitler, who was oblivious to *belles lettres,* was largely devoid of a genuine feeling for language. In his public speeches he used homely vernacular expressions only for oratorical effect, remaining first and last the propagandist

[2]For extracts in translation of the stenographic protocols of Hitler's military conferences during the years 1942–1945, see *Hitler Directs His War,* edited and annotated by Felix Gilbert (New York, 1950).—ED.

[margin note: PERSONAL ASPECT PARANOID]

who knew exactly what the masses wanted to hear and who understood how to move them with stirring slogans. But he never succeeded—as Bismarck, on the basis of his literary culture, was often able to do—in fashioning an enduring phrase or a memorable epigram.

According to the testimony of Dr. Hans Karl von Hasselbach, one of his personal physicians, Hitler regularly had English, American, and French magazines delivered to him. "Apart from some French he had learned in school, he had picked up on his own a working knowledge of the languages. Primarily for this purpose, before the war he often had French and English films shown to him in the original version." This knowledge was naturally far too slight to penetrate the spirit and structure of the foreign languages. But it did not deter Hitler from claiming that the English language was incapable of expressing thoughts which went beyond generally proven ideas and matters of fact[3]—a cliché once popular with the ideologists of German nationalism.

As he explains in one of the *Conversations,* in his youth Hitler was a lonely outsider with no desire for company: "But now I simply cannot stand to be alone. . . ." Even in Munich he had preferred to go to an inn he liked, rather than eat at home alone. During the war he had a particular need for companionship as a means of relaxing, and generally took a full hour for lunch. His evening meal occasionally lasted more than two hours.

Hitler loved jokes. Since he had a phenomenal memory, he was able to tell a great many of them, revealing a striking ability to imitate expressions, voices, and dialects. But he never told off-color stories, let alone dirty jokes. His personal photographer, the south German Heinrich Hoffmann, who occasionally did tell such stories and jokes, was quite an exception in Hitler's circle. Apart from Hoffmann, the restaurateur Kannenberg, who had been brought to the Führer Headquarters on account of his organizational ability, sparkled with native Berlin wit. Hitler also enjoyed the practical

---

[3]Hitler could also express himself differently. According to the testimony of Dr. Karl Brandt, one of his personal physicians, he considered the English language as something special—the simplest and clearest in expression and at the same time the most masculine in tone.

jokes that his table companions occasionally played on each other; he would slap himself on the thigh as he laughed or hold his hand in front of his eyes or mouth.

Company at meals was the sole "luxury" Hitler allowed himself during the war years, for his style of living was otherwise quite Spartan. In peacetime he had enjoyed visiting the *Skala* and the *Wintergarten,* though he had never had any use for the circus. The cinema had been his chief means of relaxation. After the beginning of the war, he never again visited a theater except for one production of *Die Götterdämmerung* at Bayreuth. As for films, he looked only at newsreels, since he regarded them as an important medium of propaganda and would often give instructions for revising them before distribution. But after the newsreels he would leave the room, preferring not to watch the screenplays shown for the entertainment of his staff. He did not want to be better off than German soldiers on the front. Since he did not smoke, avoided both coffee and alcohol, and subsisted solely on vegetarian fare, he felt he could certainly look any soldier in the eye in respect to diet as well. To this extent Hitler even outdid William II, who in his wartime headquarters at Pless had strictly limited his eating and drinking.

Throughout his life Hitler remained an inland-oriented German, his imagination untouched by the sea. He had never been exposed to the uncanny power of the storm, the pulsing rhythm of the rolling waves with their foam and spray, the shimmering sunlight on the placid surface, or the sun descending into the deep; nor had the struggle of mankind against the primeval element water and the dauntless courage of the mariner ever penetrated the deeper levels of his consciousness. But Hitler was not only inland oriented; he was completely rooted within the cultural boundaries of the old Roman Empire. He clung to the civilization of the Mediterranean world and took no part in his followers' grotesque glorification of the Teutons. He had no use for pine forests, and once even declared, "I would rather walk to Flanders than bicycle to the East. It is only the force of reason which dictates our moving eastward."

Hitler had great plans for Berlin, which, as capital of the "Greater German Empire of the German People," he was planning to rename

"Germania." But his heart was not in the idea. He thought Berlin unsuited to be a center of the arts: "For this purpose it simply lacks the atmosphere." A grotesque judgment if one thinks of the Reich capital in the twenties—Berlin was the first city of Europe in theater and music, and set the tone for all Germany in every branch of the arts.

Hitler had skied when he was younger, and he continued to love the mountains. But in his mature years he lost the desire to climb them and to be rewarded for his effort by the view. In fact, he ceased to participate actively in any sport, and walking became his sole exercise.

2. Hitler's Ambivalence

Hitler's associates were impressed by how concerned the "Chief"— as they referred to him—was about their welfare and what an active interest he took in their individual joys and sorrows. He would, for example, devote serious thought to what sort of birthday gifts would be particularly appreciated. In this regard, the summaries of Hitler's *Table Conversations* by Dr. Henry Picker, the young lawyer responsible for transcribing them, are quite revealing. Picker, who previously had known Hitler only as a distant political figure, was greatly impressed by the human qualities Hitler revealed in the inner circle of his associates: by the good will he showed the younger among them, by his readiness to laugh, and by the magnanimity he demonstrated when someone committed a faux pas in his presence. Within this circle, in fact, Hitler, the man without family or friends, was a good "comrade." He had learned the meaning of comradeship in the First World War and had never forgotten it.

Hitler's associates also knew how strongly he reacted to beautiful and cultivated women. They knew of his affection for children and for his German shepherds, Blondi and Bella, and what pleasure he got out of watching the animals. In the *Wolfsschanze,* or "Wolf's Lair," as his headquarters near Rastenburg in central East Prussia was called, he had an obstacle course constructed, similar to those used in the training of infantrymen, where the dogs had to demonstrate whether they had intelligence as well as courage.[4]

The friend of women, children, and animals—this was one face of Hitler, neither acted nor feigned, but entirely genuine. There was, however, a second face which he did not show to his table companions, though it was no less genuine.

In his *Table Conversations* Hitler said that he would personally shoot down whoever dared to commit certain offenses. Knowing that he had never personally fired a shot at a political enemy, his guests did not take his warning at face value. At times Hitler would get carried away and make terrible threats. But he rarely spoke of the hideous orders he was giving precisely during the months when the *Table Conversations* were being recorded, and which in the end cost millions their lives. To point out only a few examples from the months in question:

September 16, 1941: Stopping General Hoepner's armored column short of Leningrad, with a view toward eliminating the population of the city by starvation; similar thoughts about the fate of Moscow.

October 21, 1941: Execution of fifty French hostages by firing squad because of the killing of a German officer; thenceforth, in all theaters of war, strictest application of the policy of breaking terror with terror.

January 20, 1942: Wannsee conference, initiating the deportation of the Jews to the East and beginning their systematic annihilation.

February 1942: Integration of the steadily burgeoning concentration camps into the German war economy.

March 21, 1942: Authorization for *Gauleiter* Sauckel to incorporate foreign slave workers into the Germany economy.

---

[4]Once I had an opportunity to observe how well trained one of Hitler's dogs was. On a walk near the *Wolfsschanze* one day I came across a noncommissioned officer who was responsible for the dogs' care and was taking one of them for a walk. Since I used to have shepherd dogs myself, I observed the dog with interest, whereupon the soldier showed me how quickly she obeyed every command to sit, stand, and so forth. I had the impression not of a dog but a machine, and wondered whether Hitler in the training of his dogs was not motivated by a desire to extinguish the individual wills even of these animals.

April 26, 1942: By special act of the Reichstag, Hitler invested with unlimited judicial powers, making him supreme judge of the Reich with no limitations or controls whatsoever.

June 10, 1942: Destruction of the Czech village of Lidice, where, without knowledge of the population, Heydrich's assassins had temporarily hidden.[5]

August 23, 1942: Orders to Field Marshal von Manstein: "Phase 1: Cut off Leningrad and seek contact with the Finns. Phase 2: Occupy Leningrad and level it to the ground."

In order to appreciate the *Table Conversations* as an historical document, one must consider the character the war assumed as these monologues of hubris were being transcribed. After the winter of 1941–42, the condition of the army in the East was as follows:

By April 30, 1942, the casualty total had risen to 1,167,835; one out of three men who had marched on June 22, 1941, when Germany attacked the Soviet Union, had fallen. Of 162 infantry divisions on the Eastern Front, eight were fully combat-ready and three more would be after a rest pause. Forty-seven divisions were ready for limited offensive operations and seventy-three could be used for defensive operations, while twenty-nine were only conditionally suitable for defensive action. Two divisions, at least for the time being, were useless. On April 4, 1942, the component units of Army Group South were up to about 50 per cent of their full fighting strength, but only because, in view of their role in the coming campaign, they had been given priority in the assignment of replacements. Army Groups Center and North had only about 35 per cent of the infantry fighting strength they had had in mid-1941. The number of combat-ready aircraft had declined to somewhere between 50 and 60 per cent of the strength of May 1, 1941. There were good prospects for improvement in all these areas through the return of men who were still convalescing, new recruits, and the exploitation of the previously untapped reservoir of those who had just turned nineteen. Nevertheless, the overall picture was very

[5]Reinhard Heydrich, one of Heinrich Himmler's closest associates, who had assumed command in Prague in September 1941, was fatally wounded by assassins on May 26, 1942. In retaliation the Germans leveled the village of Lidice near Prague and summarily executed all its male inhabitants.—ED.

serious. The survey report of the Operations Staff of the High Command of the Wehrmacht, in which these figures appeared, concluded that, "because of the impossibility of fully replacing losses in men and material, the overall fighting power of the Wehrmacht is less than it was in spring 1941."

This conclusion was all the more grave because there was no prospect whatever for change in the adverse factors that had brought it about. In an address to officer candidates of the Wehrmacht on May 30, 1942, Hitler explained that the rising birth rate stimulated through National Socialist propaganda would far outstrip the number of dead. This sort of calculation, in an entirely different context, might have been appropriate for a bank or an industrial concern, but it was nothing less than monstrous when applied to human life. Moreover, it proved to be patently false, for the war resulted in the net loss of many millions of German lives.[6]

There was no getting around the fact that during the winter of 1941–42 the war had entered a new phase. Hitler, who was precisely informed about events, was fully and deeply aware of this, no matter how he tried to think otherwise. When General Alfred Jodl, Chief of the Operations Staff of the High Command of the Wehrmacht, finally was free to speak at the end of the war, he made a revealing statement. On May 15, 1945, shortly after Hitler's suicide, he said at a staff conference in Mürwik in Schleswig-Holstein that it had become clear to Hitler and himself, after the catastrophe of the winter of 1941–42, that "victory could no longer be achieved."[7]

[6]The text of Hitler's Berlin Sports Palace speech of May 30, 1942, to ten thousand officer candidates is appended to Schramm's edition of the *Table Conversations*. Schramm has estimated that approximately four million Germans died as military casualties and another half-million as civilians (as a result of air raids and other war-related causes).—ED.

[7]After the German capitulation early in May 1945, the High Command of the Wehrmacht was permitted to function at the headquarters established at Mürwik near Flensburg in Schleswig-Holstein for another two weeks, providing continuity in the transfer of control to the victors. The staff conference records kept by Major Joachim Schultz-Naumann report General Alfred Jodl as having said on May 15, 1945, that although the General Staff accepted Hitler's argument that the war against the Soviet Union was necessary, yet "we all . . . entered this war against Russia with anxiety at the thought of its outcome." Jodl added that it was clear, in particular to Hitler

By the end of 1942, reverses in North Africa, Allied landings in Algeria and Morocco, and the imminent encirclement of Stalingrad clearly showed a deteriorating situation on all fronts. Then " . . . it was clear not only to the responsible soldiers but to Hitler himself," Jodl acknowledged in his Nuremburg cell, "that the god of war had now turned from Germany and gone over to the other camp."[8] It all added up to this: At the very time the *Table Conversations* were being recorded and Hitler was describing to his listeners what the world would look like after Germany's victory, he knew very well that all his plans were unattainable. Yet he admitted this to no one, not even the narrow circle of "comrades" who were privileged to join him at meals and were pledged to absolute discretion.

If we find no reference to these grim facts in the *Table Conversations,* it is not because they have been omitted or suppressed, but

---

and himself, that when the catastrophe of the winter of 1941–1942 occurred, when the German armies were stopped before Moscow, "victory could no longer be achieved. The point of culmination had been passed, and the new and initially successful attempt to turn the hand of fate in the summer of 1942 also failed."

[8]On reading this passage in the *War Diary,* revealing that Hitler as early as 1942 had realized the war could not be won, Hans Kehrl, formerly with the Ministry of Armaments and War Production, wrote to me in June 1963: "At that time (i.e., fall 1943) I participated in a conference with Hitler which had been arranged by [Armaments Minister Albert] Speer. In addition to Speer there were, to mention only the most important, [Coal Commissar] Paul Pleiger, leaders of the iron and steel industry, and (I do not remember exactly) [Economics Minister Walter] Funk or General von Hanneken.

"Briefly, it was a matter of convincing the Führer that there was not enough steel for the armaments program, but that steel production could be expanded if sufficient coal and coke were made available. The question, in other words, was where the buck was going to be passed next.

"The discussion was carried on primarily by Hitler and Pleiger. Hitler, incidentally, was businesslike and well informed. He knew the production figures per man-day from England, America, France, and so on. Pleiger conceded that a limited increase in output would be possible if enough Russian prisoners of war were made available, but even so the desired production figures could not be reached. To my boundless surprise, Hitler in the course of the conversation quite dryly said, 'Pleiger, if we cannot produce more coal and more steel, the war is lost.' I very clearly remember these words which Hitler spoke in the presence of a group which was by no means small or particularly intimate."

rather because Hitler was altogether silent about them. He understood, as well as anyone who ever lived, how to keep his own counsel.

Hitler's capacity to live at several levels simultaneously made a strong impression on Dr. Picker, who transcribed Hitler's *Table Conversations:* "The striking thing about it was that even on days of the most critical tension, he hardly even referred to the problems of the war, but would chat about the harmfulness of smoking or the like—even when the most bitter arguments had occurred during the military staff conferences. . . ." Dr. Picker notes further that no matter how animated he became, Hitler intuitively never forgot to camouflage "those things for which he would find no resonance among his table companions or among the great masses of the [German] people."

Yet those familiar with Hitler's radical utterances during the last completely hopeless months of his life early in 1945 will be able to perceive in these discussions with his table companions during 1941–42 an occasional sentence that reveals the kinds of thoughts Hitler was struggling with in the deepest recesses of his mind. At midday on January 27, 1942—at the height of the winter crisis, when the Eastern Front was gravely threatened by Russian units which had broken through or infiltrated the German lines—Hitler explained that the burden of responsibility lay with the leadership, that as long as there were still a thousand people in a country who were ready to go to prison for the sake of an idea, the cause was not lost. "It is only lost when the last man comes to doubt. As long as there is one stronghearted man to hold up the banner, nothing has been lost. In this respect, I am ice-cold:[9] If the German people are not prepared to give everything for the sake of their self-preservation, very well! Then let them disappear!"

On April 12, 1942, as a new offensive in the East was being prepared and the question arose whether the Wehrmacht was in condition to make another swift advance or whether it would soon

[9]It sounds no less self-conscious and stilted in German than in English for a person to speak of himself as being *"eiskalt"* ("ice-cold") in his determination or attitude, but Hitler consciously used this term, as Schramm points out later. As in other direct quotations cited by Schramm, I have attempted to approximate as closely as possible the style as well as the content of Hitler's often willful but never bland German.—ED.

grind to a halt, Hitler led a discussion of the plans for an Olympic stadium with the observation that "[we Germans must learn] to overcome our halfheartedness and always strive for the total solution with a view to achieving the greatest possible success." This was something, he continued, which Wallenstein had grasped, but not Hjalmar Schacht, who created one problem after another when it came to raising funds for rearmament. "Especially in this war we must bear in mind constantly that in case of defeat we're done for. No matter how ruthlessly, we've got to put everything we have on the line for the sake of ultimate victory."

"One way or another" *(so oder so)* was an expression Hitler often used. During the period of his triumphs this had meant that if the enemy did not cooperate freely, his resistance would be broken by force. From 1942 on it came to mean that if the first try was not successful, then the second or the third would have to be—but there would be no capitulation, no surrender! On January 10, 1943, as the fate of Stalingrad was already becoming clear, Hitler explained to the Rumanian dictator Marshal Antonescu that in contrast to the First World War, the issue was now one of "existence or nonexistence." In the event the "Anglo-Saxons" (as he called the English and Americans) prevailed, they would be victors in a limited sense only, since they would be confronted with the power of Soviet Russia. "The result would be a mighty Bolshevik empire with a powerful industrial plant, boundless raw material resources, and vast manpower reserves, which would pursue the old expansionist goals of Russia with these masses and energy. . . ." He went on to emphasize that with Germany and her allies forced to fight under such circumstances, it was "not a war over the possession of territories, but a struggle for existence." During the subsequent visit of Marshal Antonescu on April 12, 1943, Hitler expressed the matter even more clearly, saying that he was "firmly convinced that there were only two possible outcomes of the present war: either a clear victory or absolute annihilation." Hitler's model became Frederick the Great, who had also been saved from an absolutely hopeless situation because he had held on. That had to be the task of the German "Leader" now, no matter how anxiously the hearts of his followers might quake. Hitler held to this view with grisly pertinacity to the very end. At the high point of the crisis of 1944 on the Western

Front, following the Allied breakthrough after the successful establishment of the Normandy beachhead, Hitler pointed out the steadfastness which he had demonstrated during the winter of 1941–1942.

A leader of indomitable character could rely, Hitler believed, on the "eternal laws of nature," according to which the more valuable person, the man superior in character, had to triumph in the end. Consequently, when in defiance of "nature" Hitler's Greater German Reich crumbled, he blamed the Germans. "The German people had proved themselves to be the weaker," and the stronger Eastern peoples "alone should inherit the future. Whoever survived the struggle would in any case only be the inferior, for the good had fallen." This conception was, as we can see in the *Table Conversations*, already implicit in the positions Hitler took during 1941–1942, and had its origins even earlier. Greek mythology tells of the face of Medusa, which is said to have petrified those who beheld it. Had the members of Hitler's circle of mealtime companions ever been able to see his true face, even the most loyal and devoted of them would have turned to stone.

Whenever anyone tries to understand Hitler, the final result somehow never adds up correctly. His contact with children and dogs, his joy in flowers and in culture, his appreciation of lovely women, his relationship to music were all quite genuine. But no less genuine was the ferocity—morally uninhibited, ruthless, "ice-cold"—with which Hitler annihilated not only real but even potential opponents. Hitler's two faces explain why he had such differing impacts upon people, arousing enthusiasm in some, aversion in others. He could switch these faces from one moment to the next, so that people whom he had just charmed, or had just repelled, were utterly confounded.[1] Alternately driven by reason, by temperament, or by dark instincts, Hitler was more enigmatic than anyone in German history had ever been before him. But this man, who had so uncanny an ability to draw others into his sphere of personal influence and

[1] See, for example, the memoirs of Dr. Peter Kleist (*Die europäische Tragödie*, Göttingen, 1951, p. 199), who had first been employed in the Bureau Ribbentrop and then in the Ministry for the Eastern Areas, concerning a conversation with Hitler in the *Wolfsschanze* during the summer of 1943: "I had an opportunity to study his face carefully. It had always amazed

then to dominate them, also understood how to master himself. As awkward, and even embarrassing, as were some of the scenes that occurred during his staff conferences (General Guderian in his memoirs precisely described one such clash with Hitler), Hitler hardly ever lost control of himself completely, even though in time his nerves were taxed to such an extent that most men, operating under a similar burden, would not have been physically equal to it.

Consequently, it is very difficult to come to grips with what Hitler really thought and perceived, difficult to clarify the extent to which he was motivated by logic or impelled by instinct. In this essay I shall attempt to draw together what the *Table Conversations* reveal in this respect. To begin with, we discuss Hitler's immediate environment, focusing on his personal relations with his associates, his family, and women. Next we turn our attention to his prejudices and animosities. Then we briefly examine his views of foreign countries and of the world of economics and administration. With these general political and social considerations behind us, we shall be in a position to explore more fundamental aspects of Hitler's personality and intellect, turning first to his artistic bent and his relationship to the arts in general. I shall further attempt to reconstruct his intellectual world, particularly his concept of history and biology. This leads to the question whether Hitler was religious in any sense at all or whether he should be considered nonreligious. Hitler as a military technician and his relationship with the professional military leadership is a dual theme of central importance, but is only touched on in this essay because it is explored in detail in the study of Hitler as a military leader printed in the second half of this volume. A discussion of his will power, the most uncanny and extraordinary of his characteristics, is followed by notes on his health and concluding reflections on Hitler as an historical problem.

---

me because of the multiplicity of expressions it contained. It was as though it were composed of a whole series of individual elements without adding up to a single total. . . . Photography, by selecting only a single moment out of context, could show only one aspect, thereby giving a false impression of the duplicity or multiplicity of being which lay behind this image. I tried to find some explanation for the hypnotic effect of those eyes without arriving at any explanation."

3. Hitler's Relations with His Associates

During the years before the war, so much information about Hitler's more intimate associates had already become common knowledge that even people who admired the dictator began to question the personalities in his inner circle. How could he tolerate around himself men who clearly were not equal to the responsibilities of the offices they held, or who provoked misgivings on moral grounds, or who were possibly even unsuitable in both respects? One answer to this question was given by Dr. von Hasselbach, Hitler's personal physician, several months after Germany's defeat.[2]

"Hitler repeatedly asserted," Hasselbach reported, "that one of his essential capacities, which he could depend upon absolutely, was the ability to judge men. Even a brief impression was sufficient for him to be able to say what sort of person a man was and how he could best be used.

"The selection of his associates makes this conviction seem dubious from the very beginning. One would like to assume that a man in Hitler's position would have done his utmost to surround himself with particularly intelligent and experienced men of character who were beyond reproach. Yet, to cite only a few examples, Hitler made Martin Bormann his closest associate, Schaub his chief adjutant, and Morell his personal physician.[3] He tolerated people like Heinrich Hoffmann, Hermann Esser, and Adolf Wagner as frequent and welcome guests in his private household. All were men of a kind the German people, insofar as it knew them, would much rather not have seen in the company of their Führer. Often enough Hitler had pointed with pride and satisfaction to the 'Guard' comprised of his *Reichsleiter* and *Gauleiter* [the highest echelons of the

---

[2]Hasselbach was "the most critical and reliable of Hitler's doctors," according to H. R. Trevor-Roper, who notes, on the basis of a credible source, that he was " 'probably one of the few people associated with Hitler who did not fall under his spell' " (*The Last Days of Hitler,* p. 120). For their captors, Drs. Brandt and Hasselbach prepared memoranda on Hitler and his associates, of which Schramm acquired mimeograph copies.—ED.

[3]Hitler had several personal physicians, as Schramm explains later, but most of the others were finally dismissed when they warned Hitler against the strong preparations Dr. Theo Morell was giving him.—ED.

National Socialist leadership], whom, in terms of personal character and extraordinary ability, he claimed to be virtually without equal in history. He continued to speak this way when the failure of a great number of these men in many different respects, but particularly in their personal style of life, was notoriously clear to the German public. The most important posts of the Reich were occupied by such unsuitable men as Ribbentrop, Hess, Frick, Rust, and Axmann, while Hitler meanwhile underestimated many of his opponents in an ominous fashion.

"If we ask how such blunders were possible," Hasselbach continues, "we can hardly find a single satisfactory answer. In the first place, we must consider that although Hitler was indeed convinced of the reliability and competence of his corps of political leaders, he by no means found the personal composition of the group constituting his immediate environment particularly felicitous. Yet he was not able to bring himself to make any basic changes in these positions.

"Throughout his entire life, and particularly since the First World War, Hitler was dominated by a strong feeling of comradeship, loyalty, and gratitude in his relationship with the men who in the time of his struggle and persecution had been faithful and devoted comrades in arms—even at the cost, in some cases, of serious physical injury and great economic sacrifice. Consequently, he had no sympathy for Mussolini's method of frequently and, so far as he was concerned, faithlessly changing his associates. For his own part, he felt obligated in his relationships with old supporters to put up with a great deal before finally drawing the line, and only very rarely did it come to that.

"Clearly, an important factor in this outlook was Hitler's extreme conservatism in his personal life. He wanted no changes in his daily routine if they could be avoided. He took the same walk every day. He wore the same old-fashioned kind of cap, and held on to his old Munich flat. By the same token, wherever possible he avoided cutting himself off from people he had grown accustomed to. Nevertheless, he would certainly have decided to do so more often had he been capable of making an objective appraisal of those of his associates who were incompetent or had serious character deficiencies.

Occasionally he in fact acknowledged that he knew his old comrades in arms were not all angels; but he would dismiss these shortcomings as understandable in light of their competitive personalities. The real problem arose when Hitler saw weaknesses which he believed he could accept as the price of having men around him whom he had long been used to, who would be loyal, and with whom he could feel at ease. Yet the all too gross character deficiencies of some of them had the most fateful consequences precisely because of the positions they held. . . . Ribbentrop and Morell in particular, to neither of whom, in view of their background, Hitler had reason to feel obligated, are resounding proof of his poor ability to judge men. Otherwise it would have been impossible for Hitler to call Ribbentrop a second Bismarck and Morell an unusually competent physician and scientist.

"In many cases we do have to assume, however, that Hitler managed to suppress an entirely correct judgment which was uncongenial in order to justify persons who seemed to him useful and devoted. His attitude toward others was also conditioned by the fact that he had an extraordinarily high estimation of his own capabilities and consequently measured his fellow men by far more modest standards—despite the great demands which he now and again might make. And when he insisted that a great man had to have an insignificant wife because he would not be able to devote himself to her sufficiently, he may also have harbored similar thoughts regarding his immediate associates."

There is only one point to add to Hasselbach's analysis: Hitler did have an amazing ability to judge people to the extent that he was able to sense immediately whether the person standing in front of him was for him, could be won over, or would be immune to his personal dynamism. In this respect he had a sort of "sixth sense." There was only one person whom Hitler had not been able to see through, and this was Admiral Canaris, chief of the Wehrmacht intelligence service. Canaris was so perfect an intelligence officer that in his dealings with Hitler he was able to dissimulate successfully enough to deceive Hitler's intuitive sense about people being with him or against him. Consequently, Canaris was arrested only in 1944, when the facts spoke all to clearly against him.

It is almost impossible to convey to those who never experienced it the personal impact of Hitler. Such could be its strength that it sometimes seemed a kind of psychological force radiating from him like a magnetic field. It could be so intense as to be almost physically tangible. As widely attested as this strange power of Hitler's was, there were nevertheless many people upon whom it had absolutely no effect. A colonel once described to me how, when he was reporting to Hitler along with several others, he felt a steadily rising aversion to the man as he watched him at close hand. (It is worth noting that Hitler dismissed this colonel and the others very quickly.) The reverse reaction was provoked in a sophisticated lady of aristocratic background and Christian convictions, who abhorred Hitler. By chance she met him on the boardwalk of a Baltic Sea resort, was grazed for a brief moment by his glance, and declared, as though struck by lightning, that while she still did not like him she felt that he was a great man. Those whom Hitler tolerated close to himself were of course more than just grazed by his glance, and they were transformed into his willing satellites.[4]

4. Hitler's Views on Family and Women

Many photographs exist showing Hitler with happy children. These pictures were liberally exploited in party propaganda; they documented for the masses how kind and good the "Führer" really was, and how he had sacrificed any family life of his own to be able to

---

[4]At the end of the war, an atmosphere developed around Hitler which was described shortly after the catastrophe by an elder General Staff officer. He had experienced it while briefing Hitler during March and April 1945, and found it repulsive. He wrote: "My impression—and as I determined in conversations with others, by no means mine alone—was that a person was not merely spiritually crushed by this atmosphere of servility, nervousness, and untruthfulness, but that one could even sense it as a sort of physical sickness. Nothing was genuine there except the fear. There was fear of all shades and degrees—from being afraid of somehow provoking the displeasure of the 'Führer,' or annoying him by some ill-advised comment, to naked fear for life itself in view of the impending end of the drama. The external forms of life were still scantily preserved, but even they disappeared after the middle of April." [Schramm does not identify the man.—ED.]

devote himself night and day to the welfare of the German people. Hitler's joyful expression in these pictures was not a mask put on for the photographers. He truly loved children, and made genuine contact with them as they swarmed about him.

Public welfare support for children, particularly illegitimate children, was a subject to which he gave considerable thought. He was also genuinely concerned with the problem of providing security for the family, which he regarded as the natural unit of social existence, as well as with making it easier for newlyweds to get a start in life.[5] This was not something he talked about only in his public speeches, but a theme he frequently returned to in his *Table Conversations*. Many of the expressions he used in this connection had something almost homespun about them, and many things he said could be accepted even by those who might otherwise despise him.

Hitler felt that premarital intercourse was not objectionable, but rather that it assured that a man and his "maiden" really belonged together. This no longer provoked much opposition in 1941, particularly as he needed only to cite the customs among the country people of his own homeland, and as there was no denying much of what could be pointed out about the double standards of morality of the "upper ten thousand," Hitler's term for the aristocracy together with the wealthiest members of the upper middle class. On this subject, then, Hitler seems the kind of man who accepts life as it is and merely wishes to replace a crumbling façade with "natural" ethics dictated by reason.

Beneath this, however, lay other thoughts which Hitler did not, and could not, express publicly if he wanted to retain the esteem of the masses. Here the *Table Conversations* give us a deeper insight. In them we see unveiled the conclusions which Hitler drew from the fusion of his basic views with his biologically oriented conception of

[5]Schramm could presuppose, on the part of many of his German readers, a certain familiarity with the Nazi policy of granting marriage loans and baby bonuses. Not a few of them, as a matter of fact, could attribute the circumstances of their birth to the calculated largesse of the state during the 1930's. These policies not only had the effect of increasing the birth rate but also of removing women from the labor market, thereby reducing unemployment.—ED.

selective breeding. He saw nothing wrong in a racial elite having illegitimate children. Indeed he welcomed it. After the French campaign in 1940, for example, Hitler observed that he had seen much better "human material" among the youth in the combat areas of 1914-1918 than he had found there during the First World War. He felt that "German and English soldiers had brought about a Nordicizing process,[6] the results of which are today incontestable."

In Hitler's eyes, this Nordicizing process was justified not only in enemy territory. On the contrary, he thought that it was desirable within Germany as well. When he bought his mountain retreat near Berchtesgaden, he explained in 1942, he had found such a mongrel population there that he really felt something had to be done quickly to improve it. "Credit has to be given to the SS Bodyguard Regiment for the fact that today there are numbers of strong and healthy children running around the area. It shows that elite troops should really be sent wherever the composition of the population is poor, in order to improve it. . . . Sometime it would also be a good idea to station elite troops in the Masurian Lakes and Bavarian Forest regions." If someone objected that such a procedure could undermine the morality of the German people, Hitler would become furious. With jibes at the Prussian princes' practice of keeping mistresses and at the upper classes' repudiation of their illegitimate children, he categorically dismissed conventional morality as hypocrisy and nothing more. He was prepared to concede only that two people in love might be bound together by their child.

This was one of the many cases in which Hitler's logical train of thought derailed into inconsistency. Had he followed through with his ideas, he would obviously have come to conclusions that were irreconcilable with his other conceptions. Clearly, protection of the family and "Nordicization" by elite troops were completely incompatible. Had he thought the matter through, Hitler would have been constrained to consider whether "Nordicizing" these areas—aside from the painful humiliation and shock of the parents and brothers —would not result in such indignation against the elite troops and

---

[6]Literally, *Aufnordungswerk,* crude Nazi racial jargon meaning "a job of Nordic upgrading by selective breeding."—ED.

the regime itself that in the end the gain of even several thousand "Nordic" children would be outweighed by the bitter alienation of hundreds of thousands. That Hitler somehow was purblind to this is almost certainly in part explained by the fact that he himself had no family and had spent many years of his life in a milieu in which the very structure of family life had seriously disintegrated.

There are a number of statements in the *Table Conversations* regarding the special problem of Hitler's relationship with women.[7] He occasionally described to his circle how strongly, as a visually minded person, he reacted to beautiful women. Before the war he had found it both delightful and relaxing to chat with a lovely young woman over tea, or to fascinate elegant ladies at a reception with his conversation. Hitler was always unfailingly gracious and correct with women. If he scorned earlier rulers who had exploited their position to indulge themselves with numbers of mistresses, he could do so in good conscience, for his own conduct in this sphere was nearly impeccable. Unnoticed by the public, Eva Braun assumed the role of a housewife at the *Berghof,* Hitler's mountain retreat near Berchtesgaden. During the war, the only other women he saw were the wives occasionally brought by his guests. Not even Eva Braun was admitted to the *Wolfsschanze,* his headquarters in East Prussia, where there were no women at all except secretaries and a cook who prepared Hitler's vegetarian fare. After he stopped taking his meals in a larger group, Hitler let his cook join in the conversation with the small gathering who ate with him, but this was only for the sake of relaxation and distraction.

Only at the very last moment, with his "Thousand-Year Reich"

---

[7]During the night of January 25–26, 1942, Hitler reflected on the fact that marriage would have been disastrous for him: "A woman who loves her husband lives for him alone. . . . Thus she demands that he in turn live for her. But a man is the slave of his thoughts. His tasks and responsibilities are his master. . . . When I consider it, I would have been able to spend only a few days of the year 1932 at home. . . . Marriage would have been a terrible burden to take on, because any man would want to please his wife. For me there would have been her sorrowful, careworn face, or else I would have had to neglect my duties. Thus it is better not to marry. . . . It is much better to have a lover. The burden of responsibility is removed and everything that remains is a gift. Naturally this applies only in the case of outstanding men."—ED.

crumbling before his eyes, when he was prepared to accept the consequences of his annihilating defeat by taking his life, did Hitler finally give undivided attention to Eva Braun. His formal civil marriage to her was perhaps the only humane scene in the inferno of the concluding act of the Third Reich. Yet it, too, was grotesque—finding the proper official to perform the ceremony was understandably very difficult at that point—and had something petty and provincial about it. With everything crashing down in ruins, it hardly mattered what posterity thought about Eva Braun.

What role did Hitler assign women in his view of the world? From the *Table Conversations* it is evident that for him woman was still the creature who wanted to be protected by man and to look up to him: "The world of the woman is the man. Only now and then does she think of anything else." She was not suitable for politics, Hitler asserted, because of her inability to discriminate between reason and emotion. She should be as attractive as she could, and might also be jealous, but she should not concern herself with philosophical questions. It was essential for her to bear children: "If a woman does not have a child, she will become hysterical or sick."

As a basis of comparison with Hitler's ideas, we can take the middle-class ideal of woman during the period before the war, when the intellectual equality of the educated woman was already a generally accepted fact and the relationship between man and wife had accordingly become far more complicated than during earlier generations. By this standard, what Hitler had to say sounds extremely reactionary: "A man has to be able to stamp his imprint on any woman. As a matter of fact, a wife does not want anything else!" Hitler simply was not aware of what had been going on during the past decades. As we shall see, this was not the only respect in which he was behind the times.

5. Hitler's Social and Philosophical Resentments

Anyone whose rise in the world had been as hard as Hitler's would perforce have been marked with strong affinities and bitter hostilities. The *Table Conversations* clearly demonstrate the extent to which Hitler was still completely dominated by such resentments almost a decade after achieving power, though in fact there was not the slightest reason for concern about possible resistance on the part of his defeated adversaries.

It would be superfluous to discuss at any length the judgments which Hitler expressed at his table about kings and princes. He thought the crowned heads and their families rotten to the core, indescribably stupid, and hence not worth being taken seriously. He spoke condescendingly of the "Hohenzollern brood" and expressed the anger he still felt at the memory of his formal reception by the King of Italy in May 1938.[8]

As for Hitler's remarks about the "upper ten thousand"—a term he often used—or the bourgeoisie, these were similarly petulant. He spoke of the Saxon burgher class as "a riffraff of idiotic stupidity." "No segment of the population," he declared, "is more foolish when it comes to political matters than this so-called burgher class." In his opinion, the German burgher desired only tranquility and order and was politically cowardly. Only the Hanseatics, the citizens of the once independent north German seaports, came in for an occasional compliment in Hitler's conversation. There is no way to account for the fact that he remained so prejudiced against the middle classes, for without their efficiency in commerce and industry Germany would never have been able to recover so swiftly from the misery of the years before 1933. Moreover, "Führer and Reich Chancellor"[9] Hitler had won over a large part of the bourgeoisie,

---

[8]On May 2, 1938, Hitler set out with four special trainloads of functionaries to visit Italy, responding to an invitation which Mussolini had extended during a visit to Germany the previous autumn. Hitler was disgusted "by the fact that protocol required him, as Head of State, to stay with the King in the Quirinal. The formality of his reception at the Palace irked him and left him with a permanent dislike of the Italian Royal House" (Alan Bullock, *Hitler, A Study in Tyranny*, p. 444).—ED.

[9]On January 30, 1933, Hitler was named *Reichskanzler* by *Reichspräsident* Paul von Hindenburg, who died on August 2, 1934. Thereupon Hitler united in himself the functions of chief of state (president) and head of government (chancellor), assuming the formal title *Führer und Reichskanzler,* an act confirmed by 84 per cent of the voters in a plebiscite on August 19, 1934. Although this figure reflects duress and manipulation, there is no question but that the great majority of the German people did endorse him.—ED.

while also enjoying social contact with important representatives of the "upper ten thousand." Undoubtedly he sensed that many burghers and intellectuals rejected him or at best regarded him with reserve, but there is really no explanation for his negative attitude other than that he never overcame the resentments which had taken root during his youth and intensified during the years of his struggle for power. He clung to these resentments with that rigidity he maintained in all of his basic conceptions.[1]

It is more difficult to account for Hitler's prejudice against professors. Since the nineteenth century they had made a vital contribution to Germany's reputation, and the results of their research—including the achievements of scholars who had nothing whatsoever to do with National Socialism—had been of great significance to the Third Reich. Certainly at the beginning of the war this was clear. But Hitler still did not like professors. "If the German professor were to be put in charge of the world for a few centuries," he declared in 1942, "there would be nothing but cretins running around after a million years—gigantic heads with hardly any

[1]Hitler's relationship with the German bourgeoisie, the burgher class, is strikingly illustrated in Edouard Calic's recent edition of two conversations Hitler had with Richard Breiting, editor of the influential Saxon newspaper *Leipziger Neueste Nachrichten,* in May and June 1931 *(Ohne Maske: Hitler-Breiting Geheimgespräche 1931,* Frankfurt, 1968). A member of Stresemann's moderately conservative party, a friend of later resistance leader Mayor Carl Goerdeler of Leipzig, and a man quite interested in the possibility of "using" Hitler and his movement as a brake against the serious menace of socialism and communism, Breiting had two long conferences with Hitler several months after the Nazis' first big breakthrough (from twelve to 107 seats) in the Reichstag elections of September 1930, but almost two years before Hitler would become chancellor. Hitler was scathingly condescending in his attitude toward the German middle classes. He did not need them; they needed him and his movement. He would make even faster work of them than of the Marxists. He would do whatever he wanted with them and they would obey unconditionally. Their talents were indispensable, to be sure, but only as specialists, and as such they had to cooperate and comply without question. The German bourgeoisie was rotten to the core. Once he reached power legally, Hitler would close down their Reichstag and convert it to a museum. Despite this sustained tirade, Breiting reacted relatively positively to Hitler. He was impressed by the man's personal stature, by his attitude toward big business, and by his determination to end the Marxist threat. Hitler might be a diamond in the rough, but he seemed to have a hard cutting edge that could be put to good use.—ED.

bodies at all." In this connection he accused professorial scholarship of leading away from instinct, from that "instinct" which Hitler accorded so important a place in his overall view of the world. Beyond this, he probably also had the uncomfortable feeling that his teachings would not stand up to meticulous analysis and evaluation at the hands of the professors.[2]

It would have been to Hitler's advantage to call in leading professionals, true experts, in order to be kept up to date on scientific research and developments. At best this was done only with medical and natural scientists, never, so far as I know, with scholars of archaeology, history, the fine arts, and so forth. If such men had been called in, however, Hitler would almost certainly have dominated the conversation. Yet it would have been very easy for him to have arranged for recognized experts to be invited from time to time to join him and his circle of mealtime companions, thereby affording a relaxed means of gaining new information. The reason Hitler did not choose to do this was suggested after the war by Dr. Karl Brandt, one of his personal physicians, in the following terms:

[2]Hitler's distaste for scholars was by no means reciprocated by the German academic community as a whole. A significant segment supported him months and even years before he came to power, undoubtedly lending him and his cause a certain respectability in the eyes of many uncertain observers. The distinguished German historian Friedrich Meinecke, a professor at Berlin, in a letter written early in December 1931, almost fourteen months before Hitler's appointment as chancellor, told a friend how he had vainly attempted to find as few as eight prominent colleagues to support an anti-Nazi public statement. People were already accommodating themselves to the "coming Nazi regime."

Even Meinecke himself, though he never wavered in his abhorrence of Hitler, could write in 1938 that the annexation of Austria had "thrust the whole of German history ahead in one leap and fulfilled old aspirations and ideals." Then, in 1940, the German defeat of France filled him with "profound emotion, pride, and joy," even though he still was unable to identify himself with the Third Reich. But at the same time (as he wrote on August 7, 1940, to the Austrian historian Heinrich von Srbik), he had a terrible sense of apprehension about the very nature of the Third Reich and Adolf Hitler: "It almost seems as if the propelling force behind great and necessary revolutions stems more from the evil than the good side of human nature. This brings us once more to the demonic character of historical life. But we will never be able to penetrate the veil entirely. There is nothing else for us to do but to be modest in our historical interpretations."—ED.

"It is possible that he felt the need, in his conversations, for a sounding board so uncritical and unpretentious that he could freely pour out his thoughts 'in rough draft' in order to reach the goal of clarifying them." This would account for Hitler's not wanting to have representatives of the educated middle classes and the intelligentsia around him but rather people, as Dr. Brandt suggests, "whose lives had somehow been disturbed or whose background as self-made men was similar to his own."

Hitler criticized secondary school teachers for failing to make clear to pupils in their history classes the broad relationships between events, and for laying stress instead on the biographies of individual monarchs and insignificant dates. In doing so, he thereby overlooked all the reforms which, at least since 1919, had successfully improved the instruction of history. Hitler had a particular distaste for elementary school teachers, most of whom, in Germany, even up to the Second World War, were men. He had a completely stereotyped conception of them, as expressed in April 1942: dirty, tainted with socialism, a "stupid and un-self-sufficient intellectual proletariat." Hitler wanted to replace these teachers with women, thereby freeing the men for the war effort. He also felt that the discharged noncommissioned officers who were entitled to civil service positions should be brought into the teaching profession, since they had been drilled in both cleanliness and leadership. If education were carried too far, Hitler felt, it would simply drive the children to idiocy by brain massage. Consequently, elementary school teachers should learn only what was absolutely necessary for elementary instruction—and nothing more. A teacher who planned to spend his whole life in a country village would not need academic preparation. Hitler found himself repeatedly angered "that in the teacher training schools a tremendous amount of material is funneled into future elementary school teachers, although afterward their only job will be to teach the elementary principles of reading, writing, and arithmetic. How much does a person need to know from every possible branch of knowledge in order to teach six-year-olds the correct pronunciation of *a, a, a . . . b, b, b!* It is sheer insanity to try to pound everything possible into the children in school. If you ask them a year or two after they have left school about all these things, they hardly know anything about them any longer. It should therefore be the responsibility of the school administration to set up curricula so that children will be taught only what they actually need to know in order to measure up later in life. Incidentally, it would also be a lot smarter to have them spend as much time as possible out in the fresh air. That way we would get a healthy younger generation which would be able, when the time came, to endure physical exertion without taking sick right away."

If these intentions of Hitler had actually been realized, it would have meant the reversal of the epoch-making reforms of Dr. Carl Heinrich Becker, the Prussian Minister of Culture from 1925 to 1930, who had established respectable educational standards for elementary school teachers, comparable to the requirement of bachelor's degrees in America, instead of the once acceptable certificates from two-year normal schools. But beyond that, Hitler's ideas would actually have set back the development of the elementary school system by still another generation, for the assignment of veteran non-commissioned officers to the schools was an old Prussian policy.

Hitler could hold such convictions because he simply did not take cognizance of the generally accepted modern pedagogical theory that no person can discover and develop his talents fully without the benefit of as comprehensive an education as possible. "Why does a boy who wants to study music," he once asked, "need geometry, physics, and chemistry? What does he remember about them later on? Nothing!"

It goes without saying that Hitler hated lawyers. After all, they had made it very difficult for him during the long years of his rise to power. Lawyers had also created all sorts of problems for him after he had come to power, constraining him again and again to hew to the letter of the law. The only really surprising thing about Hitler's attacks on lawyers is the degree of bitterness in his remarks. The expressions which he used, and which were accepted without question by his companions during the *Table Conversations,* today seem almost embarrassing, even to those willing to acknowledge that there may have been an element of truth in them. So far as Hitler was concerned, every lawyer was either defective by birth or would have to become so in the course of time. The law was not a respectable profession and led, in trying a case before court, to mere play-acting. There was, moreover, a kinship between lawyers and criminals, Hitler asserted, and "also in their internationality there is no difference between the two." Contrary to accepted legal teaching he claimed that lawyers systematically denied the concept of responsibility. To him they were simply irresponsible and useless.

From the beginning, Hitler had been inclined to regard financial experts as rogues and villains, for whenever he let them get a word in edgewise they presented him with uncongenial facts. He was similarly prejudiced against administrative officials. In his eyes they were petty and egotistical, lacking in sound common sense, men ignorant of the exigencies of daily life who thought only in abstract terms. A number of different experiences helped form Hitler's distaste for administrative officials. Until 1914, after all, he had only passive contact with the bureaucracy, insofar as he received instructions to report here or there, or when his personal life was interfered with in some minor way. After 1918, as he set out to build his party and began holding mass meetings, he had repeated collisions with "the authorities." Then, after 1933, his own bureaucracy seemed to be throwing one obstacle after another in his way by insisting that his plans violated the law or ran counter to established administrative practice in one respect or another.

The Prussian reformer Baron vom Stein had thundered against the bureaucracy early in the nineteenth century, and toward the end of the century Otto von Bismarck had also done so, but their rage stemmed from lifelong experience in administrative matters. Until he came to power, Hitler never spent a single day in a government office, and was in fact completely foreign to bureaucracy and administration.

Now and then the Freemasons are mentioned in the *Table Conversations*. Hitler was absolutely convinced that behind the scenes the Masons played a vitally important role in world affairs. For example, that Franco did not accept his bid to bring Spain into the war when they met at Hendaye on October 23, 1940, was attributed by Hitler, in the last analysis, to the "fact" that the Caudillo was a Freemason. After the SS had confiscated the records of the German Freemasons and brought them all together in Berlin, the Nazi party discovered to its great surprise that in all of Germany there were only sixty thousand fraternal members and that their political activity was absolutely harmless. Here was an instance of fighting a phantom built up by the polemics of the nineteenth century which he un-critically assumed.

The situation is much more complicated in the case of Hitler's animosity against the Church. He himself pointed out how abiding were the impressions he received in his early youth when he had been made to serve as an altar boy and a singer in the choir. In school he had been struck by the way in which the teachings of the Church and of natural science conflicted. The more he had con-cerned himself with the matter, the more alienated he had found himself, not only from the Catholic Church but from Christianity altogether. In a secret speech which he made in October 1937, Hitler declared that he had freed himself, "after a hard inner struggle, from the remnants of the religious conceptions of his childhood," adding, "I now feel as fresh as a foal in the pasture." With what-ever religious feeling remained, he built his own creed, which was essentially a variant of the monism so common before the First World War.[3]

Once in power, Hitler decisively opposed everything connected with the Church. He spoke of its promoting religious insanity and of its intellectually crippling effect on Christians. Impelled by his belief in the idea of progress, he represented the Church as a back-ward, spiritually archaic opponent whose teachings were a cultural outrage which, like the persecution of witches, simply had to be done away with. He said in November 1941, "Today no one who is conversant with scientific research can take the teachings of the Church seriously anymore." At the same time he acknowledged that the problem could not be solved simply by the stroke of a pen. The Church would have to "rot away like a gangrenous limb."

[3]Monism, teaching that there is only one ultimate reality, took the form of a dynamic (rather than naive mechanical) materialism, as represented by the famous biologist Ernst Haeckel (1834–1919), whose *Welträtsel* (*The Riddle of the Universe,* 1899) was an international best-seller, and by the physicist Wilhelm Ostwald (1853–1932), who published five volumes of monistic Sun-day sermons between 1911 and 1916. The ethical and moral teachings of this "religion" had a very strong current of social Darwinism.—ED.

Up to this point, Hitler's ideas about the Church are not uncommon. Many others have taken a similar position. What is startling, however, is the malicious condescension with which Hitler disparaged the "shavelings," including the popes, and how he attributed everything they had ever achieved to exclusively base motives. He accused them of a "cunning mixture of hypocrisy and avarice," and spoke of their "satanic superstition" as well as of the "hypocrisy" of Christian teachings about love. So profound and intense was his hatred that he was continually conceiving new phrases to give it expression. Basically, his view of the Church was rooted in the unsophisticated polemicism of the nineteenth century, which in turn had its origins in a vulgarized liberalism derived from the popularization of the teachings of the Enlightenment. Any more recent ideas about the role of the Church in the modern world were apparently unknown to him. When his ruthless campaign against both Catholicism and Protestantism in Germany led to the mobilization of both religions' full resources in defense, Hitler's reaction was to see in this nothing but a political response, requiring appropriate laws, surveillance, and arrests. He was apparently oblivious to the spiritual, intellectual, and moral dimensions of the issue.

Hitler's relationship to the Church was riven by the most obvious contradiction. Hitler regarded himself, rightly, as a master of mass psychology—as someone who not only knew the way the masses thought but also knew how to manipulate their thinking. Yet in his relationship to the Church he became a prisoner of his own prejudices. He applied precisely the wrong methods to deal with the very opposition he himself had provoked, thus clearly demonstrating his limitations. He was so badly crippled by his own narrow-mindedness on the subject of the Church that his policy can only be described, and this charitably, as obtuse.[4]

[4]The limitations of Hitler's policy toward the Church were dramatically demonstrated in August 1941. At the beginning of the war, Hitler had ordered that all persons who were incurably ill be put to death as socially worthless parasites. His compulsory euthanasia policy was top secret, but a program which within two years provided for the killing of some seventy thousand persons could hardly be concealed indefinitely. The victims were drawn from all walks of life throughout Germany. Relatively large numbers of people were directly engaged in the euthanasia program. At first suspicion and then

Only after his conflict with the Catholic Church was well underway did Hitler turn his attention to the Protestants, for whom
he had even less respect than he did for the Catholics. "The hypo-
critical bigotry of the Protestants is far worse than that of the Catholic Church," he said in December 1941. The Catholic Church had
a broader outlook, in Hitler's opinion, and was also more cunning
in the matter of forgiving sins. Describing the only conference he
ever had with the leaders of the Protestant Church in Germany,

---

alarm mounted as word spread of more and more patients dying of appendi-
citis who had had appendectomies years earlier, or of stroke, though their
families had seen them, in weekly visits over the years, as placidly feeble-
minded souls who would hardly be expected to die of such a cause.

Then, on August 3, 1941, Count Clemens August von Galen, the Roman
Catholic Bishop of Münster, proclaimed from his pulpit in St. Lambert's that
throughout his Westphalian diocese, on state orders, lists of incurables were
being drawn up in hospitals and sanatoria. These people were to be murdered
by the government. The first transport from Marienthal, near Münster, had
already left the past week. "Woe unto mankind," the bishop continued, "and
woe unto the German people, when the holy Commandment of God, 'Thou
shalt not kill,' . . . not only is violated, but when this violation is even tolerated
and goes unpunished!" Nor did Bishop Galen stop there. With the holy fervor
of an Old Testament prophet, he lashed out with example after example of
how the Germans under Hitler had flagrantly violated many other Command-
ments.

The wrathful sermon had an electrifying effect. It was printed and copies
were distributed not only to all corners of Germany but among the troops in
the field. Many Nazi leaders urged that Galen be hanged. The grey eminence
of the Third Reich, Martin Bormann, who had become head of the Party
Chancellery after Rudolf Hess's flight to Scotland, argued that such treason
deserved nothing less than the death sentence. But Hitler's shrewd propaganda
minister, Dr. Josef Goebbels, emphatically demurred, calculating "that the
population of Münster could be regarded as lost during the war, if anything
were done against the bishop, and in that fear one safely could include the
whole of Westphalia." Rather than write off the industrial heartland of
Germany for the rest of the war, Hitler swallowed his fury and accepted his
impotence—for the time being. Within a month of Galen's sermon the compulsory euthanasia program was halted.

Aside from the fact that his courage saved untold thousands of lives,
Cardinal Galen's case is important to an understanding of Hitler. His successful defiance dramatically demonstrated that although the Nazi regime had
reached an unprecedented degree of control over the country, there were still
very real limits to its power of life and death over the German people. Hitler
and Goebbels, despite their hatred and frustration, were well aware of that
fact, and accepted it with nothing more than the thought of future vengeance
to comfort them.—ED.

Hitler recalled an embarrassingly distorted picture in which frayed frocks and soiled linen played a role. It was almost as if he were intellectually allergic to Protestantism.

In the final analysis, Hitler's conception of the danger to state and culture represented by Catholics and Protestants was essentially the same. He was very clear about what he planned to do about it: "The worst influence on the people are our pastors of both confessions. I cannot give the answer now, but everything is being entered into my big black book. The time is going to come when I will settle with them without any ceremony, and when that time comes, I have no intention of letting myself be tripped up by any legalistic nets. The only consideration will be what is practical. I am convinced that within ten years everything will look entirely different. There is no way to avoid a basic solution."

This is a clear, stenographically authenticated, and therefore literally accurate statement, which should be the point of departure for any consideration of whether Pope Pius XII and the Catholic Church, as well as the "Confessing" Church (the wing of German Protestantism which did not accept the supervision of Nazi-dominated state ecclesiastical authorities), acted correctly or not during the Third Reich. This statement shows how decisive and brutal their enemy was.

No one will be surprised that the theme of anti-Semitism runs through the *Table Conversations* like a red thread. The *Conversations* offer nothing new here, since Hitler had already expressed himself on the Jews so often. But the *Conversations* do bring out more clearly than other sources the two sides of Hitler's anti-Semitism. On the one hand, he based his argument on allegedly empirical facts conjoined with a pseudo-scientific biological theory. For example, he once said about the children born of mixed marriages between Jews and Gentiles: "Experience proves that after four, five, or six generations, the offspring of these Jews always 'mendel out' pure Jews again." On the other hand, he let himself be ruled by a Semitophobia which was absolutely grotesque and appalling in its implications. Behind Stalin, he felt, stood the Jew. A small clique of Jews in Sweden had "colossal influence." It was clear to him that "the Roosevelt regime in the U.S.A. is unquestionably a Jewish organization." And so it went, on and on, tiresomely into the night. The only thing that might still evoke some sense of surprise among his table companions would be the startling manner in which an objective analysis would suddenly, as though by a sort of intellectual short-circuit, lead into an outburst against the "international brood of Jewish traders," against the Jewish-dominated world press with its lying blather, or against the alleged activities of the Jews in some other derogatory fashion. No matter what happened in the world, and no matter in what country it happened, Hitler saw the Jew behind it, and especially was this the case if the event involved something unfavorable for Germany. This anti-Semitic mania, or "tic," often prevented Hitler from analyzing a situation objectively in order to decide on a rational course of action. To this extent Hitler was almost like the medieval person who sensed the presence of the devil everywhere. But whereas in the Middle Ages a man might cross himself or—if he had the courage of Luther—hurl the inkpot at Satan, Hitler's mania led to his revenging himself on the millions of Jews who fell into his hands in Germany and the occupied areas of Europe.

Hitler's anti-Semitism had its origins in the early impressions of his youth, but it was reinforced during the five years he spent in Vienna before moving, at the age of twenty-four, to the Bavarian capital of Munich in 1913. Those prewar years in Vienna were, as Hitler himself points out in *Mein Kampf,* the period when the Viennese lower middle classes were organized by the city's anti-Semitic mayor, Karl Lueger, into political shock troops, while the nationalists under Baron von Schönerer also made use of anti-Semitic slogans. Hitler's anti-Semitism was further intensified during the long years of his struggle for power, for its very vehemence understandably provoked Jewish resistance in many forms.[5] In addition, *The Protocols of the Elders of Zion,* frequently republished

[5]The social and cultural background of Hitler's anti-Semitism is given in Peter G. P. Pulzer's *The Rise of Political Anti-Semitism in Germany and Austria* (New York, 1964), while the most complete study of Hitler's anti-Semitism in practice is Raul Hilberg's impressive—and appalling—*The Destruction of the European Jews* (Chicago, 1961).—ED.

since 1903, made a deep impression on him. There it was in black and white—the Jews were out to destroy existing states in order to rule the world! Hitler never seems to have taken cognizance of the fact that *The Protocols* had been discredited time and again as a crude falsification whose origins had been fully accounted for by serious scholarship.

Many different factors help to explain Hitler's anti-Semitism, but no matter how far one goes to account for it, something darkly inexplicable always remains. There were many people before Hitler and during his own lifetime who did not like the Jews, or who hated them, or who even despised them, but no one has ever surpassed him in the extent to which he allowed anti-Semitism to grow into so intensive a mania that it completely shattered the faculty of reason. Where has there ever been anyone who let himself be driven by his hatred to such gigantic crimes?

The attempt has been made to explain Hitler's anti-Semitism by demonstrating that there were Jews among his own ancestors. According to this theory, the church records where Hitler's family originated are supposed to have been falsified to cover up the fact that a Jewish master who took advantage of a young girl in his employ should actually be listed as one of Hitler's immediate forebears. It may sound plausible that Hitler, enraged about this illegitimate strain in himself, turned his hatred outward and took revenge on the Jews in general as scapegoats for the ancestor who escaped punishment. But when subjected to close examination this explanation has turned out to be highly questionable, especially since the chronology is dubious.[6] In the end, all attempts to explain the unprecedented and immeasurable intensity of Hitler's anti-Semitism finally founder on the inexplicable.

[6]Schramm refers to the suspicion that Hitler's paternal grandfather was Jewish. It has been discredited. For an account of the tale and its flaws, see "Appendix I: The Alteration of the Name and the Jewish Grandfather Story," in Bradley F. Smith, *Adolf Hitler: His Family, Childhood and Youth* (Stanford, 1967), pp. 157–160. According to Dr. Werner Maser, author of serious studies of the early history of the Nazi party and of Hitler's *Mein Kampf*, his "missing" paternal grandfather probably was Johann Nepomuk Hüttler, his mother's grandfather.—ED.

6. Hitler and Foreign Countries

A collection of quotations from the *Table Conversations* demonstrating Hitler's sympathy or antipathy to particular countries would not be very rewarding. The fact is that before the Second World War the only countries Hitler knew firsthand were Austria and Germany, aside from the area of France in which he had served during the First World War. In the period of his rise to power during the twenties, Hitler never crossed the German border. For a time he considered taking a trip around the United States, an idea suggested by his friends the Hanfstaengls, a wealthy Munich publishing family. But before he got around to it, he was deterred by the Munich *Putsch* and its consequences. Once in power, Hitler did become acquainted with Italy. His visits with Mussolini were a great artistic experience for him, though he had no opportunity to be exposed to the people themselves. What little Hitler saw of foreign countries after the beginning of the Second World War was through the windows of his limousine or special train. So far as foreign countries were concerned, then, Hitler remained dependent throughout his life on pictures, the cinema, and the reports of others. In this respect, he was unlike Roosevelt or Churchill and more like Stalin, who left Russia for the first time when he attended the Teheran Conference in November 1943.

One has to bear these factors in mind to understand Hitler's stereotyped conception of foreign countries. He thought in terms of clichés characteristic of the arrogant propaganda put out before World War I by the pan-German and more racially oriented nationalistic press. However, Germany's defeat in the First World War brought a change, particularly in intellectual and artistic circles, so that there came to be an increasingly fruitful exchange with foreign countries during the twenties. But this was all lost on Hitler, who had no feeling for literature and vehemently rejected the new art and architecture, suspecting that the Jewish conspiracy had infiltrated the arts completely. Since Hitler clung to the idea that the loss of the First World War had not been a genuine defeat, he saw no reason whatever to reconsider his feeling of nationalistic superiority. On the contrary, as a result of Germany's recovery under his leadership, not to mention its victories until 1942, he felt that his fundamental belief in Germany's superiority had been absolutely vindicated.

It may surprise some to learn that Hitler spoke with so much respect about Stalin. The explanation lies in his sense of solidarity and identification with another dictator. Hitler's comments about Franklin D. Roosevelt and Winston Churchill, on the other hand, are shocking. To be sure, no one would expect him to show any sympathy for them. The most intense hatred would, in fact, be understandable, for these were the men who checked his ambitions. But the notion that hatred often brings special insight was not borne out by Hitler. He not only defamed and cursed both Roosevelt and Churchill continually, but he also trivialized them—which no one should ever do with one's enemies and which, of course, Hitler paid for sorely. Thus, once again we are confronted with the phenomenon of a man who read so widely, who had so much information at his disposal, and who was able to think so sharply in certain areas, nevertheless allowing himself to be mastered by groundless delusions which blocked his clear vision.

The *Table Conversations* reveal a good deal about Hitler's attitude toward England, an attitude determined by that strangely vacillating mixture of love and hate which led so many Germans in the nineteenth century to admire the British at one moment and despise them the next. "They are incomparably insolent, but I admire them nonetheless. We still have a lot to learn from them." Before the war the film *The Bengal Lancers,* which showed English officers in the Indian Army to best advantage, arrived in Germany, and Hitler had it played for himself three or four times. T. E. Lawrence's *Seven Pillars of Wisdom* also made a lasting impression on him.

Hitler's hope that the "London Naval Agreement" of 1935 would be the first step toward a genuine Anglo-German understanding was not realized. If he had been better informed about Great Britain, the idea would never have occurred to him in the first place. As it was, however, he clung to the vision that the future would draw England and Germany closer together, if for no other reason than that their interests were linked by a common rivalry with the United States—another matter about which he was misinformed.

At the very latest, one might have been able to speculate about an Anglo-American rivalry around 1900. In a notorious article in the London *Saturday Review* in 1896, which contained the key phrase *"Germaniam esse delendam,"* the United States was cited as England's other potential enemy.[7] But in 1911 a treaty was concluded between London and Washington which assured that any difficulties that might arise between the two powers would be settled by arbitration. The First World War led to the symbiotic relationship between the two great English-speaking peoples which has been maintained ever since. Again Hitler was the victim of an antiquated delusion of his own making.

7. Hitler's Conception of Economics and Administration

Hitler seldom spoke of economic questions in his *Table Conversations*. In the main, he was simply uninterested in them; the subject of economics had eluded his otherwise very broad general knowledge. He operated on the maxim that the state gives the orders and the economy complies.

In this respect Hitler had been spoiled by the course of events. There is no telling how many Germans who opposed Hitler were absolutely convinced that he would be brought down by the realities of the economic world—or if not brought down, at least forced to pull in his horns. But they were wrong. As things worked out—with the help of Hjalmar Schacht's economic policy, which in its own way was a work of genius—Hitler seemed to be vindicated by the development of the German economy. The recovery of the economy, its consolidation in the course of his policy of achieving autarky, and

---

[7]The *Saturday Review* article asserted that in "all parts of the earth, in every pursuit, in commerce, in manufacturing, in exploiting other races, the English and Germans jostle each other. . . . Were every German to be wiped out tomorrow, there is no English trade, no English pursuit that would not immediately expand. Were every Englishman to be wiped out tomorrow, the Germans would gain in proportion. Here is the first great struggle of the future: here are two growing nations pressing against each other, man to man all over the world. One or the other has to go; one or the other will go."—ED.

the financing of rearmament were all accomplished without precipi-
tating a severe economic crisis. Even the problem of covering the
staggering outlays of the war, which had been so difficult during the
First World War, was smoothly handled in the Second, without
the public even learning how. Nothing characterizes Hitler's relationship with this sector of public affairs as well as his treatment of
his finance minister, traditionally considered the most important of
the civilian cabinet officers during wartime. The last time Hitler saw
Count Lutz Schwerin von Krosigk was in 1942. All of Schwerin von
Krosigk's subsequent attempts to reach Hitler were in vain. Hitler
almost certainly sensed that the minister would come to him with
annoying statistics and unwelcome recommendations. Toward the
end, Schwerin von Krosigk could no longer even count on his
memoranda reaching Hitler's desk. Consequently, he worked
through Dr. Heinrich Lammers, chief of the Reich Chancellery,
whom Martin Bormann was not able to block.

To his mealtime companions, Hitler advocated state monopolies
in the iron, oil, coal, and power industries. At the same time he
wanted to retain private industry, since he felt there would otherwise be a terrible bureaucratization which would bring the whole
system to a grinding halt. Individual initiative should not be
smothered, he said repeatedly. This applied, however, only to those
private enterprises that were managed by the owners, or whose
owners were in any case readily identifiable. Monopolies by private
companies were to be eliminated completely. Hitler thought of
stocks as abominable objects of speculation which channeled the
profits of labor to nonworkers. He was, accordingly, very much
against public corporations owned by stockholders, as opposed to
privately owned ones, and considered the nationalization of the
former a long-range goal. The financing could be covered with
national bonds to be offered at a uniform interest rate.

The first reaction to these naive economic conceptions may be
to associate them with Gottfried Feder, the founder of a militant
anti-capitalist league and propagandist against "shrinking money,"
who once had advised Hitler on financial matters. But in fact the
origin of these ideas can be found in the years during which Hitler
saw how Mayor Lueger mobilized the Viennese lower middle classes

against "big business." It may well have been that at this time Hitler began to equate in his mind financial speculation, "criminal profits," exploitation of the workers by the idle rich, and "filthy Jewish parasitism."

Hitler believed that paying off the debt Germany incurred during the war would be a very simple matter. The value of the conquests would be many times greater than the cost of the war, and some twenty million foreign workers would be incorporated into the economy. Since the wages paid to these workers would only be half those paid to German workers, profits here alone would far exceed the national debt. "Finally," Hitler declared, brushing aside any objections before they could arise, "history teaches that no nation in the world has ever collapsed because of its debts." Two days after saying this, he added that if the war were not ended successfully, everything would be lost anyhow, so that for the sake of winning the war no accumulation of debt could be too great. Considering this kind of financial logic, it is all too easy to understand why Hitler evaded a conference with his finance minister.

Hitler's thoughts about administration corresponded to his thoughts about the economy. The administration simply *had* to function and to be ready for whatever demands the government placed on it, because the war effort required it. Among his table companions, Hitler repeatedly spoke with understanding about the dangers of too much centralization. No attempt should be made to force everything into an arbitrary pattern of conformity. The different German states should retain their individual customs and laws. Hitler also desired a multitude of smaller, middle-sized, and larger cities that would retain their character as centers of cultural life. Decentralization in these respects would make it easier for the central administration to find good men, since the more decentralized an administration was, the more opportunity men would have to work their way up through the regional organizations. By the same token, responsibility would have to be delegated from the top down.[8]

[8]These ideas of Hitler concerning decentralization by no means represented a departure from German tradition, but they differed sharply from National Socialist policy. All the German states but one were put under control of the central government when Hitler came to power; the exception, Prussia, did

Hitler could well afford to make such concessions to the German states because he had already broken their backs in 1933. He could depend upon the new links of control he had forged, which eliminated any possible danger to the unity of the Reich. "It will make a tremendous difference that throughout the entire Reich there is only *one* military establishment, *one* SS, and *one* administration."[9]

The war led the central government to tighten its hold on the country more than ever, even though before 1939 it had already exerted a degree of control unprecedented in German history. In addition, there was the increasingly severe reign of terror against anyone even suspected of being hostile to the Third Reich, so that the formation of centers of opposition was made as difficult as possible. Whatever his inclinations in the relaxed atmosphere of after-dinner conversation, all of Hitler's ideas about preserving the identity of the individual German states and delegating authority from the central government to the regional administrations succumbed to the exigencies of waging the war.

Apart from Hitler's practice of intervening in the administrative process and of establishing new institutions of overlapping and conflicting jurisdictions, with a result that one can only describe as an administrative jungle, Hitler's complete unfamiliarity with the daily workings of government must be emphasized. He had never spent a single day of his life employed in an administrative office of government and had had contact only with the very lowest echelon of the military bureaucracy during the First World War. His experience in building the National Socialist party had been characterized by improvisation, division, consolidation, reorganization, and the continual precaution that no one under any circumstances be permitted to build a base of power which might rival his own position as party leader.

---

not need to be taken over by the Nazis because it had already been taken over in a *coup* by Franz von Papen when he was Reich Chancellor in 1932.—ED.

[9]The tradition of particularism in Germany remained strong well into the twentieth century. Hitler had served as a soldier in the *Bavarian* Army. Even under the Weimar Republic, Germans carried passports issued by the states of Hesse, Prussia, Bavaria, and so forth. Only under the Third Reich did they acquire a general German citizenship, unless they were Jewish, in which case they were accorded German nationality but not German citizenship.—ED.

Consequently, Hitler did not have the background to understand, let alone manage, a well-regulated administration. Although he believed he was able to run things on the basis of his own experience, in fact his experience was not really applicable, since it had been gathered in areas in which entirely different conditions obtained. That Hitler despised "the bureaucrats" is a well-established fact. Why he despised them is now also clear.

8. Hitler's Taste and Interest in Art

Hitler considered the highest form of art to be architecture. Next he ranked sculpture, and after that painting. During his Vienna years, before moving to Munich in 1913, he had tried his hand at painting, and he would have given anything in the world to have become an architect, or so he told his listeners in May 1942. But the First World War had thrust him in another direction. Nonetheless, Hitler rated his own potential architectural talent very high, and boasted that he "probably would have become one of the first architects if not *the* architect of Germany"—a pipe-dream, surely, for architecture requires not only imagination and vision but also a solid foundation of knowledge and technical skill which Hitler lacked the opportunity, and quite possibly also the discipline, to acquire. But if it was a dream, it was a bold one, and dreams are almost always revealing. Perhaps just for this reason most people seal them in their hearts in order not to risk being doubted or even ridiculed—something Hitler did not need to be concerned about.

Hitler shared in the concept of genius which had emerged at the end of the eighteenth century and which in the nineteenth led to a veritable cult of genius that accorded the great painters, sculptors, actors, singers, and concert virtuosos a place of honor in society. Hitler, certainly, conceded this place to them. His associates marveled at how many artists' and performers' names he remembered from his Vienna years. Many of these crop up in the *Table Conversations*. The word "genius" recurs repeatedly. Hitler saw a relationship between the artist of genius and the statesman of genius. In his hours of triumph the conviction grew in him that Providence had also endowed him with genius—the sort of genius which would have enabled him to become a great artist had fate not put him instead in a position to go down in history as a great statesman and military leader, one whose impact as a great builder exceeded that of any king who ever lived.

The concept of genius had also played a central role with Nietzsche, whose case revealed the close relationship between genius and insanity. Our own century has become increasingly fascinated by the question of genius as new aspects of it have been opened up by psychoanalysis. The concrete question which confronts us here is whether Hitler really had any talent at all as an architect or whether it was simply a matter of self-deception, of sheer illusion.

Hitler did have an extraordinarily clear conception of space. Two examples can be cited. After the annexation of Austria, the Nuremberg chief of police told Hitler he had attended the theater in Graz. Asked what his impression of the building had been, he was able to talk only in very general terms. Thereupon Hitler mentioned that the transition from the stage to the auditorium had been poorly executed. The point of the story is that Hitler, at this time, had never been in Graz and knew the design of the theater only from sketches and illustrations. Then there is the incident of Hitler's visit to the Paris Opera in 1940, where he asked to see the oval room. He was told that there was no such room. Then Hitler pointed to a door, behind which he said it lay. It turned out that the large oval room had been subdivided into a number of smaller chambers so long ago that no one had remembered the original form, even though it could be deduced from the design of the ceiling. The Frenchmen present were rather disconcerted, the Germans greatly impressed.

As a painter Hitler never got beyond dabbling, and as an architect he never had a chance to prove himself at all. But he did have enough buildings erected to give some idea of what he might have done had he become an architect.

The Reich Chancellery in Berlin was so contrived for monumental effect that it was without any sense of proportion. The relationship between man and building, which has always been the basic problem of architecture, was clearly forgotten. Inside, the design and furnishings represented the superlative of the slightly modernized castle style of interior decoration affected by certain hotels. The Reich Chancellery was more imposing than the Palazzo Venezia, where Mussolini had his giant workroom. For sheer monumentality it also overshadowed anything in America. All things considered, it was a building of boundless pretentiousness, proclaiming to visitors from all the world: "Note well that you are now entering the place where the Führer of the Greater German Reich resides!"

Characteristic of Hitler as a private person was his own south German retreat, the *Berghof* overlooking Berchtesgaden. It was situated on a mountain slope and blessed with one of the most magnificent vistas in Germany. When Hitler acquired it, it had been a modest enough place, thoroughly in keeping with the style of the region. As he added on to it, he retained the old core intact as a side building. From the outside, consequently, the resulting complex was not architecturally significant.

After passing through the hallway, which led onto a spacious balcony, one entered the main room, where Hitler received distinguished guests and held conferences. It was a large room with a huge picture window, comfortably furnished with carpets, furniture, and flowers, much in the manner of the summer home of a cultivated industrialist. There was nothing to offend good taste, but neither was there anything which rose above bourgeois conventionality, and certainly nothing that was the slightest bit modern or that might have suggested any individuality on the part of the owner.

Hitler loved beautiful carpets, and on the walls he had a number of pictures he liked, which he changed every few months. There was a large drawing by Albrecht Dürer in the *Berghof,* a magnificent portrait of a man, which has probably been lost. But he also owned other, much less distinguished pictures, such as a painting by the Viennese artist Alt. A multi-volume encyclopedia was placed in a convenient spot.

Hitler preferred old furniture, but was willing to accept new furniture that was not too modern and had pleasant lines; he disliked clumsy club chairs. The revolution in furniture introduced by the

"Dessauer *Bauhaus*"—characterized by functional design and new materials—had to be sharply rejected by him insofar as he even took cognizance of it, since it contradicted his sense of beauty.

Hitler appreciated natural materials and was particularly fond of natural stone. He did not like stucco. He criticized the addition of balconies and the practice of framing windows with columns and the like. In this, as in other things, he had a point of view which was quite common in the period before the First World War.

Hitler loved flowers. Large bouquets adorned his rooms, and at the banquets he gave in peacetime they were used lavishly. He also liked giving away flowers. He cherished orchids, but he had no particular favorite flower and no appreciation for gardening. He regarded a bouquet rather as a beautiful still-life in the spirit of the Viennese Makart style, according to which arrangements of natural, dried, or artificial flowers had been an essential aspect of interior decoration.

Hitler was anything but revolutionary in the physical environment he created for himself. He adhered to tastes which were already being abandoned, even before the First World War, by those who set the style. They had been interested in the impressionists and even the expressionists, had been fascinated by Chinese lacquer work and the colorful prints of the Japanese (particularly because of the striking facial expressions), and had begun to decorate their homes with strange and expressive works from Africa and the South Seas. But there was no trace of any of this with Hitler, who was not even ready to recognize the art of all Europe.

One might expect that Hitler would have had a weakness for Germanic art, since so many Nazis outdid themselves in their enthusiasm for anything associated with the Germanic peoples. Indeed, ever since the publication of the much reprinted cultural call to arms by Gustaf Kossinna, *Die deutsche Vorgeschichte, eine hervorragend nationale Wissenschaft (German Prehistory: A National Science Par Excellence),* the serious academic study of German prehistory had become a part of German nationalism. It proved increasingly attractive to dilettantish dreamers, and as the party functionaries generally lacked the background to distinguish between solid researchers and charlatans, party-subsidized studies of early Germanic history account for one of the most dismal chapters in the history of German scholarship.

Hitler ignored all this. In fact, he dismissed it with the observation that while the Teutons were making their pots, the Greeks had already built the Parthenon. On another occasion he spoke of the "beautiful clarity of the ancient world." He considered the Pantheon, which he saw during his visit to Rome in 1938, one of the most perfect buildings of all time, and while viewing it he sent his retinue outside so he could concentrate on it undisturbed. He also wanted to be left alone in the Colosseum, and the grandiose dimensions of the Baths of Caracalla impressed him as well.

The Romanesque style of architecture had a certain similarity with that propagated by Hitler; although he was not fond of any particular building in this style, he did approve of its clear proportions, practicality, and force. The Gothic, on the other hand, he rejected altogether, judging it senseless in its exaggerations and in the excess of its ornamentation. Its upward thrust made him uncomfortable. He was willing to accept only the Strasbourg Cathedral, because its nave, in his opinion, was not so narrow as in other Gothic buildings. He was enthusiastic about the cathedral's famous angels' columns, presumably because the horizontal subdivision stood out and the figures were worked out of the stone in almost full relief. Hitler was, as is known, thinking of making this cathedral, after the final victory, into a monument for the Unknown Soldier of World War II. It is a frightful thought for those of us who survived the war that he might just have been able to do this.

Hitler regarded the pictures by the old German painters as important historical documents, but he ridiculed Göring for collecting them, contending that he did so because his father had bought a castle in Austria. Hitler explicitly rejected the early sixteenth-century German artist Matthias Grünewald because his paintings were "ugly."

For Hitler, the Italian Renaissance represented, as it had for Gobineau,[1] "the dawn of a new day, the self-discovery of Aryan

---

[1] The French diplomat and Orientalist Joseph Arthur de Gobineau's *Essay*

man." As he had put it earlier, "Basically we should be grateful to Jesuitism. Who knows whether without it we would have moved from the building style of the Gothic to the light, open, and bright architecture of the Counter-Reformation?" Hitler had no reservations about recognizing the greatness of Italian architecture; in this respect he was quite without nationalism. He praised the proportions of the Palazzo Pitti in Florence, with the great hewn stones of its foundation walls and its broad windows. In Naples he was impressed by the court of the royal palace, and in Venice by the monument of the Colleoni. In general he liked the height of the rooms.

Italy was a great experience for Hitler, as it was for many Germans. But he looked at it through the eyes of the nineteenth century. Since Heinrich Wölfflin's famous book *Renaissance and Baroque* appeared in 1888, the eyes of the educated traveling public had been opened to the Italian baroque as well as the Renaissance. But Hitler, on the whole, was not drawn to it, though he liked the large and colorful designs, and he approved of Versailles, to which he had been indirectly exposed by the copy that the Bavarian king, Ludwig II, had erected on the island Herrenchiemsee. Of the Belvedere in Vienna, the baroque palace of Prince Eugene of Savoy, Hitler could bring himself to appreciate only a few details—but then, the French baroque was so much more "classical" than the Austrian.

Hitler appreciated Rembrandt and Rubens, but more as great historical figures than as artists. He also accepted Poussin, but there is no evidence that he was really moved by these masters.

As a neoclassicist chiefly interested in clarity and grandeur, Hitler was unable to make anything of the art of the rococo, and he criticized the lack of powerful lines in the Empire style. He had ambivalent feelings about the painting of Romanticism and the Biedermeier style. He appreciated Blechen and Waldmüller, liked to look at pictures by Caspar David Friedrich, venerated Rottmann, the painter of heroically interpreted landscapes, and liked Schwind and Feuerbach. Adolf von Menzel he considered a God-inspired

---

on the Inequality of Human Races (1853–1855) propounded the theory that the white races, particularly the Aryans, had created civilization.—ED.

artist, for the content of his work as well as the diligence and precision of its representation.

While still in Vienna, Hitler acquired an interest in the *Jugendstil*[2] which he never entirely lost. Characteristically, he retained a preference for painters who had been esteemed during his youth, such as Makart and Alt in Vienna and Lenbach and Stuck in Munich—artists whose importance was already dubious before the First World War, and whose reputations have declined ever since.

The main purpose of the art gallery Hitler planned for Linz was to present a worthy display of nineteenth-century painting. He was proud that he had already acquired so many paintings by Defregger and his students that he would be able to fill a large display hall with its side galleries. He envisioned limiting the National Gallery in Berlin to Germanic and German painters and displaying its other holdings elsewhere. The consequence would have been a sort of compromise whereby the art of the Mediterranean world would by and large have been able to claim its due, but "Nordic" (and particularly its core, German) art would have received the place of honor it deserved in Hitler's eyes.

Hitler's appreciation of art ended with the nineteenth century. He was unable to make any sense out of impressionism and held Liebermann to be a dabbler. Although he found Corinth's youthful pictures excellent, he had many objections to his later work. In the plastic arts Hitler accepted sculptures that had a classic touch, for example, Adolf von Hildebrand's Munich fountain with its bulls; and he was enthusiastic about Kolbe's "Dancer" (1912), though he rejected his later work. Klimsch, on the other hand, became in Hitler's judgment "ever greater and more significant"—although today the very opposite is thought to be the case.

During the war Hitler took the time to go through back issues of the art magazine *Die Kunst,* which had once been quite authorita-

[2]More commonly known outside Germany as *Art Nouveau,* the *Jugendstil* emerged shortly before the turn of the century, achieving considerable prominence at the Leipzig Art Exposition of 1897. Self-consciously modern, the decorative "youth-style" theoretically advocated simplicity of design, but soon developed an egregious ornateness which contributed to its early oblivion.—ED.

tive but had come to be regarded with increasing circumspection. He came to the conclusion that "if one considers the niveau of art even in 1910, it is shocking to see—taking 1930 by comparison— how far it has declined." He regretted the languishing of the colorful weekly journal *Jugend (Youth),* which Georg Hirth had founded in 1896 to propagate the *Jugendstil.* Hitler saw nothing but "one single deformed blotch" in what had been created after 1922—a conclusion entirely consistent with his conception of the function of art: accurate portrayal, presenting what was beautiful pleasantly and what was magnificent grandly.

Hitler's support of artists was something of a "transvaluation of all values." Painters who were merely competent craftsmen were suddenly hailed as great masters. Artists with real ability were corrupted by Hitler's commissions, for they had to devote themselves to a strained monumentality and paint the desired themes in the approved fashion—"correctly" sketched, clearly painted, and pleasing in content. Worse still, a number of "artists" who deserved nothing more than general ridicule suddenly found themselves the subjects of great acclaim.

Hitler was nonetheless convinced that he was beginning a new and better chapter in the history of German art. For the exhibition in the "House of German Art" *(Haus der Deutschen Kunst)* in Munich there was a virtual flood of from ten to twelve thousand entries. From this number, 1,200 works were selected; these were all, as Hitler explained in July 1942, "in every respect first-class"— certainly an improbably high percentage. High standards of selectivity were guaranteed, according to Hitler, by the fact that the choice was made not by artists, who might have been biased, but rather by his personal photographer Hoffmann—a crass layman with petty bourgeois tastes—and the museum director Kolb. The fact that the undertaking was appreciated was said to have been demonstrated by the attendance of millions. What is so astounding about these remarks is the brazen self-confidence with which Hitler and his associates, whose credentials consisted of nothing more than antiquated prejudices and pretended expertise, decided what was good and what was bad.

As Hitler openly said, he would have liked to send "bad" painters to prison, to insane asylums, or possibly even for "rehabilitation" to concentration camps. What a conception of the struggle of the artist is revealed by this remark! But the fate of the versatile artist Ernst Barlach, who was forbidden to go on working, shows that Hitler was not making an empty threat.

In 1937 and 1938, Gert H. Theunissen wrote critical reviews of exhibitions at the "House of German Art" for the leading Cologne newspaper, *Kölnische Zeitung;* they were ostensibly favorable, but subtly and with remarkable skill they managed to suggest between the lines the state of atrophy in which German art found itself. Theunissen saw in German art produced under the Third Reich old, wrinkled farm wives, but without "the smell of poverty as in naturalism"; fresh, sun-tanned maids identified as heiresses to the family farm by the aluminum milk can in the background; women offering their well-rounded breasts to infant children; families gathered around the cradle in merry domesticity; and other paintings appealing to the innermost feelings and moods of the German people. But there were also many pictures of factories, inspired by the principle of the "beauty of labor," and a large number of more militant ones, such as "Thus Was the SA," showing a band of strapping brown-shirted rowdies marching down a lane formed by subhuman Communists. Last but not least, the exhibition included a lot of nudity.

Writing with feigned admiration, Theunissen ridiculed Josef Thorak's "massive monumentality" and "muscular tension" (rooted in biological insight), and Ferdinand Liebermann's giant female figures, which had even been given a "certain sacred consecration" by gilding the plaster. He noted that most visitors responded very favorably to the Gothic imitation represented by the greater-than-life-size oak figure by Margarete Hanusch—because it was already somehow familiar to them. But otherwise the critic did not note any imitations of earlier works or styles: "Generally a point of view is maintained which was worked out by the elder generation of living sculptors"—in other words, that of the end of the nineteenth century.

Moving idylls prevailed in painting: "Schwind and Richter are very influential," Theunissen wrote, "while the trailblazing work of the early romantics, to cite one case, has not yet been recognized to the extent, for example, that the Nazarenes have influenced the painters in this exhibition. Thus everywhere the attempt is made to follow the offshoots of different traditions in order to achieve a certain structure." Theunissen's ridicule is hardly even veiled when he remarks that Ziegler's female nudes, painted with the precision of photography, had enjoyed the strongest response—for the fact is that it was only a small step from his paintings to nude photography, which can always count on having its admirers.

In summary, Theunissen noted that the pleasant and passive predominated, for the basic principle had been observed that a painting above all should be suitable as a decoration for the home. The painting of Hitler's day was therefore characterized by a charming nostalgia and freedom from experimentation. In the graphic arts it was not important *how* the artist saw the world, but rather that he gave a precise duplication of *what* he saw. The hallmark of the exhibition was an optimistic representation of reality.

One Reich, one people, one Führer—and one art! A practical art which honored the political guidelines and by its philistinism corresponded to the lowest common denominator. An art which strove to turn history back thirty years or more while garnering raucous praise for being wholesomely progressive despite its corrosion of what was truly vital and creative. It was an art full of the trivial sentimentality of *Kitsch*,[3] and its "masterpieces"—insofar as they have not been destroyed or lost—have silently disappeared into the attic. In the meantime, real art, defamed as perverse and dumped overseas at giveaway prices, at best served the purpose of improving the balance of payments.

Today it would seem that such an attitude is—as a glance eastward shows—all but inevitable under totalitarian regimes, where men who have risen from below, encumbered with prejudices shaped by the art of the past, demand of art either that it serve them as a political tool or that it afford them pleasant relaxation. To this

---

[3]*Kitsch* is an untranslatable term which suggests an intellectually vacuous, often lugubrious, and tastelessly ornate style that gushed to its florid apogee in the latter nineteenth century.—ED.

extent Hitler, Khrushchev, and Ulbricht, however different they may otherwise be, constitute a reactionary clique attempting to arrest the development of art, and if possible set it back.

9. Music, Dance, and Literature

Like art, music played an important role in Hitler's life, though he never mastered any instrument. He had found, as a choir boy, that he sang badly, and he never tried it again. During his Vienna years, however, he became familiar with both opera and operetta, the *Fledermaus* and Lehár's *Merry Widow* being his favorites. There were many names from the musical world of the time that he never forgot.

Chamber music meant nothing at all to Hitler. He never acquired a taste for Bach and Beethoven, or for the music of the previous centuries which was finding a growing audience during his formative years. Hitler's real love in music was the opera. Mozart seems to have meant little to him, but he appreciated Weber's *Freischütz,* Puccini's *Bohème* and *Madame Butterfly,* Verdi's *Aida,* d'Albert's *Tiefland,* and several of Richard Strauss's operas. The music of such nineteenth-century composers as Schumann, Brahms, and Reger meant nothing to him, but he occasionally showed interest in the work of Bruckner. It was Richard Wagner who held his highest admiration, not only for his music but for his philosophical outlook and his subject matter. "When I listen to Wagner," Hitler declared to his circle, "it is like the rhythms of the primeval world!" This was the bygone golden age, which in Hitler's musings had acquired an extraordinary splendor and glory.

The *Berghof* was provided with a large collection of phonograph records and excellent phonographic equipment, but Hitler made little use of it. During the war his interest in music waned almost entirely.

Hitler saw in the art of the dance, as in music, one of the most fundamental expressions of the culture of a nation. He admired dancers of stature who remained true to their art as he understood it, refraining from what he considered mere acrobatics. He was never able to understand or appreciate the art of modern dance, toward which traditional ballet was moving in a number of respects. His impression of a dress rehearsal of the Berlin Opera was that it was a group of philosophers dancing under the direction of a woman of intellect. Goebbels tried to interest him in Gret Palucca, who had been celebrated since the twenties; Hitler attended one of her performances and thought it had nothing to do with dancing, but looked rather more like so much hopping around punctuated with strenuous leaps into the air. His nineteenth-century ideal of the dancer remained the beautiful picture of a gracious creature gliding weightlessly across the stage with no other purpose than to delight the eye.

We should note at this point that just as, for Hitler, the architect and the statesman were related, so also were the orchestra conductor and the leader of the masses. Occasionally he would tell how on one occasion in 1926 he had gradually succeeded, by the power of suggestion, in bringing a group of listeners gathered in Weimar around to the very opposite of what they had expected. That had taught him "how cleverly, how slowly, and how much as a very great artist one has to move forward." Hitler had no need of Le Bon's works on social psychology to become a greater master of mass suggestion than the Pied Piper of Hamelin. He needed only the gifts he had been born with, the guiding concept of himself as the conductor, and above all a fund of practical experience which grew from year to year.

Although there is much to say about Hitler's appreciation of art and music, he had remarkably little interest in literature. His only contact with the German classics was with whatever might have become familiar to him during his youth or at the theater. It is striking how few references to literature appear in Hitler's speeches. According to Dr. von Hasselbach, Hitler had no appreciation for poems, particularly lyric poetry. Novels seemed to him to be a waste of time. This man who read so much thus chose to cut himself off from one of the most essential areas of German intellectual life. Through the novel he might have familiarized himself with the basic intellectual problems of the previous half-century, but he did not do so.

10. Memory and Knowledge

We now move from Hitler as he took in the world with his eyes and ears to the manner in which he thought and formed his convictions. We shall concern ourselves with his relationship to history and the natural sciences, as well as with the faith he developed for himself. We should consider, in general terms, Hitler's native intelligence, the knowledge he acquired in his youth, how he later extended it, and how he went about assimilating whatever he learned.

One of Hitler's capacities which impressed everyone, including those who did not like him, was his stupendous memory. It enabled him to retain inessentials exactly and to store away everything he ever saw: his teachers and classmates; the figures in the Wild West stories of Karl May; the authors of books he had once read; even the brand name of the bicycle he had used as a courier in 1915. He also remembered the exact dates of events in his political career, the inns where he had stayed, and the streets on which he had been driven. This was a capacity he took for granted, and he was not particularly impressed by it.

But with such a highly developed memory, Hitler was able to recall precisely all reports made to him, including specific numbers, so that officers had to be meticulously careful that what they said agreed completely with whatever they had told him earlier. If Hitler perceived any contradiction whatever, his suspicion that an attempt was being made to deceive him, never far beneath the surface, was instantly aroused.[4]

His remarkable memory, together with iron diligence and a strong power of concentration, had enabled Hitler in the course of the years to acquire knowledge of a scope and detail that again and

[4]A characteristic example was the case of the navy captain who gave Hitler situation briefings on the war at sea. He told me once that by mistake he gave the number of submarines in the Mediterranean as one too many. Having checked it out with the Navy High Command, he would have to casually slip in a correction during the briefing the next day. Otherwise, if one or two U-boats were sunk in the next couple of weeks, Hitler might ask about the rest. There would be the very devil to pay if the figures did not add up correctly—since Hitler would be sure to have all the numbers in his head.

again amazed persons talking with him, and earned him sincere admiration. For this reason alone, Hitler was in a position to assume the dominant role in mealtime conversations with his circle, since he had something to say about absolutely everything that came up. If any issue did remain in question, it usually worked out, when the encyclopedia was consulted, that Hitler had been right after all.

In order to clarify his mind on a topic, Hitler would walk back and forth alone in a room—"for kilometers," as he himself put it. But then he still needed to talk out his "rough draft" thoughts in "clean copy," so to speak. This was, in fact, one of the functions (aside from relaxation) the mealtime conversations had for him. When someone who knew what was on his mind set him going with a key word he was able to launch immediately into an almost formal lecture. In order to organize his thoughts, he inserted "in the first place," "secondly," and like phrases. Even so, he often went off on a tangent, as other thoughts came to mind. For the same reason, his formal speeches often have such sudden transitions that they cannot be reconstructed in logical terms. Yet he never lost sight of the goal he had set himself in a conversation or a speech. He would therefore finally arrive at the conclusion he had set out to reach, the acceptance of which, by the audience, he considered to be self-evident.

Hitler never achieved the type of rigidly logical thinking which the Catholic Church inculcates in its priests and the General Staff in its officers. This is shown, for example, by his Berlin Sports Palace speech in May 1942 to the officer candidates of the Wehrmacht, which displays all the typical characteristics of his way of thinking. According to what Dr. Picker learned from the stenographer, Hitler apparently dictated the entire speech in one session. Presented with the emphatically masculine gestures and the verve Hitler displayed on such occasions, and delivered in the sonorous voice that fascinated many, this speech presumably had a strong impact on the officer candidates, who would have been prepared to respond to a commander-in-chief who, in the course of the past three years, had won victories unprecedented in military history. But as effective as the speech must have seemed to the listeners, anyone attempting to follow the main thoughts or to trace the logic of their relationships with each other will become aware of how many gaps and breaks the structure has as a whole.[5]

As far as his attempt to provide himself with historical background was concerned, it must be noted that even during the war, despite the great pressures and the excessive burden of thousands of details, Hitler still managed to read. He mentioned to his mealtime companions, in connection with a history of mankind which Bormann had given him, that he had been much interested in Franz Petri's book on the Germanic heritage in the Walloon areas of Belgium and in northern France, a scholarly study which had been brought to his attention by a newsreel correspondent. In another conversation he showed that he was familiar with Karl Pagel's recent history of the Hanse. Occasionally he had General Walther Scherff, the Chief of Military History at his headquarters, provide him with the four-volume set of the speeches of William II, to see how the Kaiser had addressed the German people. Once he unexpectedly came upon General Scherff reading Ernst Kantorowicz' biography of Frederick II, the medieval Hohenstaufen emperor; yet he did not, as feared, make a derogatory remark about the emigrant author, but only mentioned that he himself had read the book twice. According to his physician, Dr. von Hasselbach, Hitler also felt "obliged to look through the principal German newspapers and magazines regularly." But no systematic attempt was made to ac-

---

[5]This is the reason why it was so difficult to reduce Hitler's speeches to a clearly outlined summary, as I was able to observe when it was made possible for me, through personal connections, to hear a speech which Hitler delivered on January 27, 1944, to generals brought in from all fronts. Its purpose was to give them all a massive "booster shot" (as it was put at the time) on the eve of the Allied landing in the West, which was anticipated in the next few months. I sat in the last row of the meeting room at the *Wolfsschanze* and made notes on Hitler's presentation, despite the fact that it was prohibited, since I was not endangered from behind and was unobserved from in front. But when, on the basis of my notes, I attempted immediately afterward to reconstruct Hitler's line of thought, I found out that this was possible only in very approximate terms; though he had never lost sight of his goal, he had gone off on many tangents and permitted himself many interjections in and interruptions of his line of thought.

quire reading material that would be of interest to him, so what came into his hands was largely a matter of chance.

When in 1944 the suspicion arose that Hitler's weakness, which greatly concerned his doctors, might not be due to the aftereffects of the assassination attempt of July 20 but rather to a case of strychnine poisoning, Hitler, before consulting his physicians, attempted to figure it out for himself with the help of medical books. He liked to examine controversial issues personally, and he always kept a number of reference works at hand in his living quarters, a practice that owed something, no doubt, to the perpetual suspicion of this man who never fully trusted anyone.

Hitler occasionally observed, as Dr. von Hasselbach reports, "that hardly a day passed when he did not work his way through the essential contents of a book." He did this during the late night and early morning hours, the only time when he was alone. Hasselbach goes on to say that Hitler could not possibly have read his books page by page, but at the same time the expression "work through" cannot simply be dismissed as conceited exaggeration, for he did grasp and retain the essential content. Hitler himself confided that he read books from back to front, a procedure that served the purpose of assuring him that the content of the book at hand was worthwhile. If not, he either laid it aside or got only as much out of it as he needed to polemicize against the author. The more convinced Hitler became of the unassailable validity of his *Weltanschauung,* however, the less question there could be of his entering into an intellectual dialogue with an author, calmly evaluating and reflecting on what he read. Consequently, it seems futile for the purpose of discovering the cultural and intellectual influences on Hitler's thought to reconstruct a list of books which he may have read.[6] Considering the intellectual violence with which he adapted whatever he read to his preconceptions, one can at most speak of certain intellectual affinities or parallels.

It would certainly have been conceivable for a man of such om-

[6]It is sufficient here merely to note Hitler's remark of May 21, 1942, "that during [his] youth no two other men had interested [him] as much as Fridtjof Nansen and Sven Hedin."

nivorous reading habits to have invited recognized figures in German intellectual life to share their views with him. But Hitler simply did not rely on others to answer the basic questions that concerned him. He shunned the scholarship that would have put him in a position to select what seemed best to him from the arguments presented. Anyone of caliber whom Hitler received had already been screened for his ideas, and if a conversation ensued, it was dominated by Hitler; the only use he had for such visitors, aside from gleaning certain definite information, was to confirm him in his basic opinions. In one of his books William II was able to refer to a number of leading personalities of intellectual stature with whom he had contact. The corresponding list which a biographer of Hitler might compile would include only names which mean nothing at all any more or are remembered with disdain or scorn.

School had done little for Hitler's education, and during his period in Vienna before the First World War he read only what he came upon by accident. He drew together his store of knowledge from conversations, newspaper and magazine articles, brochures, and books he chanced to borrow. He lacked the money to buy books, but even if he had had it, he might well have spent it on works of dubious quality, for he knew no one who would have been able to give him serious guidance or help him make critical evaluations. Until he became a soldier at the age of twenty-five, he had probably never had the opportunity for discussion with a cultivated, well-educated person, and therefore never experienced a genuinely intellectual exchange; nor did he acquire a systematic way of thinking.

The knowledge which Hitler had when he became a soldier and with which he began his political career after the defeat in World War I—almost certainly he had not added to it significantly during the war—was therefore that of a self-educated person. The determination and diligence with which he went about acquiring whatever he knew was nothing short of amazing. But the basic disadvantages associated with self-education remained characteristic of Hitler's thinking until the very end. Once he had come to power, it was, according to Dr. von Hasselbach's testimony, no longer possible to persuade him to change his mind. "Even mild objections were far more apt to be taken wrongly and lead to a further hardening of his position, the very opposite of what was intended by them."

Hitler's knowledge, then, based on his retentive memory and assiduous reading, was remarkably extensive, but it retained a fortuitous and arbitrary character as the result of his self-education. It never developed and matured, because the rising politician was not willing to expose himself to qualified specialists and professionals. In the end, at the height of his power, his mind became completely rigid, because he was convinced that he knew best in all matters, intellectual and otherwise.

There emerges the picture of a half-timber house, the framework of which was constructed of the cheapest lumber because the builder could afford nothing better. Moreover, since he had no competent craftsman to help or counsel him, he put it together in whatever way seemed best to him. To fill the spaces between the timbers he had picked up bricks wherever he could find them—old and new, oversized ones which he had broken to fit, firm ones, but others already crumbling, completely at random as chance would have it. Nor did the builder change his approach when he finally got the chance to acquire the very best materials. Least of all did it occur to him to replace the soft pine framework, even though it was already splitting badly in places, for he was unshakable in his conviction that the basic structure of his house was sound. At most he would consider a few small additions to it.

Thus we find in Hitler a great eagerness to learn, coupled with the most intractable intellectual rigidity and arrogance. The *Table Conversations* clearly show the extent of this intellectual arrogance. The most ridiculous information is presented and uncritically accepted whether originating from Hitler personally or from his satellites. It was, for instance, reported to Hitler in July 1942 that of the rebels apprehended in connection with recent disturbances in Serbia, between 95 per cent and 99 per cent had criminal records. Hitler never thought to question how it was possible to arrive so quickly at such a remarkable assessment. None of the apprehended rebels who had criminal records were apt to have volunteered the information, and it is unlikely that the confused Serbian bureaucracy, even if so disposed, could have provided documentation on even as many as 30 per cent. But Hitler declared that the very high percentage did not surprise him at all; it merely confirmed the impression about insurrectionists which he had developed in Germany in 1918–1919.

He was also prepared to accept a report that coincided with his concept of the Roman Catholic Church, whereby Franco had accorded to St. Tununcisla the full military honors of a field marshal, because she had protected the "Whites" in Segovia. A call to a specialist in Hispanic literature and culture would easily have established the fact that there never was a saint in Segovia with that un-Spanish-sounding name. In any case, immediately following this revelation one of the members of Hitler's circle produced a similar tale—an example not only of the uncritical acceptance of what Hitler said, but also of the manner in which his followers echoed him.

11. Hitler's Relationship to History

It was in history, according to Dr. von Hasselbach, that Hitler was most interested: "In long conversations he would repeatedly make it the basis of his political reflections and projections."

"Whoever has no sense of history is like a person without hearing or without a face; he can live that way," remarked Hitler in July 1941, "but what kind of a life is that?" This sounds a bit like an allusion to Goethe's remark that anyone unable to account for four thousand years would spend his lifetime as a fool. But the similarity is mere accident, for Hitler had no intellectual affinity with Goethe.

Hitler liked to consider himself and his lifework in the stream of history; he saw himself as someone who gleaned examples and warnings from the past regarding what he had done and was undertaking. It should therefore explain much about Hitler's vision of himself if, by summarizing his judgments, we can reconstruct his picture of the course of world history.

Hitler's knowledge of primeval times appears to have been slight, despite the fact that even in the nineteenth century a plausible picture of the stages of development and a reasonably precise chronology of the prehistoric period had been formulated. He questioned whether it might not be necessary to conclude from the myths of the Greeks and the Germanic peoples that there had once been a natural catastrophe that destroyed an earlier erect form of mankind. To the objection that this was not archaeologically demonstrable, he replied with the contrived thesis that metal, as opposed to stone, is transitory, so that any traces of such an extremely early bronze- or iron-age civilization would in effect have rusted away. In any case, this culture could have flourished in areas which today lie beneath the sea. These and similar thoughts of a "Golden Age," including the myth of the lost continent of Atlantis, are, of course, not unique to Hitler.

As a neoclassicist, Hitler had serious reservations about the glorification of the early period of the Germanic peoples—unlike many of his followers. For all the Germanic prejudice of many Nazis, Hitler recognized the greatness of the culture of antiquity and the statesmanship of the Romans: "The real centers of culture, not only during the last millennia before Christ but also in the first thousand years after his birth, were the lands of the Mediterranean." The decline of classical civilization preoccupied him as an example of what he felt he had to prevent in his own time. "I often reflect on what caused the fall of the ancient world," he said in conversation in January 1942, and he then proceeded to give as reasons for that decline the degeneration of the ruling class, which produced fewer and fewer children, and the growth in the number of slaves. At another time he explained that it was not the Huns and Germans who had destroyed the Roman Empire, but rather Christianity, to which he attributed a corrupting influence similar to that of Bolshevism—a variation of a hypothesis propagated in the eighteenth century by Edward Gibbon and thereafter advocated in a number of different forms.

After the fall of the Roman Empire, according to Hitler, Europe had been continually threatened from the East. This had happened during the time of the Huns and the Mongols, and the danger would have been renewed by the Bolsheviks if action had not been taken against them. Hitler had only the most naive conception of the Slavs, who were so important in this connection. He derived the Bulgarians from the Turkomans; the Czechs, he decided on the basis of appearance, were descended from Mongolian tribes. Historically speaking, this was sheer nonsense. But no one contradicted him—in this case probably not even out of cowardice, but rather out of ignorance.

During the Middle Ages the threat from the East was successfully averted by the "German emperors," as he called them, ignoring the fact that the Holy Roman emperors were not primarily concerned with Germany at all. At their head, so far as Hitler was concerned, stood Charlemagne. The defamation of the great Frankish leader for slaughtering the Saxons, which had been carried on by Himmler and other prominent Nazis in league with amateur historians, had already drawn Hitler's criticism before the war in a speech in Erfurt. In the *Table Conversations* the name of Charlemagne comes up repeatedly, and always with an expression of veneration.[7]

Hitler also admired Charlemagne's successors, who in his eyes had enjoyed the uncontested mastery of the world for five hundred years: "Aside from ancient Rome, the history of the medieval emperors is the mightiest epic the world has ever seen." The personal stature of the emperors was "undoubtedly something quite different than that of the petty farmer Henry the Lion." Here again he repudiated his party comrades, who held up the Guelph Duke Henry, together with Henry I and Lothair III, against the emperors with their fateful Italian policy, and regarded Henry the Lion as a pioneer in national settlement of the East. Considering the structure of Europe at that time, Hitler found it understandable that the emperors moved south rather than eastward.[8]

[7]Charlemagne, known in German as *Karl der Grosse* (Charles the Great), is regarded by many Germans as no less French than German. This position is historically valid, insofar as a division between France and Germany occurred only after his reign, while no separate German state even began to emerge until more than a century after his death.—ED.

[8]Henry the Lion, duke both of Saxony and Bavaria and a twelfth-century contemporary and challenger of Emperor Frederick Barbarossa, was the leader in Germany of the anti-imperial Guelph (or Welf) Dynasty. Frederick established the power of the Hohenzollern Dynasty (known in Italy as the Ghibellines), suppressed Henry the Lion, and vigorously sought to assert

The fact that the medieval empire was electoral rather than hereditary was regarded by Hitler, contrary to general opinion, as an advantage. He felt that hereditary monarchy automatically led to degeneracy. In this respect the medieval empire seemed to him to be more like a republic, though of course a Germanic one (perhaps an early form of the "Führer-state").

On occasion Hitler acknowledged that the papacy was a grandiose organization. Naturally, however, he was opposed to medieval Rome no less from his extreme German nationalism than from his anticlericalism. Consequently, he regarded the period from the third to the seventeenth century as an epoch of cultural impoverishment, brought about by the spiritual narrow-mindedness cultivated by the Church in its quest for power.

It was in this context that Hitler came to praise Luther, even though he stood further from the Protestant Church than the Catholic. Hitler recognized the German reformer as a great man, but at the same time criticized him for not having gone further. After him, however, there were only followers and imitators in his Church.

From Hitler's biological perspective, the various civil wars in the course of history generally turned out not to be regrettable at all, since they were a necessary phase in the growth and maturity of peoples. According to him, the German people, seen as a nation, were the "combined product of violence, ideas from antiquity, and Christianity."

Hitler praised Rudolf of Habsburg because this petty prince from southwest Germany acquired Austria, then on Europe's eastern frontier, as a base of power for his dynasty, defeated Ottokar of Bohemia, and restored unity to the empire which had lacked firm leadership during the generation following the death of Emperor Frederick II in 1250. Hitler also had kind words for the

---

imperial power in Italy rather than to develop a strongly centralistic kingdom in Germany. Long before the National Socialists came along, this "sacrificing" of German national interests for the sake of an international imperial ideal had been excoriated by German patriots who singled out Henry I and Lothair III, together with Duke Henry the Lion, as lonely examples of the kind of leadership which might conceivably have brought Germany out of the Middle Ages as a strong and united nation-state rather than a weak and fragmented federal empire.—ED.

empire under Rudolf's successors, who brought it to a number of "truly high points." The Habsburg Monarchy must be given full credit "for having upheld the German idea even in a period when the medieval Reich had disintegrated into individual states and was literally being torn to shreds by dynastic interests."

The fact that he had been born in Austria and that his first strong impressions were from the imperial city of Vienna meant something to Hitler throughout his entire life. But he consciously tore himself free from such fond sentiments and acknowledged that Prussia, after all, had won the Austro-Prussian War in 1866 and renewed the Reich. It is understandable that among the Hohenzollern kings of Prussia, Hitler favored Frederick William I, that "bull of absolutism," because of his strict training methods. Hitler identified himself more and more with Frederick the Great, who despite all his defeats held out until he got what he wanted, for Hitler's own position seemed to become more and more similar to that of Frederick *before* the surprising change for the better. There is no need to elaborate here upon how false the analogy was.

Naturally it was Bismarck whom Hitler regarded as the most important historical figure of the nineteenth century, but there is no evidence that he made any attempt to study the speeches and writings of the chancellor, though they might have profited him. What had a lasting effect on Hitler from his own experience was the memory of how England, France, and Russia had joined together in 1904–1907 in a policy of "encirclement." He must have read many articles about this during those years, since the patriotic nationalist press was full of alarm. Almost certainly Hitler knew the book of the retired General Friedrich von Bernhardi, *Germany and the Next War,* which appeared in 1912, and in which the author suggested that, in view of the threat, Germany should smash the ring by a preventive war before it finally closed. The thought that he—once risen to the position of "Führer of the Greater German Reich"—would have to act decisively in time to prevent a new encirclement became one of the basic principles of Hitler's policy.

In this respect he "learned" directly from history. But as in the case of Frederick the Great, the analogy which he sensed was false. As a matter of fact, by his very advances beyond the borders of the

German Empire as established by Bismarck, Hitler himself forged the ring that finally choked him. It is a terrible enough fate for people not to learn from their history, but more frightful still when they misunderstand it.

Again and again one sees how fortuitous and unbalanced Hitler's understanding of history was, despite his mastery of so many individual details and facts. But though we are dealing with the undisciplined knowledge of a self-educated mind, we can nonetheless attempt to determine where Hitler stood in the development of historical understanding.

In the year 1841 Thomas Carlyle's book of lectures *On Heroes, Hero-Worship, and the Heroic in History* appeared, a book that Hitler probably read at some time or other. In 1842, King Ludwig I of Bavaria dedicated the temple-like "Walhalla" near Regensburg, in which the busts of all great Germans were to be displayed. The basic conception that it is men who make history was adhered to by idealistically oriented German historiography until the beginning of the twentieth century. Emperor William II, with widespread public approval, set up the "Siegesallee" ("Victory Boulevard") in the Berlin *Tiergarten,* characterizing all the Hohenzollerns as benefactors and heroes.

Nevertheless, the fact that this approach to history was already questionable by 1900 was shown by the considerable agitation surrounding Karl Lamprecht's conception of history, which was by no means limited to specialists in the field, and which continued throughout the decade before World War I. Taking into account the new insights of psychology, Lamprecht advocated a form of cultural history which left the previous foundations of the hero cult in question. It was the First World War, however, that delivered the final verdict on the role of the hero in history. With the possible exception of Lenin, neither among the victors nor the vanquished did any single individual achieve the kind of stature that would make it possible for anyone to speak of him as a "maker of history." From this point on, whenever historical figures were presented biographically, primary attention was apt to be given—witness the case of Bismarck—to the imperfections in their life work, the instances in which they had not reached their goals, and the extent to which they were limited by the perspectives of their own times. Systematic research in social and economic history had already begun in the nineteenth century in response to such thinkers as Karl Marx, while since the turn of the century the protagonists of intellectual history had been directing attention to the influence of ideas. In 1908, the German historian Friedrich Meinecke published *Weltbürgertum und Nationalstaat,* an epoch-making study of cosmopolitanism and nationalism. William II's "Victory Boulevard" was therefore a relic of the past not only in artistic terms but for the entire conception of history which it represented. In sum, by 1900 it was no longer possible to plot the course of history in terms of a series of history-making figures.

But Hitler appears to have remained oblivious to everything scholarship contributed since the beginning of the twentieth century to broadening the scope of historical understanding. He clung instead to the ideas of another era—to King Ludwig and his "Walhalla." Though the relationship between Hitler's conception of history and his *Führerprinzip,* the basic principle of leadership with which he sought to overcome democracy, is very clear, it would be a mistake to conclude that his study of history led him to this conclusion. It is more correct to say that because he advocated it he discovered its advantages in history.[9]

In Hitler's understanding of history, the great events brought about by great men stood in the foreground. Yet he regarded the course of history as being predetermined in two respects. In the first place, he thought that international power politics was inexorably influenced by geopolitics, as spelled out by Rudolf Kjellén in his book *Die Grossmächte der Gegenwart (The Great Powers of the Present),* which had first appeared in 1914 and had found such a responsive audience that by 1930 it was in its twenty-third printing. Second came his understanding of the pseudo-Darwinian idea

[9]The *Führerprinzip* or "leadership principle" was a rigid, hierarchical conception prescribing absolute obedience to those above, demanding absolute obedience from those beneath. Thus it reversed both the democratic flow of authority from below and the corollary idea of the consent of the governed, and instead dictated the absolute rule of the Leader over everyone below him.—ED.

that in the struggle between peoples, no less than between individuals, might makes right.

The presence of Germanic blood was Hitler's explanation for the greatness of other nations. According to this view, the English ruling class came from Lower Saxony and the majority of the soldiers who had led England to victory in her wars were also of German origin. The United States was partly established by German blood, and American technology flourished because its founders were almost exclusively of Swabian-Alemannian background. So far as Italy was concerned, Hitler's observation was that one can still see the German influence in Lombardy. Germans had also helped the tsars of Russia set up their empire. Even Atatürk, the father of modern Turkey, was "a blue-eyed person who certainly had absolutely nothing to do with the Turks." Hitler would probably have liked to claim him also as a crypto-German.

To Hitler these facts were proof for his thesis that the German people were capable of establishing themselves as a world power: "All of these organizing activities in connection with other nations [trade, industry, colonialism, and so forth] can be attributed to this unconscious desire to expand . . . [the German] base of power."

Insofar as Hitler was not dealing with matters of common knowledge, none of the historical judgments which he makes in the *Table Conversations* can be accepted at face value—though they were not always entirely false. But whether his historical knowledge was well founded or not cannot in itself be a consideration in judging his personality. There have been many politicians who never even acquired so much as false information about history. One should have a clear impression, however, of the incontrovertible certainty with which Hitler presented his version of history to his patient and indeed admiring circle of table companions, for only then can one appreciate the implications of Hitler's conception of the past. Fortuitous and uninstructed as it was, and distorted by hero worship and glorification of the Germanic, Hitler's relationship to history was a major influence on both his thinking and his actions. He transformed the historical information he gathered into an explosive of terrible power.

12. Hitler's Interest in Medicine and Natural Science; His Pseudo-Darwinism

Hitler was free of superstition and spoke with scorn of the "horoscope swindle" in which so many Nazi party functionaries, from Hess and Himmler down to the grass-roots level, believed. For tactical reasons he did go so far as to make some concessions to the continuing superstition of the masses on various points, for example, with measures involving the number thirteen.

We have the testimony of his personal physician, Dr. von Hasselbach, that Hitler's knowledge in the medical field was above average. "He saw to it that he was regularly informed about the progress being made and solicited literature on it. Nevertheless, he did not venture to measure his judgment against that of the professional, nor did he attempt to influence his decisions. He asked for an explanation of the reasons [for the doctor's decisions] and wanted to have explained as precisely as possible the way in which the various medications would work. It was entirely in accord with this critical attitude toward medical questions that he ridiculed nostrums, but fully recognized the triumphs of scientific medicine [such as] the success of vaccination in preventing smallpox epidemics throughout World War I. In other respects, he harbored prejudices which he refused to change, for example, the erroneous opinion that the human body is fundamentally vegetarian, and that it consequently will perform better with vegetarian nourishment than with a mixed diet of meat and vegetables."

Hitler's interest in medicine stemmed largely, of course, from his concern with his own health. If a question disturbed him, he referred to professional reference works which stood at his disposal, as for example when he came down with jaundice during the summer of 1944. Even in areas in which the layman normally relies on the physician, he had his own opinions. He regarded cancer, as he once explained to his listeners, as the result of a sustained poisoning of the human organism, presumably caused by improper nourishment.

Hitler was interested in astronomy and passed on the impressions he had picked up in his random reading as irrefutable statements of fact. The craters on the moon were brought about by the crashing of smaller moons, there were other inhabited planets, and so forth. Hitler had read much to extend his knowledge in other natural sciences, but here he also remained self-educated insofar as he was educated at all. Even in this area he scorned the thought of allowing himself to be informed by recognized authorities. This led, in one instance, to his being taken in by the *Welteislehre,* the world-ice theory, which had originated with the Austrian engineer Hanns Hörbiger, a conception which the SA, following Hitler's lead, attempted to propagate. Though anyone with a working knowledge of the subject could have pointed out that the theory was an absolutely untenable fantasy dreamed up by a man who was not taken seriously by responsible scholars, Hitler went on from this abstruse theory to the most unlikely speculations. Perhaps around the year 10,000 B.C. the earth had been rammed by the moon, and the possibility could not be ruled out that the earth at that point thrust the moon into its present orbit.

The area of natural science which interested him most and had the greatest impact on his philosophy of life and consequently also his politics was biology. It is difficult to identify his thinking in this field with any particular school of thought. His ideas were based on Gregor Mendel's laws of heredity, which by about 1900 had come to be generally recognized, but he thought of them in rigid terms and was oblivious to the fact that since the beginning of the twentieth century research in mutation had led to alterations in and a sophistication of the earlier theory. Hitler's other touchstone was Charles Darwin, whose teaching he applied in the vulgarized form in which, by the end of the nineteenth century, it had become common knowledge. What this amounted to was "Social Darwinism": Darwin's biological insight cited as the rationalization for a theory of government and statecraft which attempted to justify the power politics of the strong against the weak. How could the smaller nations complain about being overpowered by the larger ones, considering that precisely the same thing had been going on in nature since the beginning of time?

Aside from this doctrine of "natural selection in the struggle for existence," Hitler also liked to avail himself of the biological principle of "selective sexual breeding," according to which the female's attraction to the strongest of the males would preserve the best and strongest of the species. In this manner, the rigid laws of heredity could be reconciled with the trend toward breeding a better race.

In addition, there is the concept of "development," which played a dominant role in Hitler's thinking. In Hitler's view, nothing was right except "what corresponds to the processes of nature," for nature had already given us examples to follow. Presumably on this basis, Hitler came to the conclusion that the bicycle was correctly constructed, but that Count Zeppelin's dirigible was not, and that the design of ships would also have to be changed. One evening Hitler explained: "Just as the bird represents, in comparison to the flying fish, a higher stage of development, the ship is a preliminary stage of the airplane. The future belongs to the airplane." In the field of technology, Hitler was so obsessed with the thought of development that he said he felt it was a shame to live in a time when people were not even conscious of what the new world could look like.

Hitler considered man, no less than nature and technology, to be caught up in the process of development. The purpose of education he thought to be the application of appropriate measures to give this development wholesome guidance while warding off any pernicious influences. This was the purpose of the *Hitler-Jugend* (Hitler Youth organization) as well as the responsibility of the teachers, many of whom were still doing a far from satisfactory job of ideological indoctrination. The task of reaching those who were already older lay with the political educators, particularly statesmen in public life.

For the forging of a successful people, however, education alone was not enough: "There is not a thing in the world, no substance, and certainly no human institution which does not sooner or later begin to weaken.... The hardest steel shows fatigue; all the elements decompose." This inexorable consummation, "racial death," could be postponed only by hardening. The stronger triumphs and is thereby justified. It is well that it is so, for only in this manner can what is vital be built up. A people following these laws is charged by nature with the task of multiplying itself, even if it does not have sufficient space in which to live *(Lebensraum)*. If it consequently attempts to expand by means of force, that is only just, for that is the intention of nature, which forces conflict in order to strengthen the superior and lead them to victory. One night late in January 1942, Hitler formulated this thought as follows: "According to the eternal law of nature, the land belongs to whoever wins it, because the old boundaries do not leave enough room for the expansion of the population." For this reason alone the stronger must be more prolific. This creates hardship and forces them to move in order to avoid the danger of racial death. That one devours the other is frightful, but that is the way things are.

The following July, Hitler said he was "an ardent advocate of the belief that in the struggle between peoples, those with the better-than-average quality will always be the victors." In his opinion, "the natural order of things would be disrupted if the inferior should master the superior."

Frederick the Great had once observed that "the dear Lord is on the side of the stronger battalions." If Hitler, who often enough cited Frederick as his example, had also subscribed to the view that numerical superiority is decisive in war, he would have had to acknowledge that ever since the entry of Russia into the war, or, at the very latest, that of the United States, the odds were clearly against him, the more so as raw materials and industrial capacity also had to be considered. But Hitler countered this calculation with the simplistic statement that the stronger would prevail over the weaker: just as in nature the stronger creature overcomes the weaker, in human affairs the people of stronger character win out over those whose character is wavering or unwholesome. Just as in nature one can predict with certainty the victory of the hound over the hare or the lion over the gazelle, Hitler believed that he could prophesy the victory of the Germans over their inferior enemies.

Thus one link was joined to the next in what seemed to Hitler to be a logical and scientifically irrefutable series. Thus was forged the horrible chain that shackled millions, threatened all Europe, and dragged Germany into the abyss.

It is not unique to Hitler's Germany that the work of Darwin should have been exploited to legitimatize political violence. Pseudo-

Darwinistic arguments have played a more or less important role in the political polemics of all civilized countries since the nineteenth century. But no one before Hitler had actually made the principles deduced from Darwin the basis of state policy, and no one before Hitler so consistently and ruthlessly carried those biological premises to their ultimate conclusions and then put them into practice. This chain of false conclusions, beginning with the false analogy between events in the realm of nature and the relationships between nations, was welded in the imagination of a man who scorned the thought of being informed by real experts or by experienced diplomats or other professionals about the actual strengths and weaknesses of other nations. The greater Hitler's successes, the more condescendingly he regarded those who actually knew better than he, and the more confirmed he felt in the pseudo-scientific doctrines with which he justified his policies.

From the terrible disaster at Stalingrad in the winter of 1942–1943, six months after the last of the *Table Conversations* was recorded, Hitler learned nothing at all militarily. He no more heeded the warning of this, the first of his major defeats, than of those that followed, that he should re-examine his doctrines, which were more and more clearly disproved by harsh reality. As the course of events ever more clearly refuted his expectations, he finally deluded himself with the biological sophism that those with stronger character would have to win.

13. Hitler and Philosophy; His Religious Monism

We now have to deal with the question whether or not Hitler, who was convinced that he was a serious thinker, actually had any philosophical talent or ever concerned himself earnestly with philosophical matters. Dr. von Hasselbach affirms that Hitler was intensely concerned with the great philosophers and felt a particular affinity for Schopenhauer and Nietzsche: "An edition of Schopenhauer's works accompanied him throughout the entire war of 1914–1918." In his *Table Conversations,* Hitler occasionally did refer to Schopenhauer, but only in reference to his exemplary use of langauge. He had a copy of Nietzsche's works transcribed on parchment for Mussolini, but by the time it could be sent to Rome, he had already been overthrown.

Mussolini was one of the many admirers of Nietzsche who had read him and thoroughly misunderstood him. To the degree that Hitler had actually read his works, one can assume that the same thing happened in his case. The titles of Nietzsche's books, particularly *Beyond Good and Evil* and *The Will to Power,* were, of course, peculiarly appealing to Hitler's main sentiments. Nietzsche's conception of the "transvaluation of all values," his struggle against Christianity, his cult of the unbroken instinct, his vision of the superman, and, above all, his damnation of conventional morality could hardly have been any less attractive. But by way of mitigating Nietzsche's historical responsibility, if indeed Hitler read enough of him to suggest anything of the sort, we can certainly assume that with or without the philosopher's ideas, Hitler would have been the person he was. Nietzsche was never more than an abused and exploited witness whose testimony was used to support the Third Reich. And there seems to be no evidence that Hitler was seriously influenced by any other philosopher of note.

It might be thought that given Hitler's basic orientation, both historical and scientific, there would be little room for religious convictions. Yet, though Hitler had clearly turned away from the churches and even opposed them openly, he was not irreligious. Dr. von Hasselbach describes him as a "religious person, or at least one who was struggling for religious clarity." In support of this, he points out that before the war Hitler repeatedly concerned himself with religious questions, and that he freely acknowledged the religious needs of the masses. Unlike such figures as the coarse Martin Bormann, he did not regard Nazi ceremonies as a substitute for the Church and rejected the idea of being idolized after his death like Lenin. "He went on for hours discussing the possibility of bridging the confessional division of the German people and helping them find a religion appropriate to their character and modern man's understanding of the world." He had no wish to assume the role of reformer himself, but he was interested in the prospect of seeing reform arise. No suitable movement in this direction took place, so far as he was concerned, and to his intimates he spoke very critically of the *Gottgläubigen* or "Believers," who counted on his support.[1]

For Jesus as Savior there was, of course, no room in Hitler's view of things, but he recognized Jesus' human greatness. Hasselbach testifies: "Hitler saw Christ as a unique person whose life work was dogmatically reinterpreted in essential respects during the following centuries in the interest of the Church and has therefore been handed down in a distorted form. [Hitler thought that] as a Galilean, Christ was of Aryan descent, and quite apart from his ethical values, he had to be admired for the genius he showed in leading the struggle of the people against the power and pretensions of the corrupt Pharisees." Hitler was not the first to propose this naive and contrived "rehabilitation."

Instead of "God," Hitler used the word "Providence," which had become common in the eighteenth century and continued to be used by religious liberals, or else he spoke of "the Creative Power."[2] Whoever looks through a telescope or a microscope, he thought, will recognize the laws of nature: "Then a person really does have to become humble." When Hitler survived the assassination attempt of July 20, 1944, he attributed it to Providence, which seemed almost blasphemous to people who thought in Christian terms, but there is no reason to question Hitler's sincerity about this interpretation. In a conversation in October 1941, he took an explicit stand against pure atheism: "The fact is that we are weak creatures, but that there is a creative power. It would be stupid to try to deny it. The person who believes in something which is untrue stands higher than the one who believes in nothing at all."

To the degree that Hitler had any concrete conception of what he called Providence, it was related to his biologically oriented view of life: "The only thing to do, then, is to study the laws of nature,

[1]The so-called *Gottgläubigen* or "Believers in God" rejected conventional Christianity but insisted they were not atheistic. Many National Socialists were *gottgläubig*.—ED.

[2]When Hitler on occasion spoke of the "Almighty Creator of this world," this was undoubtedly a calculated concession to the sensibilities of his audience.

so as not to attempt anything which might be contrary to them. To do otherwise would be to rebel against the firmament! If I want to believe in a divine commandment, it can only be this: preserve the species."

These convictions were derived from no single author or school, but emerged from the intellectual milieu in which Hitler was rooted. One of the most important figures of the day was Ernst Haeckel, the self-proclaimed disciple of Darwin, advocate of the "Basic Law of Bio-Genetics," and author of the widely read *The Riddle of the Universe* (first published in German in 1899). Important also were the German Monistic League, founded in 1906 on the basis of Haeckel's teachings, and his disciple Wilhelm Bölsche, who, in a popular series of works, among them *From Bacillus to Apeman* (1899), promoted evolution as a philosophy of life.

This faith in Providence became more and more intertwined in Hitler's mind with a cult of himself. According to Alfred Jodl, he was dominated by "an almost mystical conviction of his infallibility as leader of the nation and of the war." Dr. Brandt, one of Hitler's physicians, reported that he was convinced he was "a tool of Providence. He was . . . consumed by the desire to give the German people everything and to help them out of their distress. He was possessed by the thought that this was his task and that only he could fulfill it."

Hitler's self-confidence was in large measure based upon his idea of Providence, and the more clearly the facts contradicted him, the more strongly he embraced it. According to an old saying, one learns to pray in the hour of need. Hitler, while he did not, perhaps, pray, did fall back on his own peculiar form of monism, a belief in a Providence that could not fail him.

14. Hitler's Morality: An Infernally Logical Consistency

Hitler's religious convictions came to have monstrous historical importance because he used them to justify what he considered to be morality. But there were other factors in his conception of morality from quite different sources.

At the beginning of the First World War Hitler, under the conditions of military service, acquired his first practical experience in leadership. His first political model was thus the company commander—sustained by the confidence of his men and demanding unconditional obedience. This officer's own responsibility was, in turn, equally simple: to act precisely in accordance with his orders, and to be prepared to react instantly to a new or unexpected situation. For the power struggle Hitler undertook when he entered the political arena, this military experience of elementary leadership was not sufficient.

The *Table Conversations* contain many revealing statements about the principles Hitler followed and the measures he took in building up his party, fighting his opponents, establishing a subservient press, and negotiating with the Reich Chancellery before coming to power.[3] What we see is that the more Hitler, as a politician, outgrew the role of a company commander, the more he became like a *Landsknechtsführer* of the Thirty Years' War, like the captain of one of those mercenary bands who regarded any means as justified and was prepared to defend the most ruthless conduct of the men in his command.

In his conversations, Hitler was occasionally very candid in revealing details, such as tactical tricks employed in disrupting meetings and rallies of political opponents, or the systematic defamation of women who dared openly to oppose the National Socialists. But with all parties attempting to win over the masses, these details were apt to be similar, differing perhaps only in degree. In the context of political competition, Hitler and his party comrades were certainly not inclined to be fastidious in a moral sense. Later, after they had come to power, the fact that they were responsible for the Reich was no reason in their eyes to return to the conventional morality of civilian life or of the military, which was sheer hypocrisy so far as Hitler was concerned.

In the course of his struggle for power, Hitler accumulated a rich

---

[3]It should be noted, however, that in Hitler's memory things always got sorted out in such a way that they fitted in with his preconceptions. Thus Hitler the historian should be consulted as a witness to the facts only with the greatest care.

store of experience in methods of dealing with enemies as well as with opponents and rivals in his own camp. He no longer followed even the example of the *Landsknechtsführer,* who was at least bound to his men by reciprocal loyalty and the ethical code of the military. What guided Hitler was purely a sense of power, that age-old instinct, given clear theoretical formulation by Machiavelli. It is hard to imagine that Hitler ever read a line of *The Prince,* but he would not have had to in order to become a master Machiavellian, even more a man of naked power than was described by the great Florentine himself, whose ideal ruler was really not devoid of all moral inhibitions.

It was during the so-called "Röhm Revolt" of June 30, 1934, that Hitler first demonstrated in public that he did not shrink from having his opponents murdered. In the course of this bloody episode, not only opponents and persons who might conceivably have become opponents were killed, but also individuals who were guiltless even in the view of Hitler's party, victims of mistaken identity or some other unfortunate error. Among those gunned down was Hitler's old comrade, a friend to whom he was much indebted and one of very few with whom he ever stood on a first-name basis, Ernst Röhm. To have Röhm shot before he could strengthen his position as a potential rival might be an understandable motive from the point of view of naked Machiavellianism. What remains astounding, however, is that neither at the time nor later did Hitler show the slightest evidence of emotion or concern about the separation from Röhm and other old comrades. In this respect Hitler remained absolutely unmoved and uninvolved. "I have never heard a word come over his lips," wrote Helmuth Greiner, who occasionally joined Hitler's circle of mealtime companions, "which even suggested that he had a warm or compassionate heart."[4] It was as though in his soul several strings were missing which even in the most hardened and violent men can at least now and then be heard reverberating. As we have already remarked, one of his characteristic, often-used expressions during the war was "ice-cold."

[4]Greiner was Schramm's predecessor as war diarist in Hitler's headquarters. —ED.

In his *Table Conversations,* Hitler once explained on the basis of his biological theory of life why compassion was not necessary: "A person can be horrified at the way one creature devours another in the realm of nature. The fly is killed by the dragonfly, which in turn is killed by the bird, which then falls victim to a larger bird. . . . One thing is certain: nothing can be done about it." But this is only a retrospective intellectual rationalization for a psychological phenomenon which must have been very deeply rooted in Hitler's mind.

Whatever can be cited about Hitler's life, such as his lack of firm roots in a real family or social group, fails to explain adequately how—without so much as batting an eye—he could order millions killed and millions more to fight on after it had become utterly senseless to continue the war. Though there may be no adequate psychological explanation, there is an historical parallel. Robespierre and Hitler, great as the differences were between them, and great as the difference in the sheer magnitude of their crimes, do belong together as *terribles simplificateurs,* terrible simplifiers who sought to reduce the complexity of life to the dogmas they had worked out. Determined to lead mankind to felicity, both brought about the most hideous terror.

For Robespierre, the student of Rousseau, as for Hitler, conventional morality had to be subordinated to another. Traditional standards of goodness could not save the condemned who were not "Friends of the Justice of the People." The principles of Humanism, on which the Revolution was based, were perverted to the uses of Terror. With no more pity than Hitler, the "Incorruptible" had ordered the wagons driven to the guillotine till he himself became its victim. Hitler, however, was more successful in evading his enemies—by suicide.

In his public speeches, Hitler could not dare to reveal his own conception of morality, but to his mealtime companions he could and did speak more openly about such questions. At the height of his power he did not mince words about the fact that he felt more than ever fully justified in taking the most drastic measures with absolute ruthlessness whenever it seemed necessary. If he found a group of saboteurs in a plant, he would have them hanged in the factory courtyard where no one could miss seeing the example. Anyone who turned against the social order would be shot down ruthlessly. If he was confronted with a mutiny such as that which occurred at the end of 1918, he would have "all leading figures identified with opposition tendencies, and definitely including those of political Catholicism," executed immediately, as well as all the inmates of the concentration camps.[5] The mutiny would then "collapse for the lack of mutinying elements and fellow travelers." Hitler felt that his moral right to order such executions—in this case he was thinking in terms of hundreds of thousands—derived from the fact that at the time all German patriots would either be at the front or in the munitions factories giving everything for the victory of Germany.

It would be an oversimplification to characterize Hitler as a hyper-Machiavellian no longer inhibited by law. His concept of legality came from what he saw as "the eternal laws of natural events." He recognized codified law only to the extent that it agreed with these "eternal" laws. He felt entirely justified in overthrowing or violating the law whenever in his eyes it was retrogressive, that is to say, when it did not yet correspond to the "eternal" law. He would have been unable to grasp the reproach of amorality, and would probably have raged that he, Hitler, was the champion of the morality of tomorrow, conceived according to nature, and that he would not stand to hear anything further of the obsolete ethics of yesteryear.

The nation's existence was prior to all individual rights, and these could exist only if they remained compatible with that interest. Judges should be guided by the conviction "that the primary purpose of the law is not to protect the individual from the state but rather to provide that Germany not be destroyed." Consequently, everyone had to come to terms with the fact that, depending upon his usefulness or danger to Germany, he might at any time be up-

[5]Although millions died in concentration camps throughout Europe, the greater number by far were killed in the specialized extermination camps, particularly Auschwitz. Only at the end of the war were the inmates of many of the other concentration camps murdered in cold blood. Consequently, Hitler's statement in April 1942 about killing the inmates was a real threat, considering that at that time many could still reasonably hope to be released by the German authorities sooner or later.—ED.

rooted or transplanted, circumscribed in important matters, humbled or commanded, and possibly even subjugated or exterminated.

According to Hitler's conviction, a people had the right to exist only if it were racially valuable. If it were, then it also had the right to expand at the expense of weaker peoples. That this amounted to subjugation did not even occur to Hitler; in his view, "subjugation" did not exist in the realm of nature. The lion does not "subjugate" the gazelle, but only makes use of the right he enjoys by virtue of his superiority.

So far as Hitler was concerned, mankind differed from the animal kingdom only to the extent that men are able to think and consequently to provide for the survival of the species in the struggle for existence. The lion ages, may become sick, is threatened by the hunter, and possibly may procreate degenerate descendants. Similar dangers—the most serious among them being "racial death" —also threaten mankind. Those responsible for leadership therefore have the duty—in this context Hitler might have spoken of "sacred duty"—to avert these dangers with every means at hand. In this situation no misgivings of any sort are valid and compassion is inappropriate. The significance of personal suffering or individual agony pales when the survival of the race is at stake.

Thus Hitler arrived at his own ice-cold, ruthless categorical imperative, which completely reversed Kant's. The guiding principle for National Socialist legislation was not to be the standard of moral relationships between men, but rather what was seen as the laws of nature. Whoever objected that they were ruthless missed the point; whoever regarded the new standards of morality for human behavior, derived from "eternal" laws, as brutal, failed to realize that all living beings are subject to the harsh laws of nature. The first commandment of Hitlerian morality was therefore the preservation of the collective vital force of the German people; the misgivings of an older culture were simply brushed aside.

In the *Table Conversations,* Hitler the Leader continually reverts to the theme of the ideal follower. The expression "fellow citizen" was almost spontaneously replaced by the revealing slogan "comrade in arms." This comrade had to be brave, tough, ruthless, personally above reproach, of iron perseverance, prepared to assume the responsibilities of command but at the same time capable of comradeship, and characterized by the virtues of preparedness, tenacity, selflessness, and optimism in all circumstances. To this catalog of ideal National Socialist virtues one would have to add the necessity of being "fanatical" in pursuit of one's goal—a term which together with "absolute" acquired ever-increasing weight in Hitler's usage during the war.

The morality Hitler worked out for himself was well grounded and consistent within its own frame of reference. Hitler pursued its conclusions to the bitter end, taking up the struggle against the Communists, against the clergy of both confessions, against the Freemasons, and against the Liberals. Such logic led inevitably to the extermination of the mentally handicapped and the gypsies, and above all to the annihilation of the Jews. These things happened not because Hitler was a terrible amoralist, unafraid of the Furies, but precisely because his logic, which was otherwise so frequently undermined by instinct, functioned with a virtually infernal consistency in the systematic application of this "morality." Who before Hitler could have taken upon his conscience the murder of millions? The cruelty of Genghiz Khan or Tamerlane looks small in comparison with what was carried out on Hitler's orders. Only Stalin yields a worthwhile comparison.

Yet the most hideous aspect of Hitler's morality is that it was directly and conclusively derived from the philosophy of life he had arrived at by his reading and his thinking as he walked back and forth in his room alone. Given Hitler's premises, his ethics could not have been different. The only question he had to decide was at what stage he would carry out what his morality prescribed, and whether it would be done openly or secretly—mere tactical considerations, but not matters of principle, since those were settled once and for all.

15. Visions of the Future: The Translation of Theory into Practice

In his description of a typical day at Hitler's headquarters, Dr. Henry Picker, who transcribed the *Table Conversations,* speaks of

Hitler's vivid imagination, of breathtaking visions which he conjured up before the eyes of his listeners, of "glances through the side door of paradise." As a frustrated architect, Hitler personally concerned himself, even during the war, with visions of glorious building projects like the Nuremberg Stadium, which, with seats for 400,000 persons, was on a "scale such as the world has never before seen." Plans for Nuremberg and Berlin are extant which demonstrate how far Hitler's imagination carried him in reducing human beings to mere ants, all but lost in vast superstructures. The motivating force was the same as with the architectural monstrosities which Stalin not only planned but actually built—a megalomaniacal urge to outdo the United States, which until the twentieth century had been recognized as the land of unlimited possibilities. The endeavor was already historically obsolescent by 1933, because a new breed of architects—including Walter Gropius and Mies van der Rohe, whom Hitler forced out of Germany—showed Americans how architecture even on the largest scale could retain a sense of proportion and thereby remain humane.

On the basis of his ideas about breeding, Hitler foresaw 150 to 200 million Germans someday, a population, in other words, on a scale comparable to that of North America or Russia. The thought that Germany might not be able to hold her own in competition with the superpowers and their vastly increasing populations had, after all, been a matter of concern to Germans since the days of Friedrich List in the first half of the nineteenth century, and had seriously troubled some of the more nationalistic groups. Such an enormous increase in population could not have been achieved merely by encouraging large families. As a mealtime guest of Hitler's, one evening in April 1942, Himmler suggested a biological "fishing expedition" in France to find racially suitable young French women who would be brought to boarding schools in Germany, in order "to divert them from the accident of their French nationality and point out to them their German blood and consequently their membership in the greater German community." "The Chief," as Picker referred to Hitler, following the usage of his staff, "commented that he was actually not particularly favorable to all sorts of attempts at Germanization unless they could be put on an ideologically sound basis."

These 200 million Germans of the future, and those who permitted themselves to be made Germans, would, as Hitler conceived it, be able to be not only bred but also transplanted. He pictured how one day a hundred million Germans would be "deployed" in the East, twenty million of them within the next ten years alone. Entirely consistent with this strand of thought was his plan to resettle the South Tyroleans, who were a liability in his relations with Mussolini, in the Crimea. In both climate and landscape, Hitler thought, the peninsula would be entirely suitable for the Tyroleans; in fact, it would be an improvement over their previous homeland. There would be no transportation difficulties. "All they need to do is sail down a German river, the Danube, and they would already be there"; a transplantation that would cause "neither physically nor psychologically any particular difficulties"—at least not in the imagination of this self-appointed breeder of humans.

In Hitler's visions of the future, the new possibilities that would emerge from the perfection of means already at hand played an important role—it could hardly have been otherwise, considering his sense of technology. Hitler's daydream was a railroad line to the Donetz Basin deep in southern Russia, with tracks four meters wide on which two-story cars would speed back and forth at two hundred kilometers per hour. One or two supplemental tracks would also enable normal trains to travel the route. In addition, he would build dual-lane superhighways toward the East with lanes eleven rather than seven meters wide. In his mind's eye rose new cities with imposing governors' palaces. Inhabited by Germans, these cities would have nothing at all to do with native building styles. Up to that time, even the maddest of nationalists had not had the audacity to think in such terms.

Were such visions stimulated by reading the works of Jules Verne, Kurd Lasswitz, and other authors of science fiction and futuristic novels, which Hitler would have read in his youth? In technical terms, many of his visions were more or less realizable. But what of the political circumstances which would have been necessary not only to establish such German settlements in the East but to maintain them in the long run? As can be seen from many passages in the *Table Conversations,* Hitler had already developed a clear idea of how this was to be done. Russian villages surrounding the new

German cities were to be kept deliberately at a low level of culture, and the Russian cities which already existed were not to be improved, "not to mention their being beautified." The trade in birth-control devices was to be encouraged in every possible way in order to cut back the expansion of the native population. Considering their prolificacy, "it would be perfectly all right with us for the women and girls there to have as many abortions as possible." To try to set up a public health organization along German lines in the occupied Eastern territories "would be sheer madness," and vaccinations and other preventive measures were not even in question. As a matter of fact, even the desire for such measures should be suppressed. "One should go right ahead and spread the superstition among them that inoculations and the like are very dangerous." Even dental care would be limited.

A parallel chain of thought led Hitler to the conclusion that the Eastern populations should not be permitted to enjoy advanced schooling. Instruction would be limited to fundamentals such as traffic signs, the acquisition of a limited familiarity with the German language, and sufficient geography to know that Berlin is the capital of the Reich. "Instruction in arithmetic and the like would be superfluous." For this reason, Hitler noted, one should "above all not set German schoolmasters loose in the Eastern territories." It need hardly be added that the inhabitants would have neither their own government nor armed forces.

Hitler's talk about his plans for the East was more than idle chatter, for what he envisioned corresponded to the measures which had already been initiated in the so-called *Generalgouvernement,* the portion of Poland not directly annexed by Germany or the Soviet Union, a program that was being further refined at the time of the *Table Conversations.*

As early as October 18, 1939, General Franz Halder, Chief of the General Staff of the Army, made the following notes in his diary after he had been briefed on Hitler's plans for Poland: "We do not want to restore Poland. . . . Base for future German expansion. Poland to supply its own [local] administration. It is not to become a model state according to German conception. Prevent Polish intelligentsia developing itself into a new leadership class. Lower standard of living to be maintained. Cheap slaves. All the rabble has to be cleared out of the German area. Administration of Poland shall unite in itself all command authority except military. Only one command authority—the Governor General. Creation of total disorganization. No coordination with Reich authorities! The Reich is to enable the Governor General to complete this work of the devil. Military requirements: highways—railroads. Garrisons like fortresses of Teutonic Knights along the security line or forwards."

The cultural achievements of Hitler's viceroy in Poland, Dr. Hans Frank, were recently summarized in a stark and factual account:

"The possession of a radio receiver was punished with death. Permitted and encouraged were a few cultural products of demonstrably inferior value. . . . In the few public libraries that were made accessible, all works on geography, including maps and atlases, were taken away, as well as all books in English or French regardless of their content, and all dictionaries. Also removed from the shelves [except possibly at the State Library in Cracow] were most classical and Polish literary, historical, philosophical, and ideological works. Only a few politically collaborating Polish theaters were re-opened, to present superficial entertainment: sex skits, moralistic pieces from the nineteenth century, and revues. Drama, opera, and the like were forbidden. In the concert halls, classical music, folk songs, and national songs were banned. The music of Chopin stood at the top of the blacklist. Even the musical selections in the coffee houses had to be approved. Every form of sport was prohibited. . . . Mandatory deliveries by the Polish farmers and scrap metal collections in the Polish schools were paid for with brandy. Alcoholism and abortion were encouraged in accordance with official policy directives."

The feasibility of Hitler's plans for the Russian areas, leaving aside all ethical considerations, confronts us with a maze of questions which none of his table companions—whether out of blindness or cowardice—knew how to pose. How would it be possible to reduce millions of persons to illiteracy, to eradicate their sense of historical tradition, and to degrade them to a completely servile status? How could the Germans—even if tens and hundreds of thousands were prepared to occupy and guard these outer areas—assert themselves in the long run against a population larger than all the German-speaking peoples together? By way of analogy, Hitler and his followers cited India with its 400 million inhabitants held in check by sixty thousand British. But this comparison was based on a false conception of Britain's relationship to the subcontinent, demonstrated by her postwar understanding with India and Pakistan. Even the feasibility of setting up a similar arrangement in the Ukraine would have had to be recognized as being out of the question had Hitler listened to experts on Eastern affairs. His picture of Russia as a land inhabited by servile peasants accustomed to the lash and unable to think far beyond eating and drinking was totally distorted and, since the emancipation in the nineteenth century, not to mention the Russian Revolution, no longer relevant.

To think like Hitler, one would have to be possessed of that ambivalent love-hate (*Hassliebe*) attitude toward England characteristic of so many Germans in the nineteenth century. One would have to be a European whose imagination was still fired by the example of America sweeping across the continent to the Pacific in its struggle against the Mexicans and the Indians; who still believed, in Kipling's sense, in "the white man's burden" of spreading European culture, and who had no notion whatsoever of the changes which had taken place in Russia since Gogol, Tolstoy, and Dostoevsky.

In reality there were clear signs after the First World War that the time was past when other continents would be dominated by Europe. As early as 1916, the Indian National Congress and the All-India Muslim League had joined forces at Lucknow, brought together by the desire to free India from the British yoke. In 1926, England attempted to head off the self-determination of segments of the Commonwealth with the "Balfour Formula," which conceded the dominions autonomous equality. In 1933, the United States promised the Philippines independence. One could go on and on. It was not necessary to be particularly perceptive to recognize that the age of colonial domination, when one people might rule over another, was coming to an end. Hitler's plans for the East reveal that he had no conception of the new realities which had been taking shape since the end of the First World War beyond the frontiers of the Reich, and that his dreams of territorial expansion were still completely dominated by nineteenth-century conceptions.

16. Hitler's Technical Knowledge and Military Ability

We have reached the end of the part of our analysis that may be drawn from the evidence of the *Table Conversations*. So far we have attempted to deal only with the cultural and ideological sides of Hitler's personality and development. The often discussed problem of Hitler as a politician and statesman would have required an entirely different point of departure and the consideration of countless protocols, documents, and contemporary statements of all sorts. While the subject of Hitler as a military leader will be dealt with in the second essay of this volume, there are a number of observations on this and the related subject of his technological role that should be taken up at this point.

On the subject of Hitler's technological talent and its limitations, we have information from three witnesses who prepared their statements independently after the defeat and who, moreover, may be considered free of the suspicion of having curried favor for personal advantage. Dr. von Hasselbach summarized his observations in 1945:

"The officers who had contact with him were continually astounded how precisely Hitler was informed about the caliber, mechanism, and range of a field piece, about the armament and speed of German and foreign warships, and about what could reasonably be expected of fortification lines. When new weapons or vehicles were demonstrated, Hitler showed astonishing intuition concerning the advantages and flaws of their construction, and he often made helpful suggestions for improving them. He had a good understanding of the technology of truck and airplane motors and was intensely interested in other technical questions, such as the production of synthetic materials."

General Alfred Jodl, who for years was able to observe Hitler daily, has given us concrete details on the innovations in military technology directly attributable to Hitler's personal orders. Jodl reports that Hitler intervened hard-handedly in the armament program of the army, because he regarded the military technologists as lazy, bureaucratic, and backward. As a consequence, Hitler depended upon civilian professionals. "He created the Ministry for Weapons and Munitions under [Fritz] Todt, leaving only the building of airplanes and ships with the air force and the navy. From then on Hitler determined the monthly quota as well as the direction and scope of all production of weapons and munitions down to the last detail. All the Operations Staff [of the High Command of the Wehrmacht] had to do was to give him the exact figures: inventory, utilization, and production during the previous month. But beyond this, Hitler's astounding technical and tactical vision led him also to become the creator of modern weaponry for the army. It was due to him personally that the 75-mm anti-tank gun replaced the 37-mm and 50-mm guns in time, and that the short guns mounted on the tanks were replaced with the long 75-mm and 88-mm guns. The *Panther,* the *Tiger,* and the *Königstiger* [i.e., *Tiger II*] were developed as modern tanks at Hitler's own initiative."[6]

Jodl's observations are confirmed and complemented by Field Marshal Erich von Manstein, who was critical of Hitler and therefore not inclined to overpraise. As a military technologist he evaluates Hitler in the following terms: ". . . Hitler's memory and knowledge were astounding with respect to creative imagination and technical questions and to all problems of armaments. He could display a staggering grasp of the effectiveness even of new enemy weapons as well as of our own and enemy production figures.

[6]To substantiate Jodl's statement, it is sufficient to cite merely one striking example from H. Heiber's edition of *Hitlers Lagebesprechungen* (where many other examples may be found)—the record of a situation conference on the evening of June 18, 1944, shortly after the invasion of Normandy. Hitler points out that immediately after the occupation of Czechoslovakia, the most valuable guns were scrapped. "That was done out of a mania for uniformity. Only just barely were [at least] the Czech howitzers saved from being scrapped! At the demonstration, the Czech howitzer was presented as a monstrous abortion. In fact, it was better than ours. Unfortunately I made a major mistake then. From the very beginning I should have had the production of those guns continued. . . . [Ellipsis due to gap in text.] The same with the 210-mm gun! The Skoda guns were disparaged because the new German 210-mm guns were going to shoot further, up to as far as 33 kilometers, while the Skoda only shot 30 kilometers. But they were there and tested, an outstanding piece, and could fire in any direction, which in *this* case certainly is an advantage. I do not need to keep running around with the trail [i.e., support of the gun carriage], but can continually turn in any direction. For coastal defense especially, for our purpose, it is an excellent piece. The best proof is that everyone is trying to get it. The Turks want it and also the Swedes. . . ."

He was particularly fond of making use of this ability when he wanted to change the subject from some topic that was not congenial to him. There can be no question but that in the area of armaments he initiated and expedited a great deal with understanding and extraordinary energy."

Two further details can be added to this general picture on the basis of reports made to me by eyewitnesses:

When it became necessary in 1940 to supply the infantry isolated at Narvik on the northern coast of Norway with anti-tank guns, the only form of transportation that could be considered was the submarine. The navy had to report, however, that the type of anti-tank gun used by the army, mounted on a two-wheeled carriage, would not pass through the entry hatch of a submarine. Hitler recalled, however, that during the march into Austria in 1938 he had seen an anti-tank gun mounted on three legs which ought to fit into a submarine. After a series of long-distance telephone calls, the anti-tank gun was found, and it did in fact go through the hatch.

After the Allied landing in the West in the summer of 1944, the infantry complained again and again that because of the blanket of fire laid down by the enemy ships off the coast, they were unable to move. When this was reported to Hitler at a situation conference, he asked how far inland the ships' guns were able to reach. There were three naval officers present, but none knew the answer. Quite displeased, Hitler said he expected to have this information by the next day. In calculating it, he added, it should be borne in mind that the different enemy ships drew different depths of water and because of this difference in draft could come unequally close to the shore. Furthermore, the depth of the water before the coast as well as the differences in caliber of the enemy guns—Hitler recited them by memory—had to be considered. Thus the procedure for making a fairly complex calculation flashed before his mind's eye on a moment's notice.

This degree of technological aptitude is all the more remarkable considering that Hitler had never had any technical education nor the opportunity to gather practical experience in industry. His astounding memory as well as his unusually keen visual perception helped him in this area; he may not have had a photographic mind, but certainly he was visually oriented to a high degree. Moreover, Hitler's ideological prejudices had no inhibiting influence in technological matters. Nonetheless, it is difficult to find an adequate explanation for his phenomenal ability in this direction.

The principal limitation of Hitler's technological understanding was his lack of serious training or inclination for the exact sciences. His comprehension stopped where simple technology could go no further without physics, chemistry, and the like. In his statement on Hitler, Dr. von Hasselbach continues: "He had little interest in other technical questions, particularly in the area of physics, such as high-frequency technology or atomic physics and the like, even though they were brought to his attention. Consequently he came to recognize their significance in warfare only when enemy progress in these areas had already won a decisive influence in the sea and air war."

Even in technological questions, Hitler was his own worst enemy as he became more and more firmly convinced that he knew more than anyone else. According to Field Marshal von Manstein, Hitler's belief in his own superiority in technological questions had fateful consequences: "By his interference he prevented the steady development of the air force at the right time. In the development of rocket propulsion and atomic weapons he undoubtedly had an inhibiting influence." Many of Hitler's decisions in matters of technology were recognized by the experts at the time as having been mistaken, and today they can clearly be seen as false. Such was his decision about the construction of jet aircraft, for use both at the front and against enemy bombers, which had the effect of vitiating a great opportunity. What is clear is that even in the area of military technology, about which Hitler understood a good deal, his prejudice against the professionals, his suspicion of all who did not agree with him, and his inability to change his mind once he had made it up, combined to hinder his capacity and talent.

But technological knowledge and a good understanding of the procedures of modern warfare placed Hitler on solid ground in his discussions with the generals and General Staff officers. These were areas in which he was equal to them, and indeed often superior; and we should once more point out Hitler's uncommonly clear conception of spatial relationships, which enabled him to visualize buildings that he had never before entered and which was not irrelevant to the task of directing operations on several fronts at the same time.

None of this, however, explains how it was possible for Hitler— as a corporal who in World War I had not so much as led a company and consequently, in matters of military strategy even more than in military technology, was self-educated—to assume the role of a military dictator. Field Marshal von Manstein does concede to Hitler "a certain eye for operational possibilities," which is frequently found among laymen, though he qualifies this by adding that it was an eye dimmed by a tendency to overestimate the technological means at hand and by an inadequate sense of proportion regarding possible results. General Jodl spelled out more precisely the successful operations in which Hitler played a decisive role, such as the extension of the attack in the North up to the Norwegian port of Narvik beyond the Arctic Circle, and the attack in the West against the center of the enemy front rather than against the right wing, both in the spring of 1940.

It is not to be denied, therefore, that Hitler—contrary to the expectations of the professionals and presumably even to his own surprise—developed certain talents in military leadership. To dismiss Hitler as "the corporal from the First World War"—as was done at first after the catastrophe in 1945—or to think of him merely as someone who seized control and made one mistake after another, contributes nothing to the evaluation of him as an historical phenomenon. Hitler is difficult enough to understand at best, and in the military area perhaps most difficult of all.

However, there can be no question but that Hitler did make military decisions that were disastrous mistakes. In the second half of the war he followed a strategy based on fundamental principles against which the gravest objections must be raised. The final reckoning must be made no differently than when any military leader is defeated or gives orders which end in disaster.

In terms of our concern in this essay with Hitler's personality, the important thing is to point out the difference between his way of thinking and that of the General Staff. This is well brought out in a study on the Ardennes Offensive, also known as the Battle of the

Bulge, which the author prepared in 1945 while in postwar captivity, and which General Jodl reviewed in his Nuremberg cell, adding his own marginal notes. The tried and proven manner in which the General Staff made its objective calculations and then developed its operational planning in the light of the cold facts was contrasted in this study (further excerpts from which are reprinted as Appendix I) to Hitler's radically different approach, not only to planning but even to his initial evaluation of the situation:

"As a former corporal he had very real sympathy for the common man, the 'poor worm,' and with his vivid imagination was able to see clearly before him the difficulties of the battle actions, even though they had been so greatly transformed since the time of his own deployment at the front. On the basis of his personal experience in the First World War, he held fast above all to the basic principle that the troops should never be given occasion for uncertainty by offering them the option to retreat. This was the reason for his resistance whenever he was advised to approve a request for orders to evacuate a position or fall back to a new line of defense. He was convinced that, if only enough willpower had been brought to bear in the first place, most such requests would not even have been necessary.

"Willpower was to Hitler the dominating factor everywhere. This reflected the experience he had gained during his revolutionary rise to power. He thought that if he had ever learned to think in the terms of a General Staff officer, at every single step he would have had to stop and calculate the impossibility of reaching the next. Consequently, he concluded, he would never even have tried to come to power, since on the basis of objective calculations he had no prospect of success in the first place. Once in power, he remained a revolutionary no less in his way of acting than in his way of thinking. He regarded it as self-evident that his initial successes had created the prospect of further triumphs, insofar as they encouraged his followers and intimidated his adversaries. The Führer regarded it as proper in his military leadership, as he had in his political activity, to establish goals which were so far-reaching that the objective professionals would declare them impossible. But he did this deliberately, convinced that the actual course of events would leave those more modest calculations far behind. As soon as the first breakthrough was achieved, the unleashed energy of the victorious Germans and the paralysis on the side of the enemy would make it possible to achieve the improbable in the end. This was what Hitler meant when he so often spoke of fanaticism and repeatedly demanded it of the Wehrmacht. A good many of the military successes during the first part of the war had, after all, been achieved despite the predictions of the General Staff. Consequently, Hitler felt fully justified in counting on this incalculable factor of fanaticism as the decisive consideration. Had the Bible meant anything to him, then it would certainly have been the verse about the faith that can move mountains which would have been closest to his heart.

"Perhaps the most decisive of all the problems of the supreme German leadership in the war was that Hitler, because of his initial successes, could say that he and not the General Staff, which on the basis of its calculations had not established such far-reaching goals, was the true realist. He had foreseen actual developments more clearly, precisely because he had taken the incalculable into account. But then the situation changed again, and in the end the General Staff was correct in its calculations."

A striking demonstration of these observations is to be found in the private diary which Major (later General) Gerhard Engel, Hitler's army adjutant, kept during the period of the grave crisis of the winter of 1942–1943, which was to reach its climax in the disastrous Battle of Stalingrad.

On November 7, 1942, Hitler declared that "it was his repeated experience that the General Staff overestimated the enemy. In this connection, Poland and France had been one long fiasco." He was immediately proved wrong. On November 19, the Soviet offensive began against which General Zeitzler had warned; from then on, the thinking of the General Staff proved to be increasingly superior to Hitler's. But by now Hitler was firmly convinced of his superiority over these "experts" and did not let himself be shaken in this conviction by reverses—no matter how grave they were.

In contrast with other historical events, the course of military operations permits clear judgments in retrospect, since successes and failures, victories and defeats can be clearly differentiated. The tally for Hitler would show both plus and minus points, but the final total would be negative.

General Jodl, in his Nuremberg cell, begins his reflections on Hitler as a strategist (translated in full as Appendix II) with the thought that, in modern war, strategy includes foreign and domestic policy, economic mobilization, propaganda, and leadership of the people, so that "no general but only a statesman can be a strategist." Any final judgment of Hitler's leadership must consider his effectiveness in all these peripheral areas—a task beyond the scope of this book.

17. Willpower: The Dominating Force

At the end of August 1944, as the breakthrough in the West became apparent following the landings in Normandy and in southern France, Hitler expanded on the subject of willpower in a conference with two generals:

"My task, especially since the year 1941, has been never to lose my nerve under any circumstances, but rather, if there is a collapse somewhere, always to find solutions and expedients in order to set things moving again. . . .

"For the past five years I have cut myself off from the other world. I have neither visited the theater, heard a concert, nor seen a film. I live only for the single task of leading this struggle, because I know if there is not a man in there behind it who by his very nature has a will of iron, then the struggle cannot be won. . . ."

Not to lose one's nerve, to have a will of iron—these two phrases are keys to the understanding of Hitler. Everyone who had the opportunity to observe Hitler closely agreed that the most conspicuous thing about him was his will. But for the conduct of the war this will had a dark side, as more than one of Hitler's generals bear witness. General Alfred Jodl describes Hitler's actions after Stalingrad this way: "From then on, he intervened more and more frequently in operational decisions, often down to matters of tactical detail, in order to impose with unbending will what he thought the generals simply refused to comprehend: that one had to stand or fall, that each voluntary step backwards was an evil in itself." General Heinz Guderian, speaking of Hitler in the final phase of the war, gives an even stronger description: "With the grim tenacity of a fanatic, he clutched at one last straw which he deluded himself into imagining would save him and his work from going under. His compelling willpower was entirely devoted to this thought which dominated him completely: 'Never yield and never capitulate!' He had said it so often; now he also had to act accordingly."

Field Marshal Erich von Manstein characterized this overestimation of will as nothing less than the "decisive factor in Hitler's military leadership." In Hitler's view it "would only have to be transformed into belief down to the youngest grenadier in order to demonstrate the correctness of his decisions and to guarantee the success of his orders." In itself, Manstein points out, willpower is a positive characteristic without which no military leader can sustain his position. In the case of Hitler, however, it was linked to his belief in his "mission." "Such a belief leads inevitably to rigidity as well as to the opinion that one's own will can reach even beyond the limitations set by hard reality. . . ."

Professor Carl J. Burckhardt, who as League of Nations High Commissioner in Danzig had personal contact with Hitler, penetrated into still deeper levels of the phenomenon. He found that Hitler would immediately adapt his actions to changing circumstances, but that in doing so he simultaneously divested himself of freedom of choice despite the power that he possessed: "In his almost total lack of freedom, he stood very close to those whom he ruled. Between himself and the overpowering circumstances, there was what amounted to a mechanical force to which he succumbed as did all those whom he had chained to himself."

What Burckhardt had in mind is illustrated by two entries in the diary of Hitler's army adjutant, General Gerhard Engel. On October 2, 1942, Hitler declared the "capture of Stalingrad not only for operational but psychological reasons urgently necessary, for world public opinion and morale of [Axis] allies." On the tenth, he elaborated on his explanation of the attack by saying that Stalingrad had to be "broken out, . . . to rob Communism of its holy shrine." One sees with tangible clarity how Hitler the strategist, who insisted on having his way despite all the warnings of the experts, almost mechanically reacted to the nonmilitary consequences of the threatening military catastrophe and thereby only made it far worse than it already was.

Here we see the reverse side of Jodl's thesis that the modern strategist must be many other things besides a military leader. The execution of a military action for propaganda reasons assumed that strategy was no longer strategy. Prestige-strategy is the poorest strategy. In the long run, one cannot maintain a bluff in military matters, and if one makes the attempt, then the battle will not only reveal the actual relative strength, but in so doing also make the next reverse unavoidable, which—if purely strategic considerations had been followed—might well have been fended off.

Hitler had the advantage of having begun the war with extraordinarily strong nerves. They held up—as the *Table Conversations* demonstrate—even in the winter of 1941-1942, when events would have broken most men in Hitler's position. On April 1, 1942, Dr. Picker noted: "In terms of health, the Führer is in very good shape." Goebbels spoke at about the same time of Hitler's having the constitution of a bear. The decisions in the winter of 1941-1942 do not, then, appear to have been affected by Hitler's health.

On January 15, 1942, after the furious battle before Moscow, during which, for the first time in the war, the German armies were stopped in their tracks, Hitler finally gave the Fourth Army permission to consolidate its front line by drawing back. (For giving the same order on his own authority eight days earlier, General Erich Hoepner—later to be executed for participation in the unsuccessful plot against Hitler—had been summarily dismissed from the Wehrmacht.) Hitler concluded his mid-January withdrawal order to the Fourth Army with the words: "This is the first time during this war that I have given an order to evacuate a substantial sector of the front." At the beginning of March, Hitler was forced to approve a new shortening of the front line, concerning which he declared that he "had insisted with deliberate obstinacy on holding every foot of ground."

After the front had once more been stabilized and the offensive resumed on the southern wing, Hitler concluded that this had been possible largely due to his not having lost his nerve; when a new and much graver winter crisis loomed the following autumn, Hitler's solution was to hold fast, just as in the previous year. General Engel, who participated in Hitler's situation conferences during the decisive weeks, notes in his diary that Hitler's willpower had locked into a cramp of such immobile rigidity that all appeals to reason were literally repelled. The sentences reporting Hitler's words and actions in chronological sequence speak for themselves:

November 19: "Bad evening situation conference. Apparently a catastrophe with the Rumanians, but still no clear picture. . . ."[7]

November 20: "A typical situation conference. Complete confusion because of the Rumanians. Everything depends on Heim [commanding general of an armored corps]. Führer himself completely unsure what is to be done. . . ."

November 21: "Job's tidings keep pouring in. Now also south of Stalingrad a crisis with the Rumanians. Jodl suggests evacuating the Volga front with Headquarters Sixth Army altogether. . . . Führer says no with the familiar arguments: that would not change the situation and the Russians would not fail to notice. . . . Führer again and again: 'No matter what happens we have to hold the [area around Stalingrad] in any case.' "

Accordingly, during the night of November 22–23, the order was given to the Sixth Army, which had meanwhile been cut off, that it had to hold its ground, without attempting to break out of the pocket. The following night, November 23–24, a report came from General Paulus that the annihilation of his army was certain if he

---

[7]The crisis which culminated in the loss of the greater part of Stalingrad (never completely captured by the Germans) and of Paulus' Sixth Army, had begun on November 19, 1942, within days of the onset of hard winter. Two overwhelmingly powerful Russian army groups (under Rokossovsky and Yeremenko) crushed the thinly spread Rumanian Third and Fourth Armies on Paulus' flanks and closed their pincers behind him on November 21, cutting off more than 200,000 soldiers of the Sixth Army, many elements of the Fourth Armored Army, parts of two Rumanian divisions, a Croat regiment, units of the Luftwaffe, and noncombatants. Having forbidden him to retreat, Hitler finally promoted General Paulus to field marshal at the end of January, pointing out that no German field marshal had ever surrendered. Paulus did, however, rather than go down fighting—or at least commit suicide, as Hitler had expected.

The literature on Stalingrad is immense. One slim volume that unforgettably suggests the human dimension of the tragedy of the Sixth Army deserves mention: *Last Letters from Stalingrad,* with an introduction (briefly explaining the great battle) by General S. L. A. Marshall (New York, 1962; paperback, 1965).—ED.

were not permitted to evacuate the portions of Stalingrad he had been able to capture, withdraw from his northern defense perimeter, and try to break out through the western and southern sides of the pocket. This recommendation was supported by Army Chief of Staff Zeitzler and the Commander-in-Chief of Army Group B, Baron von Weichs. Nevertheless, at 5:00 A.M., November 24, Hitler's categorical order to hold Stalingrad was transmitted to the Sixth Army.

November 24 (noon situation conference, as recorded in the Engel diary): "Big discussion of radio message from General Paulus; . . . Führer crassly rejects proposal, though Zeitzler supports it, . . . [and] stresses repeatedly that Stalingrad under no circumstances is to be given up. . . . Situation conference becomes increasingly agitated. Responsibility [for the crisis] is completely unclarified." The proposal of the Army Group to give the armored corps a free hand to mount a counterattack to break the pocket was also "crassly rejected by the Führer."

November 26: Long discussion with Field Marshal von Manstein, who had just been put in command of the critical sector of the front, and who recommended withdrawals elsewhere in order to free reserves for this operation. "Führer is and remains calm," wrote Engel, "but rejects everything. Reasons: it all would be interpreted as weakness; vital living space would be lost once more; impossible impact on our allies; loss of time, since one could never tell what might happen in the West, Africa, or elsewhere. Operationally, von Manstein has good ideas, but in view of the overall picture [it is, so far as Hitler is concerned] only grey theory. . . . Zeitzler asks finally that the Sixth Army be given freedom of action [implying an attempt to break out or, should that fail, tacit permission to capitulate], which the Führer rejects out of hand. Only a relief action can even be considered, and for that purpose the greater part of the Fourth Armored *[Panzer]* Army is available [to Manstein]."

Hitler relied on Göring's assurance that the air force would be able to supply the isolated army. Engel: "We are horrified by so much optimism, which even Air Force General Staff officers do not share. Führer enthusiastic about the Reich Marshal. He will take care of things just as in the old days; there [with Göring] he does not find the pettiness so common in the army."[8] The prevailing misgivings were presented at the situation conference on November 26 by Colonel Eckhardt Christian.[9] "After calmly hearing Christians out, Führer contradicts. It is all only a question of time. A particularly gifted organizer [in other words, Göring], authorized to use his special powers ruthlessly, will be able to handle it, even if he has to move against generals who create difficulties for the airlift (von Manstein, von Richthofen)."

Thus Hitler had irrevocably committed himself. The Sixth Army was under no circumstances to be permitted to attempt a breakout, despite the gravest objections of the General Staff and General Paulus, and it was to be supplied solely by airlift, on the word of Göring, despite the alarming misgivings even of air force officers attached to the Führer Headquarters.[1] The counterattack of the Fourth Armored Army was delayed until December 12. Once underway, it succeeded in approaching to within some sixty kilometers of Stalingrad by December 18, but was then stopped by the Red Army. Because the Russians had meanwhile broken through the Italian Eighth Army on the Don, threatening the relief column's flank, Hitler was forced to abandon the effort and order a withdrawal, "because the principle of holding the furthest advanced line, no matter what," was simply not applicable in this case.

December 18, situation conference in the evening: "Again von Manstein requests that the Sixth Army be permitted to break out, since only [in this way] can contact with Stalingrad [be main-

---

[8]After the victories of the first year of the war, Hitler promoted a number of German generals to field marshal, in effect, five-star rank. The ostentatious seniority of Field Marshal Hermann Göring, who had been one of Hitler's most loyal lieutenants since the early days of the struggle for power, was preserved by creating for him what amounted to six-star rank as *Reichsmarschall.* In addition to several other posts, he was Supreme Commander of the Luftwaffe. His personal influence with Hitler and consequently his power within the Third Reich declined fairly steadily during the war, until at the very end he was ejected from all his offices and from the National Socialist party.—ED.

[9]Christian was an air force officer attached to Jodl's staff.—ED.

[1]It was estimated that a bare minimum of five hundred tons of supplies would have to be flown in daily. Less than a fifth of this rate could be sustained.—ED.

tained] and the mass of the army be saved. But atmosphere is depressed. Führer has again refused breakout although Zeitzler has put it very urgently. . . ."

December 19: "Agitated discussion, since von Manstein has renewed request for breakout of army. Führer is implacable, always with the same arguments, does not believe in saving the army [through retreat]."

Continual discussions followed, in which Hitler seems to have considered the decision of abandoning the city of Stalingrad after all. The responsible officers hoped against hope that Paulus, on his own responsibility, would attempt to break out. But conditioned by the tradition of obedience, the general could not bring himself to make that decision. Probably it was already too late for him anyway.

December 21: "No one knows how things are supposed to go on with Stalingrad. Führer is very taciturn and almost not to be seen except at the situation conferences and briefings. . . ."

On December 25, von Manstein requested that divisions from the Caucasus Front be placed at his disposal. Hitler refused his request on December 27, because it allegedly could not be carried out. But on December 28 he had to approve a withdrawal of the entire Caucasus Front.[2]

It is impossible not to wonder what was going on during these days in the mind of the man who held to the crucial decision in grim opposition to all the qualified experts. Professor Andreas Hillgruber, who edited the *War Diary* for the year 1942, supplies this much of an answer:

"Whether Hitler at this point actually still believed in the possibility of relieving the Sixth Army will never—particularly considering the psyche of Hitler—be entirely clarified. As late as the situation conference of December 28, when Christian in his briefing observed that Manstein held the airlift to be inadequate and consequently impractical [as a means of sustaining Paulus], Hitler replied 'that this was a question of rationalization. . . . It would be

[2]Hitler approved the withdrawal from the Caucasus at the end of December 1942 because the Russians were driving down the Don toward the Sea of Azov. There was real danger that all of Army Group A would be cut off, compounding the disaster of Stalingrad.—ED.

better to employ export merchants than utterly ignorant administrative or General Staff officers [for this type of operation]. Concentrates had to be used. They could be gotten and he was going to look into it himself' (Engel diary)."

Completely isolated, unwilling to learn, convinced of his position, and grasping at completely inadequate expedients, Hitler held up through this crisis. Another man bombarded by so much disastrous news might well have lost his nerve and broken down or committed suicide. Hitler's willpower—though at this point one might better speak of morbid rigidity—remained unbroken. Thus we see that the acknowledgment of Hitler's positive characteristics—here we might speak of perseverance, strength of character, willpower—must immediately be qualified by the further observation that, in the last analysis, even these worked out to have negative consequences.

These citations may strike the reader as unduly detailed, but they are significant because they concern the dénouement of Hitler's military leadership and of the war itself. From this point on, defeat was inevitable. In the classic drama of antiquity, the *peripetia* was the moment at which fate would plunge the hero from his proud heights into the abyss. In the case of the war which Hitler unleashed and which at his command was extended to the Soviet Union, it would be presumptuous to appeal to fate as the explanation. Here the mover of world history was none other than that uncanny man born in Braunau on the River Inn, the son of a petty Austrian official, who made himself dictator of Germany. During those weeks which we have documented, Hitler stubbornly set his face against the fate he had provoked, implacably rejecting all reasonable advice. With this he sealed his own annihilation. Adolf Hitler would never have been able to win; but that his end should have been so disgraceful, so frightful was something which he himself brought about, beginning with a defeat on the field which was far greater than Cannae or Sedan. Stalingrad was a link in a chain which he forged precisely because he had become the prisoner of his rigidly and mechanically reacting will. *Quem deus perdere vult, dementat prius*—those whom the gods would destroy, they first make mad.

After Stalingrad, Hitler's nerves began to falter. More and more frequently he allowed himself to fly into fits of rage when things did not go as he wished—for which there was always someone to blame. General Guderian, who saw Hitler face to face after Stalingrad for the first time in fourteen months, reported that during this and the subsequent period, "he easily lost his temper and raged, and was then unpredictable in what he said and decided." Jodl speaks of his "irascible agitation," which was so feared that at situation conferences only those whose presence was absolutely necessary were permitted to attend by the Operations Staff of the Wehrmacht High Command. By the beginning of 1943, the custom of permitting officers who were being transferred, after extensive service in the Operations Staff, to take leave of Hitler personally and then, as a reward, to participate in the following situation conference, had been abandoned. There was good reason to fear that they might involuntarily witness an eruption of their "Führer," and that they would spread the word.

To judge by the observations of Manstein, Hitler sensed instinctively just how far he could go with the person to whom he was talking; he knew with whom he had to restrain himself and whom he "could expect to intimidate successfully through an outburst of rage—which was perhaps often consciously staged." So sinister was Hitler that even at the very moments when he gave the impression that he had lost all control of himself, he might only have been acting in order to sustain his domination over the person before him.

The fact that Hitler was able to keep going, despite the excessive and increasing strain on his nerves, is something of a miracle. Aside from the short walks he took, nothing in his daily routine was natural. He turned his nights into day, refused to be talked out of the vegetarian diet that overtaxed his stomach, took medicine with pedantic precision before and after eating, and from his personal physician Morell, who was regarded with suspicion in professional circles, received massive injections and doses of medicaments, without which, in the end, he was no longer able to exist. It is almost incomprehensible that Hitler's body survived such punishment for years on end. One cannot help thinking of it in terms of a poorly serviced locomotive fired up to red heat in order to barely be able to creep into the last station on its route.

At the end of the war the consequences of this regimen were

apparent. An older General Staff officer, who gave Hitler briefings during the last weeks of the war in the bunker beneath the Reich Chancellery, recorded the impression Hitler made on those who still had the chance to see him: "Physically he was a frightful picture. As he moved from his living quarters to the conference room of the bunker, he dragged himself forward slowly and painfully, the upper part of his body thrust forward, his legs drawn along behind. He had lost his sense of equilibrium. If he stopped on the way, a distance of seventy-five to a hundred feet, he either had to sit down on one of the benches provided for this purpose along both walls, or else hold on to the person with whom he was talking. He had lost control of his right arm, and his right hand trembled continually."[3]

It would be an oversimplification, nevertheless, to explain Hitler's morbid rigidity of will purely in medical terms. In his reflections on Hitler's military effectiveness, Alfred Jodl pointed out that after Stalingrad, Hitler was not able to reach any further strategic conclusions—"but perhaps there was no longer one to be reached." Jodl lays his finger on a crucial fact: Even had Hitler's nerves remained as firm as they had been in the winter of 1941–1942, even had his health not deteriorated, he would still have had no further alternatives—unless he were prepared to capitulate (the very thought of which he had always rejected) or to clear the way for others by suicide, thereby acknowledging to the world that he, founder of Greater Germany, was bankrupt and his Third Reich defeated.

Shortly before taking his own life, Hitler said to Jodl, "I should already have made this decision, the most important in my life, in November 1944, and should never have left the headquarters in East Prussia." But he had not been able to bring himself to do it. He had looked for an unexpected miracle to save him. With his wrecked body and his nerves increasingly out of control, he had been sustained by that infernal, intransigent will, which in turn was sustained by the memory of the winter of 1941–1942 and the example of Frederick the Great.[4]

---

[3]Not Hitler's right, but his left arm and hand, were affected.

[4]After a series of disastrous reverses during the latter half of the Seven Years' War Frederick the Great became despondent enough to consider suicide; but in 1762 his enemy, the Empress Elizabeth of Russia, suddenly died

Finally, Hitler's will, coupled with his pseudo-Darwinistic idea that in the end the stronger must win, became his fate. It had led Hitler in a unique rise to power to become the key figure in Europe, made him ruler of the area from the Atlantic Coast to the Caucasus, from the North Cape to North Africa, and then, finally led to a fall such as no man in history who had just concentrated supreme power in his hands had ever before suffered.

18. Notes on Hitler's Health

The treatment of Hitler by Dr. Theo Morell—whom he had consulted even before the war as a personal physician—is a special problem dealt with in a memorandum by Dr. Karl Brandt, another of Hitler's doctors. This is the memorandum I use as my point of departure in the following discussion.

Whether it was advisable or even responsible, from a medical point of view, to give Hitler the injections and drugs that Morell administered, and whether the dosages were appropriate or excessive, is open to question. Morell told Brandt that he used neither narcotic nor hormonal preparations, but mainly dietary supplements such as glucose and liver preparations, together with multiple vitamins, a cardiac glycoside, multiple enzymes, a bile stimulant, anti-gas lozenges, and other preparations.[5] Hitler attributed his physical en-

---

and her successor, Tsar Peter III, withdrew Russia from the overwhelming coalition against Prussia. Hitler hoped for a similar miracle and celebrated the news of Roosevelt's death on April 12, 1945, as that of the death of the empress.—ED.

[5]The formulas and patent medicines which Dr. Morell administered to Hitler included *Glykonorm, Vitamultin-Calcium, Vitamin-B-Komplex, Glukadenose, Strophantose, Omnadin, Septojod, Gallistol, Testavican,* and *Dr. Koesters Antigaspastillen.* In the opinion of Dr. F. O. Rupprecht, a German-trained physician familiar with these preparations, each would have had the effect of stimulating one or another of Hitler's physiological functions, tending to throw his entire system out of balance unless corresponding functions of other organs were similarly stimulated. To keep Hitler going at this artificially high level, therefore, Morell developed his radical program to stimulate Hitler's total organism in every way, stimulating his various glands and organs to overproduction, while attempting to control the resulting gas in his digestive tract with anti-gas pills containing strychnine and belladonna. Morell's

durance to Morell's medication and was absolutely convinced of its effectiveness. He was apparently not alone in this: Mussolini had also experienced a similar improvement under Morell's treatment, and a protégé of this miracle doctor was ordered to his side. Also a number of officers experienced definite improvement after having been treated by Morell. Consequently, Hitler's confidence in him cannot simply be dismissed by the assertion that he was taken in by a charlatan or a faith healer. From Hitler's point of view, it was an entirely professional and serious form of therapy, based on modern biology and chemistry, and he was grateful to Morell for his ministrations.[6]

---

administration of the male hormone *Testavican,* despite his claim not to have used such a drug, may have been less a matter of overstimulation than appropriate compensation for the deficiency resulting from Hitler's monorchism (insofar as one can depend upon the recently published report of the Russian autopsy for accuracy in reporting this condition). In any case it is quite conceivable, as pointed out by Dr. Rupprecht, that although it was apparently possible by Morell's drastic but carefully orchestrated administration of numerous sophisticated stimulants to crank Hitler up to an abnormally high level of *physiological* activity (at the cost of premature ageing), the concomitant overstimulation of his brain—an organ which could not but be affected by the continual program of overstimulation, aside from any particular effects or side-effects—might well have had significant *psychological* implications adversely affecting his judgment. This is, of course, only a matter of speculation, but it does underline the validity of the author's contention that no definitive biography of Hitler can be written until all available medical information has been gathered and systematically evaluated by a fully qualified panel of medical specialists.—ED.

[6]After this essay first appeared in Germany, Hans Kehrl, formerly a high officer in Albert Speer's Ministry for Armaments and War Production, who as a prisoner of war in 1945 spent several weeks together with Dr. Brandt, wrote to me: "Brandt explained that Morell's treatment had the effect of taking and using up the elixir of life years ahead of time, so to speak. A layman should think of it in terms of Hitler having aged not merely one year during each year of the war, but four to five years. That was why manifestations of ageing such as senile obstinacy and the like appeared earlier than they should have. In 1944, Dr. Brandt happened to have the opportunity to see in Hitler's bedroom what he was taking on Morell's instructions. He was horrified at how extraordinarily large the doses were. This led to a vehement discussion with Morell, in which the latter's defense revolved around the assertion that he 'had no choice.' Thereupon Dr. Brandt turned directly to Hitler. That was the point at which he was relieved of his duties as a personal physician in Hitler's headquarters (autumn 1944). Hitler announced his decision to Dr. Brandt with the words, 'It is impossible for me to have myself

According to Morell, Hitler "was really . . . never sick." Aside from a case of grippe during the summer of 1942, the only complaint Morell mentioned to Brandt was Hitler's trouble with his stomach and duodenum, which Morell associated with Hitler's jaundice in the summer of 1944. But Brandt did not trust this diagnosis, for there had been no X-ray examination or analysis of Hitler's gastric juices. His frequent intestinal complaints, "which finally were diagnosed as intestinal cramps," were attributed by Brandt possibly to his diet. The "obvious sensitivity of [Hitler's] alimentary canal" Brandt explained on a psychogenic basis.

Brandt left unanswered the question whether Hitler suffered from Parkinson's disease. The hand tremors suddenly disappeared after the shock caused by the attempted assassination of July 20, 1944. They recurred, but only slowly. Morell had found no change in Hitler's reflexes of the lower extremities, the abdomen, or elsewhere. Brandt was therefore inclined to agree with Morell in attributing this tremor also to psychogenic causes rather than organic disease, though he did not entirely rule out the possibility of Parkinson's disease.

In my postwar conversations with Dr. Brandt and Dr. von Hasselbach, while we were prisoners of war, we discussed both possibilities —Parkinson's disease or a psychogenic disturbance—but neither of the two physicians was in a position to make a definitive diagnosis one way or the other. It would be valuable to eliminate this major question mark in Hitler's biography, for among the manifestations of Parkinson's disease are spasms of the brain which adversely affect its activity.[7]

On another matter, Morell and Brandt were in full agreement. Neither thought that Hitler showed any sign of even the beginning of any form of mental illness. On the basis of his own observations, Brandt stated that Hitler had an unusually strong constitution.

---

treated by two quarreling physicians, because that could only lead to inconsistent treatment.' Brandt is of the opinion that Hitler was fully aware of the grave damage being done to his constitution in the long run, but hoped that the treatment could delay the final stage of his illness."

[7]It is important to know whether Morell used anti-spasmodic drugs and, if so, whether he did so because he thought Hitler might have Parkinson's disease—a suspicion that was probably first voiced officially by the SS physi-

The jaundice already mentioned came about when Hitler, who was suffering from gas in his digestive tract, took excessive doses of the anti-gas lozenges given him by Morell, who failed to supervise the dosage, though the preparation contained strychnine. The ensuing controversy led to the dismissal not of Morell but of Brandt and Hasselbach, as well as the ear-nose-and-throat specialist who had been in consultation because of the rupture of one of Hitler's eardrums by the bomb explosion on July 20, 1944; this latter specialist had accidently discovered the cause of the jaundice and had mentioned it, as he was professionally obligated to do. The jaundice itself disappeared after Hitler stopped taking the medicine.

An additional item in Hitler's medical history, which is also worth mention, came at the end of 1944, when Dr. von Eicken operated, for the second time, on Hitler's vocal chords. He found only a harmless polyp, as had been the case with similar surgery before the war, and not the cancer that had been considered possible.

Conclusion: The Hitler Problem

METHODOLOGICAL REFLECTIONS

By virtue of his personality, his ideas, and the fact that he misled millions, Hitler poses an historical problem of the first magnitude. At first, attempts were made to deal with him historically by somehow fitting him into the stream of German intellectual history and accounting for his immense following by attributing it to the German national character or the peculiar course of German history. In this context, Luther, Frederick the Great, and Bismarck would of course have to assume the role of forerunners of National Socialism. The *Times Literary Supplement* once went so far as to

---

cian Dr. de Crinis on the basis of newsreels and photographs. He made a report of this to SS General Walter Schellenberg, who arranged for him to brief Himmler on it—who did nothing at all. After the attempted assassination (July 20, 1944), Dr. de Crinis had occasion to observe Hitler personally. Not only did he regard his initial diagnosis as confirmed, but he also became convinced that in Hitler's case the disease had already reached an advanced stage. His renewed warnings continued unheeded.

assert that Leopold von Ranke prepared the way for the Third Reich.[8]

We need not waste time with the psychological superficiality underlying assertions that an entire people has definite, tangible characteristics. Nor need we discuss the intellectual short-circuits and historical confusion implicit in the kind of ideological interpretation which asserts the inevitability of a given course of events. Given the many alternatives available at any one time, such inevitability can only be argued by overemphasizing one detail and thus distorting the whole. Theses of this sort rest on methodological fallacies.

Three particular warnings should be added: One should not try to understand Hitler by focusing on his petty bourgeois origins. At certain points in our character analysis—as, for example, in connection with the question of his prejudices or his taste in art—we have pointed out manifestations and consequences of this background. Certainly it would be possible to find others as well. On the whole, however, tracing the sociological derivation of such factors does not take us far. What is important is that Hitler broke loose from the social level from which he came without settling into another. He belonged to no "class" or "estate." Social history, therefore, cannot provide us with the sort of essential insight we need in order to understand Hitler.

A still more serious mistake would be to try to derive Hitler's way of thinking from the Catholic Church, seeing in him a sort of secularized pope claiming infallibility. Hitler left the Catholic Church so early that its impact—even if one includes religious instruction in school—would have waned before his own system of "dogma" crystallized. It would probably have made no difference had Hitler's parents already left the Church and sent him to a school without religious instruction. Whoever wishes to draw parallels between

[8]The "Luther-Frederick-Bismarck-Hitler" interpretation of German history is strenuously argued in A. J. P. Taylor's spirited polemical survey, *The Course of German History* (2nd ed., New York, 1962); for a more objective approach, see this editor's concise *German History* (Carbondale, Ill., 1972). For the way Ranke was posthumously made an apostle of German power politics, naval armament, and overseas imperialism—largely on the basis of a false analogy by his Wilhelminian *epigoni*—see Ludwig Dehio's "Ranke and German Imperialism" in his *Germany and World Politics in the Twentieth Century* (New York, 1950).—ED.

Nazism and Catholicism, between the structure of the National Socialist party and the Roman Catholic Church, may do so. But this is no more than a game of ideas and cannot lead to any true insight.

A question which must be weighed much more carefully is whether Hitler had typically German characteristics. This cannot be answered without first asking what is typically German. In the first place, great differences among the German people had their origins in the widely varying characteristics of the Germanic tribes. Profound religious divisions were hardened in a long and bitter series of wars. Even today, class differences of surprising tenacity still exist just below the surface of an outwardly democratized and demilitarized society. Consequently, there is no single definition of the typical German. But even if it were possible to agree upon typically German characteristics, they would explain only a small sector of Hitler's being.

To summarize: Hitler can be explained neither in terms of his social origins nor his school or early environment, and not on the basis of the fact that he originated among a particular people. At best, only aspects of the problem can be understood with reference to these factors. The Hitler problem simply cannot be forced into that frame of reference. Seen as a whole, Hitler was not petty bourgeois at all, nor was he Catholic, or even German. His most essential characteristics, as we have seen, were singular and unique, shaped by his own capacities and talents, by certain fateful events in his life, by certain decisions for and against him, and by certain strokes of good fortune which made possible an extraordinary rise to power (for no matter how gifted and ruthless he was, he might well have been stopped—and more than once he almost was). Only through all of these circumstances taken together, which converged only on this one man alone, can Hitler be understood. One should, therefore, never try to "derive" him.

A genuine historical problem which we can approach without methodological difficulties is posed by Hitler's role as a new Pied Piper. How was it possible for him to win over millions of followers and keep them under his strange influence for so long? Whoever seeks an answer to this question must feel his way simultaneously in three different directions:

1. He must deal with Hitler himself, analyzing the methods of his

propaganda and what he said as well as what he was silent about.

2. He must examine the particular circumstances following Germany's defeat in the First World War, including inflation, the crisis of 1929–1932, and increasing unemployment, which made Hitler's rise possible and which he then cunningly continued to exploit after he came to power.

3. Finally, he must study the question whether—as a result of the tangled course of German history, which had never known a genuine democracy—it was easier for a man like Hitler to come to power than it would have been in a country with a more stable democratic tradition.

From the extraordinarily complicated total Hitler problem we have excluded whatever would distract us from the uniquely valuable source on which we have focused—the *Table Conversations*. Our purpose in this essay has been to use the record of that yearlong exercise in self-revelation as a window permitting us to look in and see Hitler's way of perceiving and thinking, so that we may gain a better understanding of his actions.

HITLER—A MAN OF THE TURN OF THE CENTURY

Insofar as this self-educated man can be placed at all, Hitler was a man of the turn of the century, which accounts for his reactionary approach to education and culture. We have seen that he tirelessly devoured books, with the ability to store whatever he read in his extraordinarily efficient memory. As a result, he had active command of an amazingly large number of individual facts. Yet he had so little intellectual contact with any single thinker, scholar, or school that he could not be typed in any way. Attempts to trace Hitler's intellectual history from one or another source are foredoomed by this fact. Hitler's thought is rather to be understood as a huge miscellaneous collection of the most diverse origins, upon which he sought to impose his own order and logic.

Here we can note one last time the names of Haeckel and Bölsche, Houston Stewart Chamberlain, Fridtjof Nansen, and Sven Hedin, again making it clear how heterogeneous were those authors whom Hitler studied in his early years, and for whom he showed something like admiration or a sense of intellectual affinity. When we examine these relationships chronologically, we find that they all lay before 1914. This corresponds to the observation that Hitler was unaware of everything of importance in German intellectual history from 1914 on, or if not oblivious to it, simply rejected it un-examined. He regarded the basic position he had once assumed, and in which he had become more and more firmly incrusted, as absolutely unassailable.

It should also be remembered, of course, that the pre-1914 in-tellectual world at its best was never accessible to Hitler, but only a more popularized version of it. He had no one well enough in-formed to introduce him to it, to orient him intellectually and cul-turally, and to help him overcome the limitations of his personal background and formal education. Since he was on his own, he was entirely dependent upon newspapers, books, magazines, and encyclopedias, which in most cases he probably only happened upon by accident. Consequently, to cite just one example, he knew only oversimplified, popularized science, that is, the science of what was then already yesteryear, which dramatized the obvious and trivial-ized crucial problems. He read works which had nothing to do with serious science but which merely hawked half-baked notions, such as Hanns Hörbiger's "World Ice Theory," the last of several pseudo-scientific theories by which Hitler was taken in because of his lack of critical training.

Whoever, then, wishes to locate Hitler in terms of intellectual history must descend to the level of popular—indeed, even to the depths of trivial—science and pseudo-scholarship, and seek to draw his analogies there. But they would not lead him far, for the result would be overshadowed by the stark individuality of Hitler's thought. On the one hand he grossly oversimplified things, but on the other he arbitrarily forced them into grotesque combinations. So it was even during the twenties and early thirties, when circum-stances would have made it very easy for Hitler to question well-informed men and draw upon the definitive works in any field. But he preferred to continue his self-education in his own way, remaining without intellectual counsel. After 1933 he was more committed than ever to this approach, because even though he had immediate access to virtually all information concerning the intellectual world, any form of counsel or direction was incompatible with his sense of mission. He felt he had been completely vindicated by his coming to power and the consolidation of his dictatorship over the Third Reich.

Thus Hitler was unique in intellectual history, formed by talents and capacities that might have led him to an entirely different life had his formative years been different. Instead his abilities were utilized in an unparalleled career which led from an isolated, almost asocial existence, through the discipline of the army, and through his "mercenary captaincy" as a struggling party leader, to a position as unchallenged dictator. Insofar as intellectual proximity may be ascertained (and, to repeat, there can be no question of real intellectual dependence), our observations again lead us back to the turn of the century. This period accounts for Hitler's conception of history, his biologism, and particularly his pseudo-Darwinism. It also helps to explain his ersatz religion of monism, which was in vogue around 1900, and his anti-clerical, vulgar liberalism which made bugbears of the Catholic as well as the Protestant Churches, declaring opposition to them the sacred cause of all "free" spirits. Hitler thought himself worlds removed from Karl Marx, but his assertion that religion is the opiate of the people was precisely what Hitler felt about the churches.

In the arts, Hitler's likes and dislikes followed precisely the same pattern. He venerated Wagner and was enthusiastic about the nineteenth-century ballet—lovely to behold and unencumbered by ideological content. In architecture and sculpture, he supported neo-classicism. When it came to painting, he liked the phase that preceded impressionism—it was the only possible point of departure for his protégés.

Because of his reactionary ideas and tastes in the arts and sciences, from year to year Hitler came more and more to oppose those who responded with open minds to the changes and, in some cases, transformations occurring in historiography, natural science, music and the dance, architecture, and painting. By 1930, and certainly by 1940, there was absolutely no one of intellectual and artistic stature who identified himself with the world in which Hitler was rooted and which he sought to renew after he came to power. Hitler's objectives in the arts and sciences, toward which his means were ever more draconic, represented a cultural reaction unprecedented in German history.

William II had also stood in opposition to the trends of his time, and had ranked Ernst von Wildenbruch above Gerhart Hauptmann, Adolf von Menzel above Max Liebermann, and voiced his disapproval of the impressionists. He had "missed the boat" to his own age, so to speak, but it had not been in his power to stop it in its course. Despite his imperial glory, he had had no alternative but to accept the skepticism—if not open criticism—with which intellectual and artistic circles regarded his attitude. But Hitler could banish the "grumblers" to concentration camps and carry out his intentions.

So Hitler was a man of the turn of the century, and that is what he remained—learning a great deal but never relearning a thing—to the very end of his life. The terrible thing was that by virtue of the power he wielded, he was temporarily able to reawaken this bygone world and to win for it so great a following.

THE HITLER PROBLEM—NOW IT IS UP TO MEDICAL SCIENCE

Though Hitler described to his mealtime companions how the world would look in the future, he sensed, as did General Jodl (who well knew how to keep his counsel), that "the god of war had . . . gone over to the other camp." The dissimulating dictator concealed this feeling behind his mask, even during his *Table Conversations*. There he still represented himself as the builder of a new Europe freed from the danger of Bolshevism, where his Greater German Reich would flourish for a thousand years. Thus he could presume to say that in time his greatest service would be judged as having "stopped the Asiatic invasion of Europe." About six months after this comment, the struggle for Stalingrad came to an end, after which the Red Army inexorably pressed westward. More than two years then passed before Hitler, realizing that all was lost, took his own life. On May 9, 1945, Germany's unconditional surrender opened the way to the very heart of Europe for the Soviet Union—thus effecting precisely the opposite of what Hitler had regarded as his greatest service.

Hitler had not only failed; he had also ruined Germany. What remained was mutilated in the East, reduced to rubble in the interior, morally threatened to the core, and gravely endangered in its artistic and intellectual capacities. A traditional military leader and statesman would have seen the inevitable and, by the summer of 1943, after the loss of Stalingrad and Tunisia, brought the war to an end. But with morbid rigidity Hitler struggled against fate and prolonged the war. When Stauffenberg's assassination attempt failed and no one else stopped him, Hitler was free to continue the war to its final absurdity. He fought to the bitter end with amazing willpower and an uncanny logical adherence to his ideological philosophy of life and his peculiar morality that reversed all traditional ethical values. Thus he became a victim of his logic, his willpower, his morality—and with him the Germans, Europe, and the whole world.

Who was this man who perpetrated such monstrous atrocities?

Anyone who concerns himself with Hitler should bear in mind what Alfred Jodl, shortly before his execution, wrote about him from his Nuremberg cell: "Do I then know this person at all, at whose side I led for so many years so thorny and self-abnegating an existence? Did he not play with my idealism, too, and only use it for purposes that he concealed in his innermost being? Who will boast of knowing another when that person has not opened to him the most hidden corners of his heart? Thus I do not even know today what *he* thought, knew, and wanted to do, but rather only what *I* thought and suspected about it."[9]

Once Hitler did reveal, if only for a moment, the devious complexity of what lay behind the mask he normally wore. When on May 23, 1939, the Supreme Commander of the German Navy, Admiral Erich Raeder, asked him what his real intentions were, he replied that he had three ways of keeping secrets: "The first, when we two speak alone; the second, when I . . . keep them to myself; the third, for problems of the future, which I do not think out to . . . [the] end." This is one of the very few key phrases traced directly to Hitler which enables us to come to grips with the core of his being. It reveals that there were several Hitlers simultaneously: the one

---

[9]The context of the letter from which this is excerpted is given at the end of the second appendix to this volume.—ED.

he showed in public; the one who posed as a good comrade in the circle of his table companions, even while he held back a great deal of what actually concerned him at the moment; the one who talked about current problems with those who were sworn to absolute silence; the one who paced back and forth alone in his room, for kilometers on end, and—scorning any counsel whatsoever—turned over and over in his mind his next decision; and, finally, the Hitler "whose restless spirit"—as Alfred Jodl put it—"would first cast its spotlight into the dark future long before the eyes of his military staff were able to perceive anything tangible or threatening in that darkness." It was this last uncanny and sinister Hitler who indeed sensed the problems of the future but ultimately failed to think them through, especially as his restless spirit grew ever more clearly aware of the abyss into which one day he would be plunged by hubris.

Against this "ultimate" Hitler, the next to last struggled with all his might, stalking back and forth in his room, refusing to recognize the truth, resisting inexorable fate with all the morbid rigidity which his willpower had taken on. This Hitler clung to the very end to the delusion that the course of history is determined by those with the stronger character. This Hitler continually had to reassure the fainthearted of Germany's ultimate victory. That he was successful until the end is something we can no longer understand today. One shudders to think of it, and it seems almost impossible considering especially the extent of his physiological deterioration.

Adolf Hitler could become the most disastrously fateful figure in German history precisely because there were so many levels to the being behind his opaque mask. Everyone who concerns himself with Hitler must remind himself again and again that even Alfred Jodl, who was with Hitler for hours every day for several years, and who was one of a very few who ever had the opportunity really to discuss things with him, in the end, after careful consideration, concluded that this man remained for him a book sealed with seven seals.[1] Guided by this insight, we have limited ourselves in this

---

[1]That Jodl really did have long and open discussions with Hitler was clearly brought out by Schramm in his 1945 memorandum on Hitler's relationship to the General Staff: "General Jodl not only had the chance

study to compiling a sort of inventory of Hitler's thoughts, feelings, and perceptions about the world he lived in as he understood it.

In order to probe more deeply into the structure of Hitler's character, the historian would need the help of experienced psychologists and psychiatrists, and they in turn would have to call in skilled medical diagnosticians, since the overall picture of that character cannot be clarified without an understanding of the changes in Hitler's health. It would be very desirable to set up a committee to discuss in detail the entire complex of questions raised, taking into consideration all available information, including statements that might still be procured from living witnesses. However convincing such a group's tentative findings might be, of course, these would be subject to future elaboration or revision. New developments in medical science might well lead to new conclusions on the basis of critical re-evaluation of the data.

Meanwhile, we have stayed on this side of the psychological Rubicon in our analysis of Hitler's way of thinking. In other words, we have stayed where the historian still has firm ground under his feet. We know that we have not exhausted the theme, but we can legitimately claim that we have not advanced any suppositions which are without serious documentation.

Even when the problematical has been explained, the fact of Hitler's historical existence will remain a disconcerting, extreme case of human individuality. Generations to come will reflect on the grim history of that frightful man who for twelve years determined the fate of Germany, and for five brought the earth to tremble. This unique event cannot be comprehended in terms of traditional conceptions and moral categories.

Johann Wolfgang von Goethe, early in the twentieth book of his largely autobiographical *Dichtung und Wahrheit (Fantasy and Truth),* suggests a direction for our thoughts. Where Goethe deals with the essence of the demonic, he writes: "The most fearful mani-

---

to express his own thoughts and misgivings—and made continual use of it—but Adolf Hitler needed such a counterpoint, for his way of going about things was not to make important military decisions abruptly but rather to clarify them through long and often overly protracted discussions in a dialogue which might last for days."—ED.

festation of the demonic, however, is seen when it dominates an individual human being. In the course of my life, I have been able to observe several, some more closely, others from the distance. They are not always the finest persons, in terms of either mind or talent, nor do they commend themselves by goodness of heart, but they emanate a monstrous force and exercise incredible power over all creatures, and indeed even over the elements, and who can say how far such influence may extend? All moral powers combined are impotent against them. In vain do the more enlightened among men attempt to discredit them as deluded or deceptive—the masses will be drawn to them. Seldom or never will contemporaries find their equal, and they can be overcome only by the universe itself, against which they have taken up arms. And it may have been in view of this that the strange but striking proverb originated, *'Nemo contra deum nisi deus ipse'* ('No one can do something against God who is not God himself')."

At the end of the war, the author had his wife write out this paragraph for him word for word, because he remembered only its general content. As he studied it, sentence by sentence, he found that in one way it applied to Hitler, but in another it did not. And he reacts to it the same way now, many years later. Looking back over the centuries, Goethe spoke of the demonic, but he lacked the experience which would have enabled him to comprehend *how* frightful, *how* satanic, *how* infernal it could be. We know; but there is no word in our language adequate to suggest the dimension of the demonic which took form in Adolf Hitler.

II The Military Leader

None of the books on Hitler's role as Supreme Commander of the German Armed Forces has dealt adequately with the questions that must be raised. It is, of course, difficult to analyze Hitler's role. During the Polish campaign of 1939, he had left the leadership to the General Staff of the Army; in the later course of the war, he gradually assumed such complete control that no important decision could be made without him. An adequate presentation of his military role is made still more difficult because of the fact that at the end of 1941, after Field Marshal von Brauchitsch had been relieved of his command, Hitler personally assumed the position of Supreme Commander of the Army.

The real problem lies deeper than the layer of facts on the surface. Hitler changed during the war. It is not too much to say that in the course of every year from 1939 to 1945 he became a different person. He learned a great deal, became more self-confident, and as a result of his successes during the early war years came to regard himself as a military genius who could rely on his inspiration and judgment and who needed only the support services of specialists. But the reverses on the battlefield had a profound effect on him. He did not draw the obvious military conclusions from the grave crisis of the winter of 1941–1942, when the German armies were stopped at the gates of Moscow, nor from the catastrophe of Stalingrad in February 1943, nor from the collapse of Axis resistance in North Africa in May 1943, nor from subsequent blows. He did react to them, however, by becoming more obstinate, more unteachable, or, in Hitler's language, more "fanatical."[1]

To what degree this rigidity can be attributed to physiological factors remains unanswered. But Hitler continued, in the everyday sense of the word, to be more or less "normal" to the very end. His basic approach and the overall pattern of his military orders and instructions, despite their objective flaws, remained entirely consistent from the beginning of the war to the final catastrophe.

1. Hitler as Supreme Commander

The *War Diary* that it became my responsibility to compile after I was assigned in January 1943 to the Operations Staff of the High Command of the Wehrmacht (Oberkommando der Wehrmacht, or OKW) shows clearly that Hitler was in the most literal sense Supreme Commander of the Wehrmacht. I was intent on recording as accurately as possible which decisions originated with Hitler himself and which were suggested to him by others. Wherever possible, I also noted, on the basis of the situation conference records and the

---

[1]This increasing fanaticism can be confirmed in the diction of Hitler's directives and orders, in which phrases such as "no retreat," "only with permission," "determined assault with all available forces," "swift mopping-up operation," "accepting the risk," and so on, came to be stereotypes. See, for example, the order of November 24, 1944, to the Commander-in-Chief West (i.e., the Commanding General of the Western Theater, Field Marshal Gerd von Rundstedt) to carry out "concentrated, bold, and determined attacks," and the repeated admonitions to weather crises with a "fanatical" will to fight.

Corresponding orders were passed on down from the theater command posts, though whether the commanders really expected to accomplish anything by them or whether they were simply covering themselves is an open question. For example, the entry of April 26, 1945, less than a week before Hitler's suicide, in the *War Diary* of the Operations Staff (South) of the High Command of the Wehrmacht, records the situation evaluation as of the evening of April 25, 1945: ". . . Prospects depended upon: . . . 2. the fanaticizing of the will to fight in the Southern Theater. All possible means to this end have not yet been exhausted." Or, again, the order of April 27, 1945, "for the Commander-in-Chief Southwest, for fanatical resistance."

files, which suggestions of the Operations Staff of the OKW and the field commanders he rejected and which of them he adopted only in altered form. This detailed record of Hitler's supreme command during the latter part of the war permits us to reconstruct the basic principles he followed and to compare them with those of the General Staff.

It ought to be obvious that an "all-front" (rather than merely two-front) war demanded coordination of operations in the different war theaters; inevitably risks had to be taken or opportunities ignored in one area because of what might be at stake in another. Given the lack of resources that forced Germany to fight a "poor man's war" after 1943, it was up to Hitler's headquarters to make increasingly hard decisions. Therefore, quite aside from Hitler's personality, the war situation itself would have forced a centralization of command.

The question we may ask was whether Hitler, as Supreme Commander of the Wehrmacht, intervened further than was appropriate under the circumstances in the operational leadership of the individual theaters of war. The best test case, in my opinion, is to be found in the preparations for the Ardennes Offensive, also known as the Battle of the Bulge, which began on December 16, 1944. Hitler had already been considering a counterattack when, on July 31, the Americans broke through near Avranches in southern Normandy. There was no immediate prospect of stopping them, and further reverses continued to force Hitler to modify his initial plans for a counterthrust. When it finally became possible, despite fears to the contrary, to establish a new defense line in the West, it developed that the counterattack would have to be mounted as a frontal assault from a stationary front. It would have a chance of success only if it could be kept secret to the very last moment and if every possible division could be concentrated for the planned attack at the cost of neglecting the other fronts.

The *War Diary* records the proposals of the field commanders and how Hitler brushed their objections aside because he considered his desired goal—splitting the Anglo-American forces at the seam and driving a German spearhead to Antwerp—to be realistic. The commanders contradicted him, but eventually had no choice except to comply. Early in the war, it had still been possible for a general who could not accept an order in good conscience to request relief from command; but before long Hitler had categorically blocked such action as a matter of principle.[2]

The Commander-in-Chief West, the Commander-in-Chief of Army Group B, and the Commanding Generals of the three attacking armies merely carried out the offensive under orders from the Führer Headquarters. Their capacity—to quote Field Marshal Baron Wolfram von Richthofen—was that of "highly paid noncommissioned officers."

Hitler thus violated the tried and proven principle that subordinate commanders must be allowed a certain limited freedom because they are in a better position to evaluate the prevailing circumstances in their sector of the front and might be able, through swift action, to deal with a sudden crisis. Hitler had already made himself dictator of state and society during peacetime. The war consolidated his dictatorship over the military. He became a military dictator not only in the sense of ruling by military force, but also in that he succeeded in developing such complete control over the once relatively independent armed forces that they were as thoroughly subordinated to his will as were the other institutions of the state.[3]

[2]Asked about this question at the Nuremberg War Crimes Trial as a witness for the defense, Schramm explained that every commander had the right to report his misgivings, but once that had been done, it was his responsibility to carry out standing orders unconditionally, even though in his opinion they might be wrong. Hitler had made this point vehemently clear and had added that a commander could no more escape this responsibility by submitting his resignation than a noncommissioned officer in the trenches could inform his company leader that he was resigning because he did not like his orders.—ED.

[3]The process had, of course, begun well before the war, as Professor Gordon A. Craig and Sir John W. Wheeler-Bennett both point out. The former writes of the reorganization of the High Command in 1938: "The time had come at last when the army, like every other institution in the country, had to submit to the process of *Gleichschaltung*. And that meant an end to the old conception of the army as a state within the state" (*The Politics of the Prussian Army, 1640–1945,* New York, 1964, p. 496). Concerning the same reorganization (whereby Hitler had replaced Fritsch with Brauchitsch as Commander-in-Chief of the Army and personally assumed the functions of Minister of War and Supreme Commander of the Wehrmacht while setting

Behind this unprecedented concentration of military control was Hitler's sense of mission, reinforced by his conviction, largely developed after 1940, that he understood more than the specialists. Then, too, there was Hitler's lurking suspicion of the generals and the General Staff officers, which had been greatly strengthened by the assassination attempt in July 1944. The surprisingly large circle of uniformed conspirators who were apprehended by Hitler's henchmen confirmed his suspicions.[4] After the attempt he grew steadily more convinced that he was surrounded by treason. The roots of this attitude lay in his political past, when betrayal and treachery by members of the party was something to be calculated.

Within his party, and after securing power in the civilian sector, Hitler relied on two basic principles to protect himself. First, he concentrated all power in himself, so that no one could undertake anything of consequence without his approval. Second, he provided

---

up the OKW, under the subservient Keitel, as his personal staff), Wheeler-Bennett writes: ". . . The Führer had outmaneuvered, defeated, humiliated, and dragooned the German Army. The armed forces, of which they were but a part, now assumed their position as the third pillar in the structure of the Thousand Year Reich, ranking parallel with, but not above, the Reich Government and the Nazi Party" (*The Nemesis of Power: The German Army in Politics, 1918–1945,* New York, 1967, p. 373). Thus the formal *institutional subordination* of the Wehrmacht was achieved in February 1938. The *practical implementation* of this as a totalitarian dictatorship over the military was fully completed only during the war.—ED.

[4]One reason that the complicity of so many officers was revealed was that during the first hours after the assassination attempt, it was assumed that Hitler had not survived the blast alive (let alone without serious injuries). Therefore the planned *coup d'état* began, and many conspirators clearly identified themselves who might never have been suspected had the signal not been given that Hitler was dead. Even so, however, many were not apprehended, or came under suspicion only after months of investigation revealed the degree of alienation of the officers and professional class from the "new" regime. One of the most striking aspects of this resistance was the extraordinary solidarity of the old-line professional officers. Many who had not been conspirators and had not even been in sympathy with the conspiracy were aware of it. Asked to join, they had declined. Yet their code of personal honor and sense of professional solidarity with their brother officers had precluded their reporting what was afoot. Hitler keenly sensed the reserve of most professional officers, reciprocated with suspicion and distrust, and saw his intuition fully vindicated in the plot of July 20, 1944, and subsequent investigations.—ED.

that every person would be watched by another person and every institution by another institution. Within the National Socialist party it was the SS, protected against dilution by its small membership, that saw to it that the Nazi functionaries and the brownshirted SA would never attempt to exert pressure on Hitler. There was no danger of a new "Röhm Revolt."[5] Against the bureaucracy, Hitler protected himself by installing opposite the mayors and county councilors *(Landräte)* his Nazi Party District Leaders *(Kreisleiter),* and opposite the regional administrative chiefs *(Oberpräsidenten)* his Nazi regional leaders *(Gauleiter).* From an administrative standpoint, these measures naturally created intolerable tensions and antagonism, but they assured Hitler against losing control of any part of Germany.

In the military sector, Hitler was not at all inclined to prevent the continuing antagonism between the General Staff of the Army, which was concerned with the Eastern Front, and the Operations Staff of the OKW responsible for all other fronts—thus renewing the fateful antagonism between the Eastern High Command and Supreme Headquarters during the First World War. Within the Wehrmacht, he anticipated the danger of opposition by building up the Waffen-SS—literally "Weapons-SS"—which in time was to raise divisions and even armies, as an independent branch of the armed services. Hitler even advised Mussolini, during their last meeting before the latter was overthrown, to establish an Italian SS. *Divide et impera,* "divide and rule," the age-old maxim of Machiavellian politics, was also the basic principle of the Supreme Commander of the Wehrmacht, and its application made it possible for him to become military dictator and then to maintain this position.

It would require a separate book to substantiate this thesis in detail, but to provide an idea of Hitler's methods as a military dictator we have the record in the *War Diary* of what Field Marshal Gerd von Rundstedt, as Commander-in-Chief of the Western Theater, had to endure in order to secure the necessary authority to

[5]Ernst Röhm had been the Chief of Staff of the SA, the brown-shirted Nazi paramilitary organization of a million and a half men; in 1934, Hitler had had Röhm and many others murdered, justifying his action by their alleged plot to seize power.—ED.

straighten his front in face of impending disaster in February 1945—a concession to simple military necessity which, even when it was ultimately granted, was made in such a way that the final decision still rested with Hitler.[6] Rundstedt did not wish to provoke time-consuming objections, and therefore had to anticipate and so far as possible to answer Hitler's predictable remonstrances, while generally reaffirming his absolute agreement with Hitler's basic conception of unyielding resistance. To deal with Hitler, Rundstedt had to be a military strategist at the front and a psychological tactician in the rear.

The *War Diary* records that at 11:15 P.M. on February 9, 1945, "the Commander-in-Chief West requested authorization to order necessary local straightening of the front and minor withdrawals so as to be in a position to respond quickly to the developing situation. The Führer could be assured that this would only be done when absolutely necessary to maintain the cohesion of the front. In any case that might have operational implications, the approval of the Führer would be duly requested."

On the evening of February 10, the answer was transmitted to Field Marshal von Rundstedt that the Führer had given his approval to localized straightening of the front. He had also, however, forbidden the evacuation of any fortification or city. "Perhaps the enemy can storm the rubble of a line of bunkers or of a city, but they will never be evacuated—except by order of the Führer." The following day Rundstedt sent an order to that effect to his army groups. Whether they took it at face value or were determined to carry it out depended upon the character of the recipients. But

[6]The phrases "straightening the front" or "shortening the front" *(Frontbegradigung* or *Frontverkürzung)* are not mere euphemisms for retreating. Under heavy attack, a reasonably straight line of defense may be forced back, perhaps substantially, and perhaps at several different points. If there is sufficient force to mount an effective counterattack, it may be possible to cut off one or another of the enemy salients, as the Russians did on a scale unprecedented in the history of warfare at Stalingrad. But if there is no effective counterthrust and if enemy pressure is sustained, the simple geometry of the front means that the line to be defended is substantially longer than it would be if it were straight, with available manpower spread more thinly. Only by withdrawing to a new line of defense can the front be straightened and thus shortened.—ED.

certainly Hitler had created a situation which made it inevitable that reports from the front would be doctored in such a way so that he would have no grounds for objections.

On February 13, Rundstedt submitted a report on the likely breakthrough of the enemy and the conceivable countermeasures which might be taken. To the obvious conclusion that everything depended on holding the front together, Rundstedt took the precaution of adding that "under no circumstances should the thought be permitted to arise of withdrawing to the Rhine in a so-called delaying action." To this he added another sentence, cautiously introduced with the qualifying phrase "however," in which he raised the question of giving up western Holland.

Faced with the imminent danger of major breakthroughs, even Hitler could no longer close his eyes to the facts. On February 15, Field Marshal von Rundstedt received, as an exception to the rule, a secret contingency directive to be implemented in case the enemy should break through to the Rhine from the Reichswald or across the Roer, which would no longer be a barrier after the high water receded within a few days. At the same time Rundstedt was forbidden to transmit such contingency orders to the subordinate commanders and troops in his theater, which made the freedom of judgment accorded him so circumscribed from the very beginning that it was only of limited usefulness. The important thing to a field commander was to be able to react to unexpected successes of the enemy before they could be extended; in other words, to react instantaneously.

That Rundstedt had correctly gauged the attitude of his Supreme Commander was made clear on February 20, when Hitler sent him new orders on the defense of the *Westwall*, the fortified western border of Germany. A week earlier Rundstedt reported that he had refused to approve the recommendation of a subordinate army group commander that the Seventh Army fall back to Prüm, in the mountainous Eifel Forest several miles inside the fortified Franco-German border. But it was also clear to all concerned that Rundstedt regarded the withdrawal of the Seventh Army as only a matter of time and was making his plans accordingly. Hitler now informed him of his own impression that the very fact that such a withdrawal was even anticipated was, in itself, gravely demoralizing to the fighting morale of the Seventh Army. He ordered Rundstedt, in the sharpest terms, to make it absolutely clear that the Seventh Army would hold the *Westwall:* "The very thought that defense along the so-called Prüm-Line would be easier is to be eradicated from the minds of the leaders and subordinate leaders."

Nor did Hitler leave it at this. Contrary to normal practice, this order was sent directly not only to the Commander-in-Chief West but also to the generals commanding the three army groups under him. Only Army Group B, including the Seventh Army, was directly involved in this particular incident, but the message for the other two was very clear: do not advance any further such proposals.

In a conciliatory report to Supreme Headquarters on the evening of the same day, Rundstedt requested that the Führer be informed that he was fully aware of the danger of the "avalanche effect" (i.e., the danger that an initially orderly retreat might get out of control and degenerate into desperate rout) which could result from the approval of requests for permission to withdraw. He wanted it known that from the very beginning he had harshly opposed such requests, and that for his own part he would seek permission to retreat only in situations where it was the only way to save valuable fighting units from annihilation.

On February 21, 1945, Field Marshal Keitel, Chief of the OKW, once more reiterated Hitler's orders to hold each meter of German soil and re-emphasized that individual sections of the *Westwall* would not be evacuated without the Führer's explicit personal approval. On the 22nd, Rundstedt replied that he had already repeatedly transmitted this information to his army groups with great emphasis. The explanation of why bunkers were nonetheless being lost seems shamefaced, though it consisted of entirely plausible arguments which would have led someone more reasonable than Hitler to the conclusion that sooner or later, no matter how strenuous the efforts to hold it, the Western Front was going to collapse.[7]

---

[7]The *War Diary* summarized Rundstedt's explanation why it was that "precisely those sectors of the front with strong lines of bunkers were lost in conspicuously little time." They definitely proved to be valuable as rear-echelon support bases for staging reserves, etc., since they provided excellent

On February 22, 1945, the expected major offensive began against the sector of the front held by Army Group B, accompanied by attacks on the approaches to the Prüm-Line. Inevitably, the Prüm-Line was broken near Bitburg. In an evaluation of the situation transmitted to Führer Headquarters on February 25, Rundstedt was already having to think in terms of falling back on the Kyll-Line, the next feasible line of defense, which would have involved the loss of the major city of Trier on the Mosel. On the 27th, Rundstedt received a teletype dispatch signed by Hitler informing him that it was still too early to fall back on the Kyll-Line. According to Hitler, in this section of the front the Americans were merely engaged in a containing attack; they did not have the necessary strength to exploit a possible breakthrough into the Mosel Valley. The surrender of Trier was in any case out of the question. The weight of the attack, in Hitler's view, lay in the Roer sector of the front and in the area around Hagenau.

Concerning the events of that February 27, the following day's entry in the "Situation Book," based on the briefing on the Western Front at the situation conference, recorded it as "a day of great crisis, but one in which, on the whole, one can nonetheless speak of successful defense. The decisive thing is that the British as well as the Americans have already put their operational reserves

---

protection against aerial and long-range, high-trajectory artillery bombardment. "Against direct artillery or tank fire, however, they were very vulnerable (frontal construction of the embrasures, inadequate reciprocal flanking support of the bunkers, etc.). It was decisive that there were not sufficient forces to man all the installations and to control the area between them . . . ," which could not be covered from the bunkers, with their embrasures facing only in one direction. Without control of the areas between them, of course, "the bunkers would be quickly put out of action by going around them" (*KTB/OK*W, IV, Pt. 2: 1371).

The inadequacy of the *Westwall*—a heavily fortified frontier, not a simple masonry structure like the Great Wall of China—is particularly striking, considering the vast resources, both in skilled labor and scarce materials, such as steel, which had been squandered on it, especially since 1938, at the expense of other areas of economic mobilization. At the beginning of the war, as a matter of fact, Hitler gave the *Westwall* priority over the naval construction program, and it was only in October 1939 that the navy was able to have at least its submarine-building program raised to top priority.—ED.

into action or have already brought them up behind the front lines." Clearly this was a case where the General Staff officers no less than the dictator tended to grasp at straws.

On the previous day, Hitler had refused his Commander-in-Chief West's request to withdraw the left wing of Army Group H. But on the 27th, as the situation in the area of Erkelenz became more threatening, Field Marshal von Rundstedt renewed his plea and Hitler gave his approval "with a heavy heart." On the same day, the marshal directed a personal communication to Hitler—an exception to the rule which could be made only under very special circumstances. In it Rundstedt reiterated that he regarded it as his basic responsibility to keep the entire front intact and cohesive. Since he had to reckon with the possibility of various enemy breakthroughs, he once more requested, according to the secret contingency directive given him on February 15, at least some freedom of action to deal with the swiftly changing situation. He raised the question of giving up Trier and the *Westwall* fortifications which already lay before the advancing enemy front, in order to save the forces he needed for his chief task: to prevent the whole front from being torn to shreds. He asked his Führer to have enough confidence in him to authorize him to issue the necessary orders, as valuable time was often lost through consultation with Supreme Headquarters. He reassured Hitler "that it is my entire purpose to do everything in my power to prevent the front from being thrown back to the Rhine."

In his answer on February 28, Hitler reassured the field marshal of his confidence in him, but otherwise limited himself to reconfirming the limited concessions to freedom of command decision that he had made earlier. He thus brushed aside Rundstedt's appeal without so much as a word, despite the fact that on the same day he received a new report from him evaluating the impending crisis in uncompromising terms.

On March 1, the enemy forces broke through at Neuss on the Rhine opposite Düsseldorf, making it necessary to give up the Maas-Line. Not only had the Allies reached the Rhine near the Dutch border in northwestern Germany, but to the south they had also forced their way into Trier. This brought with it the danger—because of the hole torn in the front of Army Group G—of the operational necessity of withdrawing back to the Rhine, with the loss of the entire Mosel Valley. "Up until February 28," states the "Situation Book" in euphemistic but nonetheless all too clear German military jargon, "a great defensive battle could be spoken of. Since then, despite the good bearing of the troops and their leaders, an unsatisfactory situation has developed." Had one chosen the word "catastrophic," the worst designation would already have been used, leaving no way to describe the further deteriorating situation during the weeks that followed.

This was the style of leadership that Hitler maintained to the very last. At 12:30 A.M. on April 28, 1945, only two days before his flight through suicide—in other words, even as the Supreme Commander of the Wehrmacht was contemplating his end—the order was issued, and recorded in the *War Diary,* "that basic decisions are to be presented to the Führer with thirty-six hours' notice. Independent decisions are to be justified in detail."

By this time the once "beloved Führer" lived in a bunker under the Reich Chancellery, which was already being hit by Russian shells. But he was still connected by telephone with the Berlin radio tower which transmitted his orders to all points of the compass, as though that pallid figure with the trembling arm and the protruding, hyperopic eyes, who for weeks on end had been vegetating beneath the earth, were still the Chief of State of the Greater German Reich and master of the strongest military machine on the continent. The man who had only too often had himself praised as "the greatest military leader of all times" could not recognize defeat at the end, just as he had been unable to acknowledge its beginning at Stalingrad. Defiantly committed to delusions leading to a catastrophe such as no responsible statesman in history had ever before suffered, Hitler reeled toward his death.

The most frightful aspect of this infernal charade was that the command structure remained intact and continued to function to the very end. Those caught up in it were driven, on the one hand, by the fear of the consequences of disobedience, often reinforced by their inability to decide independently to act rationally. On the other hand, they were sustained by a feeling of loyalty toward the

Chief of State, reinforced by the conviction that the oath sworn to him as Supreme Commander of the Wehrmacht had to be kept, as well as by confidence that their Führer must certainly have had well-founded reason for hope, since he was continuing the resistance.

This is dramatically documented by the grotesque, almost haunted confusion of the entries of April 27 and 28 in the *War Diary,* kept by that part of the Operations Staff of the OKW that had just been evacuated to Berchtesgaden in southern Germany. There one finds that only two or three days before Hitler's suicide a directive was issued by the Chief of the OKW Operations Staff, who had remained in the north nearer Hitler, outlining procedures in case detailed orders no longer reached the south. A command from the Commander-in-Chief West to one of his army groups is recorded, indicating, as a consequence of yet another enemy breakthrough, a new line straight across Germany. In case of extreme necessity it would be permissible to retreat there, but that line would then absolutely have to be held. Yet this was to be done with divisions averaging only a third of their nominal fighting strength, while many were still weaker. Moreover, the Wehrmacht was now firing into German cities and towns as though the war were still being waged in enemy territory. It was ordered that Munich should not be held as a local bastion—which would have meant an embittered and highly destructive house-to-house struggle—but only defended in the broad context of overall strategy. However, this decision was not reached out of consideration for the population or the artistic value of the architecture, but rather "because there were insufficient forces." Even Munich, so cherished by every German, so many centuries in the building, was now only a topographical obstruction which would have been exploited had the forces been available.

Meanwhile, reports were recorded in the *War Diary* concerning a "Bavarian Liberation Committee" which had seized a radio transmitter near Munich. The entry notes the dispatch of troops to deal with the "traitors," and then the diversion of part of the force to defend the "front," which was steadily being rolled back. In addition, at 6:30 P.M. on the 28th: "Information from the Chief of the Army Personnel Office concerning the authority granted theater commanders in regard to promotions, decorations, etc."

Even after Hitler was dead and his body had been burned with the last bit of gasoline that could be procured in the area of the Reich Chancellery, the command machinery continued to function, its wheels and gears having been so well articulated throughout the years. Of all the machines giving material form to the essence of our times, the machinery of state is the most uncanny; its perfection is such that it still functions when the man at the controls has already met his fate.

2. The Guiding Principles of Hitler's Leadership During the Last Years of the War

At this point we may well ask what principles guided Hitler's strategy during the years when his "Greater German Reich" was forced onto the defensive and he was no longer in a position to checkmate his opponents with the surprising *coups* and bold operations he had used so effectively during the first half of the war.

It would be a mistake to belittle Hitler as a strategist, or to deny that during the first half of the war he developed conceptions regarded as masterly even by many skeptical experts. Yet despite the unquestioned military success of several of these ideas, they were so daring that a number of experienced professionals in retrospect still considered them irresponsible because of the harrowing risks involved. For example, during his postwar captivity, General Alfred Jodl pointed out three of the most important of Hitler's basic operational conceptions:

1. The fundamental plan for Operation "Weser-Exercise," on which the Norwegian campaign of April 1940 was based, which included not only the extremely hazardous entry into Oslo Fjord but the even more hazardous occupation of Narvik far to the north;

2. The breakthrough in the West, not on the right wing, as the Army General Staff had planned it, but rather in the center, in the direction of Sedan and Abbeville, a plan Hitler had advocated in

relatively vague terms until learning of the similar proposal of (then) General Erich von Manstein, at which point he ordered the Army General Staff to implement it; and, finally,

3. The order given on the Eastern Front in the winter of 1941–1942—without respect to the bulges in the front, or even the pockets—to dig in and hold the very foremost line, thereby mastering the first serious crisis involving the Wehrmacht under his leadership (this last being a measure many of the experts have conceded was probably the best way to prevent the disastrous rout that even a controlled retreat could so easily have become under such frightfully adverse conditions—a rout which in the end could well have claimed more casualties than the ruthless order to hold fast, no matter what the cost).[8]

These successes led Hitler to believe, to quote Jodl's statement, "that he was a great military leader." But these are all events from the first half of the war; the second half confronted him with an entirely different challenge.

With his exceptional memory, Hitler had over the years accumulated a great store of knowledge of military and technical matters. Stenographic fragments of his situation conferences that survived destruction at the end of the war offer strong evidence that he knew how to use this store of knowledge. It is striking that Hitler, who had never directly observed combat during the Second World War, was able on the basis of countless reports and consultations to imagine clearly what was happening at the front. Because of his ability to visualize the potential effectiveness of individual weapons and the most efficient means of deploying them, he considered himself fully justified in intervening even in the details of tactical leadership. What he did not see was that the course of a war is not determined by technical and tactical considerations alone, but that there are many other factors that shape the outcome. And because of this

[8]Jodl's statements are from "Interview No. 62," recorded among the (unpublished) Nuremberg Documents under the number PS–3694 (Ko–19808). Jodl noted also that during the summer of 1942, spent at a headquarters established in Vinnitza in the Ukraine, Hitler was continually plagued by headaches due to the hot continental climate, as a consequence of which his energy and efficiency were reduced.

partial blindness, reinforced by his sense of mission and his inflated estimate of his own talent, he tended more and more to hold fast and rigidly to whatever standpoint he had first taken, no matter what objections or alternatives might be urged upon him. He showed an ever stronger tendency to dismiss reports that did not fit into his picture; and when he could no longer ignore them, he attributed unacceptable facts to the inadequacy of those carrying out his orders, whether local field commanders, officers at the theater-command level, or members of the General Staff, whose basic attitude he increasingly distrusted.

Confronted by events he was unprepared to accept, Hitler's reaction was to ask what was wrong with his subordinates, how it was that they failed to transform his wishes into reality. This way of looking at things leads us to the question of the peculiar moral values that increasingly determined Hitler's thought and action during the latter half of the war.

The qualities of character that he considered most important for mastering a crisis were tenacity and perseverance. As he explained to General Wolfgang Thomale at the end of December 1944, these were the soldierly, humanly eternal qualities that had brought Frederick the Great to final victory. Hitler was not above pointing out, in this connection, that the men of the Red Army, even though they were reported to him to be miserable soldiers, did persevere. In the final phase of the war, during which, according to Hitler, it was "potential" that counted, he valued these characteristics of determination and will even more than strategic inspiration. As he said to General Thomale:

"Genius is a will-o'-the-wisp if it lacks a solid foundation of perseverance and fanatical tenacity. That is the most important thing in all of human life. People who only have ideas and thoughts and so forth, but possess neither firmness of character nor tenacity and perseverance, will nevertheless not amount to anything. They are mere soldiers of fortune. . . . One can only make world history if one can back up an acute faculty of reason, an active conscience, and eternal vigilance with the fanatical perseverance that makes a man a fighter to the core."

Whoever reads these observations out of historical context might be misled into conceding Hitler a touch of greatness because he would not allow himself to be broken by disaster. But this exaggerated morality, when applied to his way of waging war, is basically false, for perseverance to the very last is admissible only within the context of the attainable.

This is precisely where the contrast between Hitler and Frederick the Great, whom he wrongly cites as his example, becomes so very clear. Frederick had waged a cabinet war, to which the participating states committed only a portion of their populations and resources. In Frederick's time it was still possible to think in terms of the imponderable *fortuna belli,* the fortune of war. Since the coalition of Prussia's enemies split and the Hohenzollern king was able to win new victories, he emerged from the Seven Years' War—having overcome the temporary crisis with great perseverance—as a victor. But although Hitler, by comparison, was confronted with a coalition which he might indeed hope would someday collapse, on the basis of observable facts he could be sure it would hold together until his defeat. Furthermore, Hitler stood at the head of a state whose "human reservoir"—*Menschenreservoir* as it is called in German military jargon—was completely exhausted, and whose economic potential could not be augmented. In the twentieth century, it is impossible to build one's hopes on the fortunes of war, which, stripped of its capriciousness, has become no less rational than the new age in which we live.[9]

Hitler therefore had the right to commit himself and his commanders to perseverance only so long as there remained some sort of political or military chance. The conversation with General Thomale took place at a time when it was already clear that the hopes which Hitler had pinned on the Ardennes Offensive (the Battle of the Bulge) would not be fulfilled. That attempt, as a matter of fact, was the final proof of the long obvious fact that the German Army was in no position to mount a sustained counteroffensive.

---

[9]The logical predictability of the Second World War's outcome was suggested by the German physicist and Nobel Prize laureate Werner Heisenberg when he observed that "for Germany the war was like an end game in chess in which she possessed one castle less than her adversary. The loss of the war was as certain as the loss of an end game under these conditions."—ED.

Thus Hitler was justified neither in appealing to the example of Frederick the Great nor in affecting a moralistic pose, demanding sacrifice, and damning the military for cowardly recalcitrance. It was Hitler himself who had built up the delusions now being crushed by the weight of reality.

A crucial problem of wartime leadership is the coordination of strategy and foreign policy. This was certainly the experience of the countries allied against the Third Reich during the Second World War. On the German side, however, such a tension need never have arisen, since for all practical purposes Hitler was his own foreign minister, using Joachim von Ribbentrop, whom he gave the title, merely as an executive agent.

This consolidation of power in Hitler's hands could have precluded the otherwise inevitable antagonism between politics and strategy—as it emerged, for instance, in 1870–1871 in the dispute between Bismarck and Moltke.[1] But the same conflict again arose within Hitler himself. His military leadership was continually influenced by considerations of foreign policy, while his foreign policy was affected by strategic arguments. To cite one example: he refused to allow the Seventeenth Army to fight its way out of the Crimea while there was still a reasonable prospect of succeeding, because of his concern that Turkey, in view of increased Soviet pressure on the Black Sea, would abandon its neutrality and side with the Allies.[2]

[1]Early in the Franco-Prussian War, the third and last of the three Wars of German Unification under the political leadership of Prussian Minister-President (and later German Chancellor) Otto von Bismarck and the military leadership of Prussian General Staff Chief Helmuth von Moltke, the French suffered a disastrous defeat at the Battle of Sedan in which the major French army under Marshal MacMahon together with Emperor Napoleon III was captured. Moltke thereupon argued that Prussia should fight on to conquer all of France and win the total victory that seemed feasible; Bismarck insisted on a more moderate policy which would facilitate the formation of a new French government willing and able to conclude a viable peace. Bismarck prevailed, not least of all because, as the late Hajo Holborn wrote, "Moltke's calm genius did not desire personal power."—ED.

[2]By November 1943, the Seventeenth Army (together with a number of Rumanian units) in the Crimea was cut off. Only early in May 1944, when the Russians had forced the Axis troops back to Sevastopol and breached their defense perimeter, did Hitler order the evacuation by sea. Some 130,000 troops were captured.—ED.

Had the conduct of foreign policy and the waging of war been handled separately, the conflicting arguments would have been rationally weighed and the military advantages of a given undertaking balanced against the political disadvantages, as was the question of the bombardment of Paris in 1870–1871.[3] After discussion of the case on its merits, the final decision would have been up to the Chief of State. In the Third Reich, however, Hitler not only held this position, but also united in himself the functions of Chancellor, Foreign Minister, Nazi Führer, Supreme Commander of the Armed Forces, and Commander-in-Chief of the Army. Consequently, the weighing of the contradictory arguments as well as the final decisions all took place in his mind alone. Here the carefully developed arguments of his military, diplomatic, and political advisers clashed with his irrational impulses—or perhaps it would be more accurate to say that rational arguments and irrational impulses clustered in a hopelessly entangled ball, in which, in retrospect, one can at best recognize some individual strands.

This form of strategic-political leadership had devastating implications, because as a born propagandist Hitler laid too much stress on the impact of retreats on world public opinion. For this reason alone, he was unable to bring himself to make militarily necessary decisions, such as the evacuation of untenable outposts or the withdrawal from the Crimea. As has already been observed earlier in another context, such "prestige" strategy is the worst type of all. In the long run it is impossible to bluff in military affairs. Whoever tries it will not only find that the battle reveals the true balance of forces, but also that the next reverse, which might have been prevented, is made unavoidable.

In itself this explanation is nevertheless insufficient to explain why Hitler ever more senselessly commanded that untenable positions should be held, while forbidding timely reconnaissance and

[3]Bismarck favored bombardment of the city in the vain hope of shortening the siege and the war, but most of the generals were rightly very skeptical about the efficiency of a cannonade. Toward the end of December 1870, the bombardment was finally commenced, but it only hardened resistance, which continued over a month longer, until starvation forced the Parisians to surrender.—ED.

the fortification of suitable relief positions to the rear. The *War Diary* proves beyond doubt that the experts again and again urged this, but that Hitler was at best prepared to accede to their judgment only after valuable time had been lost, or even when it was already too late.

The basis for this principle of leadership can almost certainly be traced in part to Hitler's experiences as a corporal on the Western Front during the First World War.[4] When in February and March 1917, the curved front between Arras and Soissons was shortened by withdrawing to the Siegfried Line, the retreat proved to be

---

[4]How very strongly Hitler continued to be affected by the memory of that time is shown by the protocols of his situation conferences. One very good example was an evening conference in June 1944:

"The Führer: 'At no place did we have (such an inferiority in the air) during the [First] World War. That I know. For example, during our offensive, during the great battle in France, we had the English completely chased away from the battle area. During the World War, we just didn't have such a pitiful situation [as now, following the Normandy invasion, with Anglo-American air supremacy]. Even in 1917 the situation was such that during the Battle of Arras, the Richthofen Squadron had completely scoured the sky. English squadrons . . . were absolutely repulsed. I myself saw, in part, how the remainder of ten planes were brought down, down to the very last one. We had complete freedom [from air attack] there. Also in the Battle of Flanders, when the first large-scale air battles, by the standards of the time, took place, where as a matter of fact seventy to a hundred planes were engaged on each side—that was a murderous struggle, but even so it could never be said that the enemy controlled the sky or flew around [at will]. Naturally they were already getting kind of fresh, and in 1918 it got worse.'

"Jodl: 'Then came the first flights of squadrons. Four hundred to five hundred.' "

Another example is a reference Hitler made in connection with the unsuccessful German attempt to break the protracted stalemate at the Anzio beachhead by heavy counterattacks. Having learned that these were stopped by enemy artillery fire, he instructed that "future attacks should be carried out according to the principles of the offensive in 1918."

In the protocol of his conference with General Thomale in December 1944, Hitler said, on having been informed of the arrival of artillery units for two divisions:

"Something just occurred to me because people are always whining about getting reinforcements too late. For the second offensive in 1918, we started out marching on the evening of the 25th. We spent the night of the 26th in a forest and on the morning of the 27th we attacked. We marched at 5:00 A.M. The afternoon of the day before, we received our reinforcements for the great offensive at Chemins des Dames."

much more precipitate than the High Command had foreseen; understandably, the retreating units did not extend themselves to fight a delaying action for land that everyone knew would sooner or later be evacuated in any case. For Hitler, this memory crystallized in the maxim that defense lines to the rear exerted a "magnetic" force on the fighting troops, and that one should never tempt them by prematurely preparing defense lines behind them.[5]

This experience was complemented by still another of the same origin. Hitler, the former corporal, never forgot how easily the troops could break into a stampede once they had been squeezed out of the trenches, and how hard it was to stop the infantryman, the "poor worm" as he called him, in open country. What Hitler had learned in 1917–1918 was that it seemed better to hold on to present positions, no matter how high the casualty rate, no matter how vulnerable to air attacks and artillery fire, no matter how weakened by localized breakthroughs, than to order the troops to fall back across open country to the next defense line, though it might be operationally more favorable.[6]

---

[5]One of the countless examples is to be found in the *War Diary* coverage of the Adriatic sector of the Italian front during the last three months of 1944. On December 15, 1944, the Chief of the OKW Operations Staff informed the Commander-in-Chief Southwest (Italian theater) that the role of the Genghiz Khan-Line seemed to be more to attract German troops than to repel the enemy. The withdrawal toward it was being justified with (what the OKW regarded as) the very dangerous rationalization that forces would thereby be conserved and that it was necessary to deploy them in depth back to the rear echelons in order to prevent a breakthrough. The Führer, made wise by similar cases in earlier years, was expressing almost daily fears of such attitudes. For this reason, there were to be no further requests for permission to effect voluntary withdrawals.

The same attitude prevailed at a situation conference late in March 1945:

"The Führer: '. . . At least fifteen effective fighting units were lost in withdrawing from the *Westwall* because one could allegedly fight better in open country. . . .' "

Then somewhat later the same evening, concerning the military leadership in the West, which had let itself be forced out of the fortifications:

"The Führer: '. . . In this case the leadership performed absolutely miserably. From the top down, they drummed the idea into the troops that one can fight better in open country than in here.' "

[6]The Commander-in-Chief Southwest (Italy) was informed on February 22, 1945, that authorization to fight a delaying action rather than rigidly

In the final analysis, however, the identification of the corporal from the First World War with the Supreme Commander in the Second—as plausible as it may be in human terms—is by no means sufficient to explain Hitler's strategy. Once more we turn to the Ardennes Offensive as a test case. In order to grasp Hitler's underlying conception of strategy, we must ascertain his purpose and motives, for he did seize the initiative, this one last time, in an offensive operation.

Strategically, the Ardennes Offensive had its origins in the attempt —thwarted from the very beginning—to strike at the right flank of General Patton's forces which were overrunning France. The loss of the approaches to the Vosges Mountains to the west of the Rhine had deprived this sweeping maneuver of its anticipated tactical base. With amazing stubbornness, however, Hitler held fast to his intention of responding to attack with counterattack, so as not to be forced completely onto the defensive. But the retreating German forces were only able to come to a stop approximately along the former German *Westwall*. This meant that Hitler could realize his ambition of carrying out a powerful counterstroke only by mounting an attack from a stable front—rather than striking a devastating blow at the exposed flank of a moving armored column, as he originally had wanted to do. Once it was decided to attack from stabilized lines, the selection of the point at which the British and American forces met was obvious; such seams have always been the favored place to try to tear open the front of an opposing alliance. But because of his underestimation of the enemy, Hitler anticipated greater command level confusion among his enemies than actually occurred.

Before the attack was ordered, the entire plan was re-evaluated and alternatives discussed. The conclusion was reached that there was in fact no front more suitable than the one Hitler had chosen, considering the purpose he had in mind. This latter was, of course, a very important consideration. Hitler not only wanted an immediate military success which would reactivate his role in the war, but was

---

holding the line would be something "the Führer will . . . never give, since at the present point in the war it would be the ruin of the troops' morale and will to fight."

also determined that it be visible enough to the eyes of the world to stabilize the dwindling prestige of the German Wehrmacht.

The recapture of Antwerp was established by Hitler as the goal of the offensive, his rationalization being that the city on the Scheldt had been the first undestroyed harbor that had fallen into the hands of the Allies, and that depriving them of it would consequently be a grave setback. Hitler thus failed to comprehend that with the help of sophisticated modern landing equipment his opponents were in a vastly better position to overcome the lack of normal harbor facilities than he assumed.

In any event, it was an elementary calculation that in case of a successful breakthrough, there would be a pointed spearhead a certain number of kilometers long on the left flank and on the right, and covering these flanks would take so many units per kilometer—an objective calculation based on repeated and carefully evaluated experience. But at the same time, the point of the spearhead could not be weakened if the attack were to reach its goal. Aside from headquarters troops there were thirty-two divisions available, and even by the most optimistic calculations it was absolutely clear that these would not be sufficient. Responsible officers pointed this out to Hitler repeatedly, but he would not let himself be talked out of pursuing the "greater solution"—the goal of Antwerp. The "lesser solution," recommended on the basis of General Staff calculations, provided first for taking Liège, and then (if the situation permitted) bearing right in order to force the British to draw back from the front they were presently holding. The objections to the "greater solution" were so obvious that Hitler, particularly after the experiences of the past months, should have been convinced of their validity. But he was not. Instead, he deluded himself into thinking that once the Americans and British started running, their effective fighting strength would drop below their nominal numerical strength, while on the other hand the strength of the German divisions, exhilarated by their wave of triumph, would actually be magnified. Insofar as he thereby transformed a strength ratio of 1 to 1 into a ratio of one-third to 1, Hitler thought he was in a position to dismiss all the experience of the experts.

In explaining how Hitler came to think in this manner, we must assume that the experience he had gained as a political party leader played an important role. He began his party with seven members. It grew in time to seven hundred, seven thousand, seven hundred thousand, and finally millions, while at the same time the millions of his opponents melted away.[7] His confidence that military operations would be similar was nourished by his successes during the first years of the war. It had to be something on the order of this "avalanche conception"—as I would like to call it—that led Hitler to establish such an unreasonably ambitious goal for the Ardennes Offensive.

To a certain extent, this avalanche or stampede effect had made the impossible possible during the years before the war. Even during the first phase of the Russian campaign, the Red Army—in the aggregate numerically superior to the Germans—had been thrown back along the whole vast expanse of the front, bolstering Hitler's belief that this principle held true everywhere, even in war. But from the moment the German armies were stopped at Moscow in December 1941, Hitler was given one object lesson after another to validate the conservative thinking of the General Staff. Its quintessence was that it is better to over- than to underestimate the potential of the enemy, since one can afford to be surprised by one's own unexpected successes, but not by his. Hitler, to the contrary, not only failed to accept realistic estimates but actually lost sight of the crucial borderline between the possible and the impossible. As Theodor Mommsen observed, "Insight into what is possible and impossible is what distinguishes the hero from the adventurer."

Hitler the warlord, who during the second half of the war accepted even less counsel than during the first, was thus more and more handicapped by the fact that he remained a prestige-conscious propagandist, that his impressions as a World War I corporal came

[7]In a conference late in December 1943, when the Army Chief of Staff expressed his concern about the poor morale of the troops in the East, Hitler responded by referring to his experience as a party leader. During the time of his rise to power, he said, he used to receive reports from the local party branches to the effect that the Socialists were unbeatable; but in every case it had turned out to be the fault of the local party leader. Hitler was clearly projecting to military affairs the experience he had gained as a party leader.

back to him with suggestive force, and that, confronted by a deteriorating situation, he was governed by the experience he had gained as a partisan politician. This must be the basis of any judgment of him as a military leader during the latter years of the war.

3. Hitler's "Wavebreak" Doctrine

Our evaluation of Hitler's military leadership, particularly during the latter part of the war, would be incomplete without considering two further points: the first, what I would like to call his "wavebreak" doctrine; and the second, his responsibility for the senseless prolongation of the war he had arbitrarily unleashed.

According to the wavebreak doctrine, any provisionally fortified place officially proclaimed to be a "fortress" was to be defended even when the enemy had thrust past on the left and right. On the basis of this idea, a whole series of "fortresses," whose fate is recorded in the *War Diary,* was established in the West, especially along the coast. But Hitler also followed the practice in the East on the assumption that the enemy required more forces for the siege than were necessary for the defense. The entire hypothesis presupposed that the enemy would have to take these pseudo-fortresses, since he would need them as road junctions and railway depots. In the actual event, this applied only in individual cases, and in those instances where the enemy needed more forces to invest a town or city that had been cut off, the job could be done by inferior units. With respect to the Red Army, in particular, Hitler made a serious miscalculation, for the German forces in the East were actually outnumbered all along. The practical consequences are shown by the account in the *War Diary* of the fighting on the Eastern Front in 1945.

On the basis of reports made in the situation conference in Hitler's headquarters, the *War Diary* records on February 16: "On the whole, it can be determined that because of the resistance in Posen [Poznań on the Warta] and in other fortresses, the enemy advance has been tangibly delayed and will be made more difficult still." In subsequent entries, however, it became all too clear that it was only a brief respite, the benefit of which was more than outweighed by the disadvantage resulting from the loss of the units defending the "fortresses," which resulted in a still greater operational inferiority in numbers.

Woe unto the commandant of a fortress who, because of a hopeless situation, surrendered the "wavebreak" entrusted to him out of a sense of responsibility to the wounded, the last defenders, and the surviving civilian population! Consider, for example, the fate of General Otto Lasch, an experienced officer whom I had given his initial orientation briefing at Führer Headquarters before he had been put in command of the LXIV Army Corps on the Vizcayan Front. At the end of January 1945, he was made commandant of the East Prussian capital of Königsberg. On April 9, 1945, the general capitulated to the Russians. Further resistance was senseless: the garrison of his "fortress" was largely wounded or otherwise incapable of sustaining the struggle. The Wehrmacht report of April 12 noted that Lasch had been condemned to death by hanging for unauthorized surrender. Because he was already a Russian prisoner, the sentence could obviously not be carried out. But it was more than an empty threat, for the report continued: "His next of kin will be made responsible." The general's daughter, who had been conscripted as a staff assistant, was imprisoned. On April 17, 1945, I recorded in the *War Diary* the report of two of Lasch's officers who had escaped capture by swimming across the Haff, the great lagoon lying before the city. They said that the general was still fighting though "enemy tanks had already appeared before his command post." I had to add that this report was "probably false," for it was clear to me that this was a case where a man of integrity had acted on the only conclusion possible in view of the complete senselessness of further resistance—and done so, moreover, in full awareness of the fact that he was not only sacrificing his reputation but also gambling with the welfare of his family.[8]

[8]The brutal practice of using a man's loved ones as hostages and punishing them as well as him for disloyalty was only too well known; to have kept it secret would have reduced its considerable deterrent value. However, a very revealing exception had to be made by Hitler in the particularly sensitive case of the dangerously popular Field Marshal Erwin Rommel. Seriously injured

The commandant of Schneidemühl had also acted on his own authority after a twenty-one day siege. On February 14 he succeeded in breaking out toward the north, "since he was no longer able to fulfill his responsibility as a wavebreak from the suburbs which still remained in his control." Against this kind of argument there could be no objection. Moreover, there had been no capitulation. A thousand men succeeded in fighting their way out. The *War Diary* recorded: "The Führer did not regard this action unfavorably."

The most harrowing consequences of the wavebreak doctrine were suffered by Army Group Courland on the eastern shore of the Baltic. It was left on the headland between Libau and Riga in order to hold down as many units of the Red Army as possible. Once the overland route had been so thoroughly blocked that an evacuation southward to East Prussia was no longer feasible, there still remained the possibility of withdrawing units by sea; some were, in fact, saved that way; others that might have been fell victim to the doctrine.

Hitler clung to this principle to the end. In Admiral Dönitz' record of the dictator's situation conference of April 4, 1945, we read that the Acting Chief of Staff of the Army, General Krebs, reported that thanks to German troops "in East and West Prussia, altogether 193 Russian infantry divisions were tied down, thereby substantially relieving the pressure on other fronts."[9] It is up to the military historians of the Soviet Union to judge whether the attack on Berlin was in fact delayed in this way. But whatever conclusion is finally reached, the findings will be irrelevant, since the delay would in no case have exceeded a few days or weeks. When the only purpose of a given strategy is to delay the inevitable, one can no longer seriously speak of it as "strategy" at all.

---

on July 17, 1944 (three days before the attempt to assassinate Hitler) when his staff car was strafed, his immediately suspected complicity in the opposition was discovered before he had recovered. Given the choice of either dying a hero and having a state funeral or else being arrested for treason, with only too foreseeable consequences for his family, he chose poison. For a moving account of Rommel's role in 1944, including the daring ultimatum to Hitler on July 15, 1944, challenging him immediately to draw the consequences of the catastrophic military situation—i.e., resignation, suicide, or an armistice (as discussed below in the text)—see Dr. Hans Speidel's *Invasion 1944* (Chicago, 1950).—ED.

[9]The figure of 193 is so high that it is probably an error.

since it would be futile to talk with Churchill or Roosevelt. He sent it to the Führer Headquarters, but found that it never reached his still beloved Führer. Martin Bormann, who had risen to become the "brown eminence" of the Third Reich, had stopped it. Goebbels then traveled personally to the Führer Headquarters in order to put it to Hitler on a man-to-man basis, but he got nowhere at all.

Goebbels was not alone in his insight. Referring to the beginning of July 1944, former Reich Minister for Armaments and War Production Albert Speer stated at his trial in Nuremberg: "All the military leaders whom I knew said at that time that the war was bound to end in October or November, since the invasion had been successful. I myself was of the same opinion in view of the fuel situation."

The seriousness of the situation had already been candidly acknowledged in Führer Directive Number 51 of November 3, 1943, which read:

"In the East the extent of the territory does, in an extreme case, permit a loss of ground, even on a large scale, without dealing a fatal blow to the vital nerve center of Germany.

"In the West it is different! Should the enemy here succeed in breaching our defenses on a broad front, the consequences would soon be unforeseeable."

The consequences of such a deterioration of the situation had in fact already been drawn by the Führer Order of November 27, 1943, which stated that "the struggle for the existence of the German people and the future of Europe is approaching its high point. The need of the hour is for all reserve forces which the Greater German Reich can muster for deployment in this final battle. The striking power of our Wehrmacht has suffered badly through the battles of this summer, particularly in the East."

In his secret situation conferences, from which nothing was leaked, Hitler made himself even clearer. What was said on these occasions has survived only in fragmentary form, but there is a fragment from December 20, 1943, that is documentary evidence for Hitler's having said that an enemy attack in the West would decide the course of the war: if the attack were repulsed, the danger would be over, and troops could once more be transferred from the West to the East.

General Walter Warlimont, one of the few participants in those situation conferences who is still alive, has confirmed to me that he repeatedly heard such arguments expressed personally by Hitler. The Assistant Chief of the Operations Staff of the OKW kept no personal journal at this time, so we cannot be certain that Hitler actually went so far as to say explicitly that the war would definitely be lost in case of a successful landing. But for General Warlimont— who originally made the point to me years ago and recently confirmed it when I consulted him while completing this study—"there was not the slightest doubt that this was the meaning of his words."

The new year brought the Anglo-American landing at Anzio-Nettuno on January 22, 1944, the danger of which had not seriously been considered. This landing behind the German front threatened to collapse the lines and open the road to Rome. Hitler ordered the most vigorous defense. Referring to the widely known book which he himself had certainly once devoured, Felix Dahn's dramatic *Struggle for Rome,* Hitler spoke of the struggle for Rome which was to begin within the next few days. It would not only be decisive for the outcome in central Italy, but was of wider importance: With this landing, the invasion of Europe planned for 1944 had begun.

The danger that arose in southern Italy could in fact still be contained, but not the landing of the Allies in Normandy that began on June 6. When it became clear that the Allied forces could not be thrown back into the sea, the time had come for Hitler—who still sought the miracle that could, as in the case of Frederick the Great, change the course of the war—finally to draw the consequences of the insight he had already acknowledged. He should either have requested an armistice or else have relinquished power, thereby freeing the way for another to initiate that absolutely unavoidable step.

But Hitler took neither course. Instead he clung to the fact that it was initially possible to hold the enemy with an improvised front, which had its historical parallel in the front that had been built by the French along the Somme and the Aisne as the "Weygand Line"— in this case minus the fortifications. To the "experts" it was clear that the German front, running across Normandy without even the support of natural obstacles, would suffer the same fate under concerted attack as had befallen the Aisne Front, which had been penetrated in several days by a frontal assault. Hitler alone closed his eyes and ears.

At the urgent request of Field Marshal von Rundstedt, and of the Commander-in-Chief of Army Group B, Field Marshal Rommel, Hitler met with them both on June 17, 1944, at a command post near Soissons. After having been objectively and unreservedly informed of the situation, he consoled his field commanders with the prospect of the new V-bombs. (Some 2,400 V-1 and 1,115 V-2 missiles struck England, all of which merely hardened the English in their resolution to destroy Germany. Operationally, the bombardment had no significance whatsoever.) After the conference, Rommel, speaking in a smaller circle, referred to the hopelessness of the overall situation. Hitler told him not to worry about the continuation of the war as a whole, but to concern himself only with his own invasion front. Initially, Hitler had wanted to see for himself how things stood at the front, but he broke off his field trip and returned to his headquarters sooner than planned after a wild V-missile struck near his bunker.

On June 29 another conference was held, but on this occasion Hitler saw to it that there was no opportunity for Rundstedt and Rommel to speak with him privately. Once more he talked about the miracle weapons. The only tangible result of this conference was that Field Marshal von Rundstedt was relieved of his command on July 2.[4] His successor was Field Marshal Günther von Kluge, who a short time before had been at the Führer Headquarters and received the initial impression that Hitler's evaluation of the situation in the West was more accurate than that of the field commanders. It was not, he thought, as hopeless as Rommel had painted it. This element of conflict between Rommel and Kluge did not last very long; after the latter had studied the front himself, he had to concede that Rommel's evaluation was correct: as of July 9, 1944, the Normandy Front could be held for a maximum of two to three weeks. On July 27, within two and a half weeks, Patton began his breakthrough. By the thirty-first he was in the clear. Rommel's estimate had been razor-sharp reckoning.

On that July 9, Hitler was building his hopes—as he explained in

[4]Rundstedt was restored to command of the Western Theater in September 1944, after his successor, Field Marshal von Kluge, had suddenly been relieved in mid-August by Field Marshal Walter Model, who then continued to serve on the Western Front under Rundstedt.—ED.

the situation conference—on the new, highly secret jet fighter program, which he thought would break the enemy's air superiority: "The enemy will be amazed when in about four months the picture begins to change so far as air supremacy is concerned." It is hardly necessary to demonstrate that this hope was vain.[5]

From July 13 to 15, Rommel made certain once more that he had the confidence of his subordinate commanders. Then on the fifteenth he sent a teletype dispatch to Hitler which left absolutely no doubt where he stood. The original text had to be destroyed, but we know the content from Rommel's chief of staff, General Hans Speidel. In this dispatch, which had originally been drafted by Speidel, Rommel specified that in the past weeks the Western Front had suffered losses of 97,000 men but had received only six thousand replacements, and that for 224 lost tanks Rommel had received only seventeen new ones. The result was a shattering picture which led to his prediction that the enemy would inevitably break through within two to three weeks. The dispatch closed with the statement: "I must ask you to draw the consequences from this situation without delay." Two days later, on July 17, Rommel was severely injured when his staff car was strafed and his driver killed at the wheel.

"To draw the consequences" meant asking for an armistice. Hitler rejected this as brusquely as he had previous attempts to dissuade him from his morbid rigidity.

Still another field marshal called on Hitler during these weeks in an effort to bring about a cease-fire. This second appeal can be understood only if the following background is explained: By transmitting to Hitler Rommel's audacious dispatch of July 15, Field Marshal von Kluge, whom Hitler had elevated on July 3 to Commander-in-Chief of the Western Front (under whom Rommel was an Army Group Commander), had in effect endorsed its contents and identified himself with its conclusions. Kluge had soon come to

[5]The fact is that jet fighters were mass produced by the Germans before the end of the war, and that they proved quite effective in aerial combat. On March 18, 1945, for example, Me-262 *Schwalben* ("Swallows") shot down twenty-five bombers and five fighters attacking Berlin, without suffering a single loss. A total of 1,294 were built, but they could no longer seriously affect the course of the war, for, as Armaments Minister Albert Speer observed at Nuremberg, "jet planes were of no use without fuel."—ED.

realize that the situation was in fact very different from what Hitler had described to him in Berchtesgaden, and the events of the subsequent weeks constrained him to become even more pessimistic. Meanwhile, because of Kluge's ambiguous stance during the hours following the assassination attempt, Hitler had begun to grow suspicious of him. Then, on August 15, as the Allies threatened to close the Falaise gap—which could have meant cutting off the Seventh Army altogether in as disastrous a pocket as Stalingrad, where the Sixth Army had been lost—the Führer Headquarters suddenly found that it had completely lost contact with the Commander-in-Chief West. The field marshal had personally gone to the front to ward off disaster, and his radio car had been destroyed by dive bombers. Hitler became convinced, however, that Kluge had been attempting to negotiate a treacherous armistice with the British. He abruptly relieved him of his command, replacing him—at the height of the crucial Battle of the Falaise Gap—with Field Marshal Walter Model.[6] On his journey back to Germany, in sight of the battlefields of the Franco-Prussian War of 1870–1871, Field Marshal von Kluge took his own life by poison, thus evading the fate of Field Marshal Erwin von Witzleben, who was hanged, or that of Field Marshal Rommel, who was forced to commit suicide.

On the day of his death, August 18, 1944, Marshal Kluge sent a long letter to Hitler, in which he informed him of his decision to take his own life and justified his recent military measures. If Model should be unable to master the situation and the long-range weapons should fail to bring the hoped-for success, Kluge concluded, "then, my Führer, resolve yourself to end the war. The German people have borne such untold suffering that the time has come to put an end to these horrors. . . . My Führer, I have always admired your greatness and military bearing in this gigantic struggle, and your iron determination to assert yourself and National Socialism. If fate is

[6]Kluge had visited, during this tour of the front, the command post of the 2nd Armored Division, whose commanding general, Baron von Lüttwitz, clearly described, mimicking his gestures, how the field marshal, sitting at a little table before the situation map, leaning his head on his hands, sighed to himself, "Where in the world is that division? What happened to it?" There is no question but that Hitler's distrust was completely unfounded.

stronger than your will and your genius, then that is the will of Providence. You have fought a great and honorable fight. This is what the historical record will show. Prove yourself now to be so great as to put an end, if need be, to the hopeless struggle.—I take leave of you, my Führer, as one who stood closer to you, in the consciousness of having done his duty to the last, than you perhaps recognized. *Heil,* my Führer! [signed:] VON KLUGE, Field Marshal."

In terms of its content, this letter, in which one must try to overlook the hackneyed phrases and ignore the awkward invocation of Providence, is one of the most frightful documents of German history. In its tone it is reminiscent of the servile praise which General Paulus addressed to Hitler in his radio message of January 29, 1943. But there is a fundamental difference: Paulus was not bound by his radio message and survived the capitulation. Kluge stood to gain nothing, and wrote his letter because he hoped, at the end, to be able to serve his Fatherland by sounding a warning which could not fail to be heard. Presumably he believed that he would make the inevitable decision easier for Hitler by addressing him in this fashion. Whether this was the point or not, however, what he wrote, with the lethal poison already at hand, concerning Hitler's greatness, his admirable military bearing, his genius, must be taken literally. Thus spoke a field marshal who was one of the most intelligent generals of the German Army and whose whole background and tradition made him a stranger to fanaticism and faith in military miracles. Even he had fallen under Hitler's spell, to such an extent that only in the hour of his death did he dare to express freely his view of the situation. Still more frightful is Marshal von Kluge's concluding statement that he stood closer to Hitler than the latter realized. From his own point of view this may well have been correct; but he was apparently unaware that had he returned home he would have faced arrest as a proven traitor in Hitler's eyes. He went to his death branded by the enemy—as he noted in his letter—as a war criminal, rejected by all those who had sympathized with the July 20 plot because of his ambivalent stance, recognizing Hitler to the very end as a genius, but knowing only that he no longer enjoyed his full confidence and, as a matter of fact—though he was spared this knowledge—regarded by him as a traitor. How many have not also become enmeshed in similarly tangled webs of overpowering circumstances! The fate of Field Marshal Günther von Kluge, terrible because of its dramatic accentuation, was tragically symbolic of the leadership of the Wehrmacht under Hitler; and perhaps the most shocking thing of all was that Kluge's admonitions, though accentuated by his death, made no impression on Hitler.

On August 31, 1944, thirteen days after Kluge's suicide, Hitler briefed the new chiefs of staff of the Commanders-in-Chief West and Army Group B on their new assignment. In the course of his conference with them, he accused Rommel of having done the worst possible thing that a soldier could do in a difficult situation, namely, "to seek other than military solutions." There was no question, so far as he was concerned, that Field Marshal von Kluge had been on the point of initiating negotiations with the British, but this was to remain secret in order not to reflect shame on the Wehrmacht. As for the demand made by Field Marshals Rommel and von Kluge, Hitler swept it aside with the back of his hand: "I said right away that the time is not yet ripe for a political decision. That I am also in the position to achieve political successes I have, I believe, adequately proved in my life. That I would not let such an opportunity pass, I do not need to explain to anyone. But to hope, at a time of serious military defeats, for a favorable political moment, is naturally childish and naive. Such moments can come when one has successes." Hitler's task, as he saw it, was to keep his nerve. If he saw the opportunity to win a respectable peace that would be tolerable to Germany and also guarantee the life of future generations, he would conclude it.

In military terms, Hitler's senseless demand that the war be continued with unyielding tenacity amounted, under the circumstances, to nothing less than a complete inversion of morality. But we must ask ourselves whether his continuation of the war could be justified by any other hope at all—for example in terms of foreign policy.

In the conference of August 31, 1944, mentioned above, Hitler, after passing judgment on Churchill and Vansittart—who had wanted war and now could no longer back out of it—declared: ". . . The time will come when the tensions between the Allies will become so great that the break will occur. . . . Throughout history, coalitions have always gone to pieces sooner or later. One has only to wait for the moment, no matter how hard the going." The historical example foremost in his mind was the withdrawal of Russia in 1762 from the anti-Prussian coalition in the Seven Years' War. In the course of the conference, Hitler continued the parallel: "Under all circumstances we will continue this struggle until—as Frederick the Great said—one of our accursed enemies grows weary of fighting on, and until we then achieve a peace which secures the life of the German nation for the next fifty or hundred years. . . ."

It was his mission, Hitler went on, to weather every crisis—unshaken by reverses—until the final moment of vindication. "My task," he affirmed, "especially since the year 1941, has been never to lose my nerve under any circumstances. . . ." In Hitler's comparisons of himself with German General Staff officers, he accused them of lacking his sort of energy: "If there is not a man in there behind it [i.e., the German struggle for survival] who by his very nature has a will of iron, then the war cannot be won. It is my criticism of the General Staff that instead of always radiating this iron will it has weakened front officers who have come to it, or when General Staff officers are sent to the front, they have spread the pessimism of the General Staff."

We are confronted here with the problem of coming to terms historically with Hitler's own understanding of his historical role, of deciding what, if anything, can be meaningfully concluded from these statements which Hitler made about himself. The first thing that comes to mind is the frequently quoted remark of the Swedish statesman Count Oxenstierna that the only thing one can learn from history is that people learn nothing from history. But the pessimism that underlies this observation does not actually go quite far enough. Certainly world history is a manual from which—if one reads it correctly—a great deal can be learned, and it is regrettable that politicians make so little use of it. It is much worse, however, when the manual is read falsely and cited in support of an abortive policy or strategy, as when the preacher quotes a verse from the Gospel as incontestable proof of the validity of his sermon.

This, essentially, was Hitler's response as his situation became absurd. He appealed to history, which he had studied with the arbitrary violence of an autodidact—and he interpreted it falsely. In the age of cabinet wars, the succession of a new monarch to the throne of Russia had indeed helped the great Hohenzollern, but in the Second World War even changes of government on the enemy side were not decisive. What could not be doubted was that the coalition Hitler had provoked against himself would hold together to complete the German catastrophe; the strength of the anti-German commitment of each ally was stronger than any mistrust or antipathy between them. Thus we see that Hitler no longer understood—if ever he had—the psychology of his foreign opponents.

The straw to which he still clung after the collapse of the Normandy Front was the Ardennes Offensive. But by the time it began, the situation on all fronts had deteriorated so drastically that even Hitler began to realize the ultimate hopelessness of the situation. Our witness for this is once more General Jodl. In the statement dictated during his imprisonment, he reports that Hitler told him on April 22, 1945, of his decision to remain in Berlin and die there. The dictator went on to say: "I should already have made this decision, the most important of my life, in November 1944, and should never have left the headquarters in East Prussia."

Hitler had not made that decision in November, however, but instead had employed his perverted logic to argue that in the end Germany would have to win. "It is only a question of who holds out longer," he said at the end of December 1944. "The person holds out longer for whom everything is at stake. For us everything is at stake. . . . If we were to say today we have had enough, we quit— then Germany would cease to exist."

At the end of 1944, Hitler still could not bring himself to the final decision, though from the latter part of December he must have been able to see that the Ardennes Offensive was a failure. He deluded himself by pretending both to himself and to others that the battle had not ended with a genuine decision that incontrovertibly revealed the relative power of the contestants. The outcome was rather the end result of a chain of unfortunate circumstances. At the end of December, he summed it up in a discussion of the next operations: "One thing has now become very clear again, and there can be no doubt about it: with the first operations we really had particularly bad luck. It was bad luck in a number of different respects." That is a shocking statement. It may at times be appropriate to use the expression "bad luck" for private calamities, though even there it often has a patronizing tone. But it was an outrage for Hitler to employ this trivializing term to the last great exertion of the Wehrmacht, which had cost tens of thousands their lives or health and which—planned and carried out as it was under the circumstances as they developed—was condemned to failure from the very beginning. The point was that by thinking in terms of mere "bad luck," Hitler once more suppressed whatever insight was building up within him and thereby enabled himself to go on with the long-since irretrievably lost war.

The abortive offensive had made clear not only the aerial but also the armored superiority of the enemy. Yet Hitler did not allow himself to be shaken; he placed his confidence in Karl Otto Saur from Speer's Ministry of Armaments and War Production. Saur was a tried and tested master of improvisation, though he did have a tendency to calculate mere possibilities as accomplished facts. In the previously cited conference at the end of December 1944 with General Thomale, who was Chief of Staff of the Inspector General of Armored Forces, Hitler said: "Today I spoke with Saur. He said he hopes to reach a production of 1,500 tanks and self-propelled assault guns this month. The important thing is that the replacements go to Model [on the Western Front] and, above all, quickly enough so that we can move again."[7] No doubt when Hitler spoke these words he was convinced by them, though at some deeper level his negative insight may already have prevailed.

In January 1945, there were new factors thrown into the balance

[7]The production figure of 1,500 tanks which Hitler cites is in itself not grotesque. What is astounding is the underlying assumption that under the prevailing conditions in Germany in the winter of 1944–1945, most of those armored vehicles would be able to reach the front, or once there, have fuel to operate. Albert Speer had succeeded in *tripling* German war production from 1942 to 1944, despite aerial bombardment, but of 1,764 tanks built from September to November 1944 only 1,371 could even be delivered to the Wehrmacht. For a concise general introduction to the problem of economic mobilization and war production in the Third Reich in the context of Hitler's ideology, see this editor's review article, "Hitler's Fatal Mistake," *Air University Review*, XXI (May–June 1970), 82–90.—ED.

that should have forced Hitler to end the war. We have already touched on the unavoidable collapse of the armaments industry, sealed by the loss of Upper Silesia, as well as the drastic reduction of fuel production. Now came the threat of the loss of the Hungarian oil fields, which at least to a certain extent had served as a substitute —though most inadequate—for the Rumanian. In establishing his strategic priorities on the Eastern Front, therefore, Hitler gave first place to the oil areas in Hungary and in the Vienna basin, "since without this oil [representing 80 per cent of the remaining production] it is not possible to continue waging war." But when Hungary was lost and the enemy drove on into the Vienna basin, Hitler once more—despite his own clearly stated appraisal of the consequences —failed to reach the obvious conclusion.

The power of suggestion that Hitler radiated to the very end, despite his inner struggle between false hopes and real insight, was uncanny. Even so shrewd a man as Josef Goebbels was unable to evade it. On May 8, 1943, he had confided to his diary: "The Führer gave expression to his unshakable conviction that the Reich will be the master of all Europe. We must still engage in many fights, but these will undoubtedly lead to magnificent victories. Thereafter the way to world domination is practically certain. To dominate Europe will be to assume the leadership of the world." Meanwhile, as we have seen, even Goebbels had changed his tune. He was seized —as his adjutant confirmed—with doubt of Hitler's genius, and from that time on he traveled repeatedly to the Führer Headquarters with the intention of speaking his mind. He never did, however, and returned each time to Berlin full of admiration.

Even as late as February 24, 1945, with the situation obviously hopeless, Hitler had the suggestive power to inspire confidence in the *Gauleiter* gathered around him for one last time. By force of his personality he was able to give them enough of a "booster shot" to hold on.[8] Even during the final phase of the catastrophe, the power

[8] It was the twenty-fifth anniversary of the first Nazi mass meeting, at which Hitler proclaimed the Twenty-Five Point Program. In addition to addressing the assembled *Gauleiter* on February 24, 1945, Hitler also published a proclamation to the German people in which he predicted a change in the course of the war within the next ten months.

of suggestion that emanated from Hitler did not fail him. This was grimly documented by Baron Robert von Greim's report to General Karl Koller, Chief of Staff of the Luftwaffe. Hitler had promoted Greim to field marshal in April 1945 and named him Commander-in-Chief of the Luftwaffe in place of Göring, the latter having been discredited for alleged treachery. Greim, whose right foot had been shattered as he flew into the beleaguered city on April 26, and whose flight out two days later was to be hardly less hazardous, told Koller during a long-distance telephone conversation the evening of the 27th that he must never lose faith. Everything would turn out in the end. "Being with the Führer and his strength," said Greim, "have fortified me extraordinarily; it is like a fountain of youth for me. The Führer sat on my bed for a long time and talked through everything with me. He retracted all of his criticisms of the Luftwaffe. He knows what our branch of the armed forces has achieved; his criticism is directed only against Göring. For our men he has only the highest praise. I have been gratified no end about this."

When he had exhausted every delusive hope, Hitler fell back on the explanation that whatever happened was preordained. More than once he adopted this attitude. On one occasion Reich Minister Albert Speer made it a matter of record. In a letter he addressed to Hitler on March 29, 1945, Speer pointed out that Hitler had once observed that the task of statesmanship was "to save a people who had lost a war from an heroic end." In a conversation on March 18, 1945, however, Hitler had taken exactly the opposite standpoint. "In the evening," wrote Speer, "you clearly and unambiguously explained to me, if I did not misunderstand you, that if the war is lost, then the people is also lost. This fate is inexorable. It is not necessary to consider the fundamental things that a people needs to sustain its

---

The scene was described to me by *Gauleiter* Rainer of Carinthia—later extradited to Yugoslavia where he was condemned to death—in the witnesses' wing of the prison at Nuremberg. Hitler's left hand already trembled so badly that he could no longer use it to lift a glass of water to his lips. He pointed this out himself, and said that one day his head might also start to wobble, but never his heart. Whoever still believed in him said to himself that if the Führer still faced the future so firmly, then he must surely have something at hand—a secret weapon or the like—with which he could hope to reverse the situation at the last moment.

bare existence. On the contrary, it is better to destroy these things oneself. For the people would have proved itself to have been the weaker, and the future would belong exclusively to the stronger people of the East. Whoever survives the struggle would in any case be only the inferior, for the worthy would have fallen!"

Objectively speaking, this statement was a pseudo-Darwinistic rationalization of the defeat, conceived in a semi-educated mind capable of distorting anything it encountered to fit its preconceptions.[9] Historically speaking, this monstrous judgment stands as one of the most infamous, hideous statements ever uttered in the long career, so rich in vituperation, of the "Führer of the Greater German Reich"—for it was no one but Hitler himself who in 1939 had unleashed the war against Poland and then, in 1941, through the attack on the Soviet Union, had extended its scope and prolonged its duration beyond all measure.

By January 31, 1945, the cumulative monthly casualty report of the Wehrmacht, which was presented to Hitler personally, showed a death toll of 2,000,699. This figure did not include the fallen who were still listed as "missing in action," or the victims of aerial bombardment.[1] To this army of millions of dead, whose numbers continued to rise steadily during the final months, were added countless numbers who perished among the columns of refugees fleeing the East in the course of the forced deportations of untold thousands more, and among those who died as prisoners. All these were for Hitler nothing but the sum total of the sacrifices in a race war which,

[9]Hitler had long since expressed this basic attitude. In his *Table Conversations,* for example, we read that on July 5, 1942, he was "an ardent advocate of the belief that in the struggle between peoples those with the better average quality will always be the victors." In his opinion, "the natural order of things would be disrupted if the inferior should master the superior."

[1]In addition to the two million dead, the records of the Wehrmacht showed that as of January 31, 1945, there were almost two million missing. As of that date—after which systematic reporting broke down—the Wehrmacht had suffered 8,333,978 casualties—dead, wounded, or missing. The war continued for more than three months longer, but dependable records could not be maintained, and therefore no exact accounting can ever be made. Schramm estimates that a total of four million Germans died as military casualties and another half-million civilians perished as a result of air raids and other causes.—ED.

having reaped its negative harvest, was now drawing to a close. Those who survived, the maimed and wounded, those still holding on at the front, the workers in the bombed-out industrial areas, the women, the aged, the children, everyone who in any way had been affected by the war—these were all dismissed by Hitler, before his own escape from life and flight from responsibility, as biologically inferior and therefore worthy of nothing but extinction. Thus we see that this man who had deceived so many through base dissimulation and vicious falsehood was no less capable of deluding himself when the incontrovertible truth threatened to overpower him.

To grasp the full significance of Hitler's appalling statement to Albert Speer, we must bear in mind that no momentary whim or fit of temper prompted it. Only twelve days before his end, Hitler most emphatically reaffirmed this viewpoint in a conference with General Carl Hilpert, the Commander-in-Chief of Army Group Courland, who had flown to Berlin to explain the situation to Hitler and to receive new orders authorizing him to conduct operations in a manner appropriate to the changed circumstances. Two days after this conference with Hitler on April 18, 1945, the general made a report of it to his war diarist, Dr. W. Heinemeyer, now an archivist in Marburg, whose written account tells us that "after General Hilpert had expressed his opinions concerning the task of Army Group Courland, Hitler leaned back and began a long lecture on the struggle of the German people. It culminated with the words: 'If the German people loses the war, it will have proved itself not worthy of me [*meiner nicht würdig*].' " At these words, according to Dr. Heinemeyer, the general felt chills run up and down his spine. He would have liked to remonstrate by reminding Hitler how badly he had underestimated the Americans; but as such a rejoinder would have been absolutely purposeless, he had merely let the statement pass in silence.

"Not worthy of me!" Whoever reviews Hitler's statements during the last year, particularly the fragments of the situation conferences that have been preserved and published, is struck by the way the word "I" replaces, in Hitler's diction, the terms "German Wehrmacht" or "German people." The statement to General Hilpert represents the culmination of this ego-cult, which had, of course, from the very beginning been implicit in the Führer-principle, but which now seemed almost to have assumed the proportions of megalomania. In cases of delusions of grandeur, physicians search for feelings of inadequacy that may have provoked the disorder. The historian might well deduce from Hitler's statement that he was no longer able to suppress the realization of what he had perpetrated, and that he found no better way to relieve his own sense of guilt for Germany's catastrophe than to try to shift the responsibility from himself to the German people. A megalomaniac whose psychosis has carried him to the point where he has lost touch with reality cannot be refused pity. Hitler had no claim to such compassion, however. He remained fully aware of the situation. When General Kammhuber remarked in his briefing at the end of March that the war was lost, Hitler, in so many words, replied, "I know that myself."

These statements of Hitler that we have cited were all made in confidential conversations which Hitler could reasonably assume would never become public knowledge. He no longer concerned himself at all with public opinion, leaving it entirely to his propaganda minister, whose voice, even in this unspeakable situation, never once faltered. But Hitler himself did make a last attempt to influence posterity by having Martin Bormann record his retrospective evaluation of his policies and what he expected the future would bring. The record of this series of statements begins on February 14, 1945, and abruptly stops on February 26. However, one subsequent fragment from the beginning of April demonstrates that until the very end Hitler remained entangled in the web of his prejudices regarding a Judaized America, a degenerate France, and a declining British Empire. In our context, it is particularly noteworthy that Hitler conceded that the German people were confronted with a total defeat which would have frightful repercussions; yet this could not shake him in his firm belief in the future. The more the people had to endure, the more magnificent would be the ultimate rebirth of eternal Germany. He himself, however, would not be able to endure living in the transitional Germany that would have to follow upon the defeated Third Reich.

Here we see no pseudo-Darwinism, no inexorable race war, not even a reproach for the German people, but rather advice as to how they should sustain their racial purity and national unity until their "rebirth." There is really no point in trying to understand the contradictions between these and Hitler's other statements in terms of mendacity, for that would presuppose that the liar somehow knew that he was lying. There can be no doubt that Hitler firmly believed these sentences when he uttered them. To the very end, he remained the consummate actor, completely identifying himself with the role he played until the very moment he shed his costume and makeup. The veracity of his presentation was only heightened by the enthusiastic reception of it by the audience before him. In time, this became so reliable, so real, that it no longer mattered when his audience could no longer hear him because of having had to creep into air-raid shelters, cellars, and bunkers to escape the bombs of the Western Powers and the shells of the Red Army; for Hitler could now be sustained by the imagined enthusiasm of posterity.

Hitler's primary means of exonerating himself of all responsibility for the unfolding catastrophe was to attribute everything to treason, as in the night of April 20–21, 1945, as the Supreme Command was being divided into a Northern and a Southern Staff. While briefing Hitler that evening—in the presence of only a single stenographer—a senior Army General Staff officer asked if Hitler really thought the most recent reverses on the Eastern Front could be attributed to treason. "Hitler," wrote the general several months later on the basis of his still vivid memory, "turned to me with an almost pitying look, as though only a fool could pose such a question, and said: 'All the failures in the East are due to treachery.'" He then cited as alleged proof the conduct of the High Command of the Fourth Army, saying that he had been a fool not to have executed the entire staff. As chance would have it, the general who was briefing Hitler had himself been a member of the Fourth Army Staff during the period in question, and knew exactly what to make of Hitler's preposterous allegations of treason. Yet he realized that it would have been futile to attempt to dissuade Hitler from his opinion.

This same general learned later, from associates who were present, that at the situation conference on the afternoon of April 22, Hitler for the first time acknowledged in the presence of a larger circle that the war was lost, railing against the "treacherous generals" and the "worthless people" of Germany in uncontrolled outbursts of rage.

The defeated "Führer" was, however, still temporarily sustained by the hope that the armies deployed against the Russian pincers closing on Berlin might be able to save the capital. On April 25, 1945, he sent an order to Admiral Dönitz, to whom he had entrusted the defense of the Northern Area, proclaiming that the struggle for Berlin was the battle on which the fate of Germany hung, "compared to which all other tasks and fronts are of secondary significance." A year earlier, Hitler—alluding to Felix Dahn— had called the attempt to hold the Italian capital the "struggle for Rome." Now he spoke of the "struggle for Berlin," which he callously and unscrupulously represented as the "German battle of fate," though he had already acknowledged that he was convinced of the inevitable outcome. The alleged "Struggle of Liberation" was, in any case, nothing but a pitiful bluff; despite the very real sacrifices which it cost those involved, it could not possibly have succeeded in view of the enemy's overwhelming strength. A temporary respite for Berlin would have changed nothing in the overall picture.[2] Consequently this last battle for which Hitler was responsible

[2]"Here only can I achieve a success," Hitler said at his situation conference on April 25, 1945. "If I do achieve a success here [in Berlin], even if it is only a moral one, at least that will mean the possibility of saving face and winning time." On April 27: "I also remain here for the reason that I thereby have more of a moral right to act against weakness. Otherwise I do not have the moral right. I cannot continually threaten others if I myself run away from the capital of the Reich at the critical hour. We must introduce throughout the entire Wehrmacht a certain code of honor. One basic principle which has always been followed in the navy must be taken over by the party and be made binding on every individual: In this city I have had the right to give orders: now I must obey the orders of fate. Even if I could save myself, I would not do it. The captain also goes down with his ship."

These passages are translated from the text of Hitler's situation conferences held on April 23, 25, and 27, 1945, in the bunker under the Reich Chancellery, as published in the Hamburg newsweekly *Der Spiegel*, No. 3/1966 (Jan. 10, 1966), pp. 32–46. These three stenographic protocols, made during the last days of Hitler's life, had not previously been published because they had not

was the most infamous of all the defeats into which he ordered German soldiers. We can say so without reservations because in the area of strategy it is entirely appropriate—in so clear-cut a case as this—to make an incontrovertible moral judgment.

At 11:00 P.M. on April 29, General Jodl, who, with the Chief of the High Command of the Wehrmacht, Field Marshal Keitel, had been ordered out of Berlin to coordinate the counterattacking columns, received five concise questions from Hitler, who had remained behind in the bunker of the Reich Chancellery. He answered them at 1:00 A.M. on April 30, his brief reply making it clear that none of the thrusts Hitler ordered had the slightest prospect of success. At 3:30 P.M. that same afternoon, Hitler took his own life.

Finally, he brought himself to make the decision that had been due for at least a year. By relinquishing his power, he made it possible to put an end to the bloodshed. That Admiral Dönitz, who unexpectedly succeeded to power, immediately initiated the surrender, remains a service for which he deserves no less recognition than General Weygand in France five years earlier.

Whether there was any other possible end for Hitler is a question that was put to General Jodl during his imprisonment at Nuremberg. Jodl's answer is printed below in Appendix II. After having been sentenced to death in 1946, he dictated an addendum to his original statement, which contained the following passage:

". . . [Hitler's] military advisers—today one often hears it said— should certainly have made it clear to him earlier that the war was lost. What a naive thought! Earlier than any other person in the

---

been among those evacuated from Berlin earlier in April, partially destroyed, and reprinted, so far as there were still legible fragments, by Helmut Heiber. Commenting on these very last protocols (which appeared the year following the second edition of his *Hitler als militärischer Führer*), Schramm is reported by *Der Spiegel* to have said that they are "completely genuine; Hitler's diction and thought are inimitable." He goes on, in the *Spiegel* report accompanying the rambling texts, to explain that "Hitler thinks the way a shepherd dog goes for a walk." The animal has the same goal as his master, but it leaves the path and runs around in loops and circles, often disappearing altogether for a time. "This shepherd-dog thinking," Schramm observed, "is . . . shown in these documents" *(loc. cit.,* p. 30).—ED.

world, Hitler sensed and knew that the war was lost. But can one give up a Reich and a people before they are lost? A man like Hitler could not do it. He should have fallen in battle rather than taking flight in death, it is said. He wanted to, and he would have done so if he had been physically able. As it was, he did not choose the easier death, but the more certain one. He acted as all heroes in history have acted and will always act.

"He had himself buried in the ruins of his Reich and his hopes. May whoever wishes to condemn him for it do so—I cannot."

It must be remembered that Jodl had known Hitler as Supreme Commander more intimately than anyone else, and that he had also come to be quite critical of him.[3] He had seen Hitler's mistakes. He had counseled him against them where he could, but at best had been successful only in peripheral matters. His relationship with Hitler had always been limited to purely official contact. Moreover, Jodl had reflected a great deal during the months of his imprisonment, as the letters he wrote from prison clearly show, and had become well aware of the consequences of the catastrophe, which had in fact surpassed everyone's worst fears. In short, he had been

[3]As head of the Operations Staff of the OKW, General Alfred Jodl was subordinate to Field Marshal Wilhelm Keitel, whom he is generally regarded to have surpassed in professional integrity and probably in intelligence as well. Although Keitel at least once contemplated suicide, he did not dare challenge Hitler's judgment openly. Jodl did. During his trial at Nuremberg, Jodl was asked by his defense counsel to recount the crisis in his relations with Hitler:

"JODL: The worst crisis was in August 1942, in [the Führer Headquarters on the Russian Front at] Vinnitza when I defended . . . [Army Chief of Staff General Franz] Halder against unjustified criticism. . . . Never in my life did I experience such an outburst of rage from any human being. From that day on he [Hitler] never came to dinner.

"DR. EXNER: To your mess?

"JODL: No, he never came to the mess during the remainder of the war. The report on the situation was no longer given in my map room but in the Führer's quarters. At every report on the situation from that day on, an SS officer took part. Eight stenographers were ordered to be there, and from then on they took down every word. The Führer refused to shake hands with me any more. He did not greet me any more, or rarely. . . . He told me, through Field Marshal Keitel, that he could no longer work with me and that I would be replaced. . . ."

He was not replaced, however, for Hitler found him indispensable.—ED.

able to achieve a certain measure of perspective. Nevertheless, even when faced with death by hanging for having served Hitler, Jodl saw in him an historical hero whom he could not bring himself to condemn.

Had Jodl remained alive, he would hardly have stood by that judgment. In the course of time he would have detached himself further from that field of tension between duty, revulsion, and reluctant admiration, and would have come to see more clearly—as well as we all do now—how heinous, how utterly unheroical was Hitler's end. First the corpse was wrapped in a blanket and carried out of the bunker of the Reich Chancellery; next gasoline, procured only at the greatest pains, was poured over the body and ignited; and then for hours the wretched pyre was guarded by sentries spelling each other in their exposure to the risk of being hit by Russian shells in order to see that absolutely nothing—if possible, not even bones—remained of the Führer, Reich Chancellor, and Supreme Commander of the Wehrmacht. Having seen how Hitler thought, how he governed, and how he led the Wehrmacht, we can see that this mortifying death brought his life to its appropriate conclusion.

Jodl's postwar statement was very much conditioned by the atmosphere of the time. But one point still deserves our close attention. Even a year after Hitler's death, Jodl regarded him with a quality of respect similar to that expressed in Field Marshal von Kluge's farewell letter acknowledging Hitler's "genius." In personal style and intellectual background, these two senior officers had nothing in common with Hitler. Much about him they found repulsive. Their training and service in the Army General Staff had cultivated in them a way of thinking that was diametrically opposed to Hitler's. Yet they had submitted to him not simply out of obedience to the Supreme Commander and Chief of State but also because they respected Hitler, despite his flaws and inadequacies, as superior to themselves.

This is one of the keys to Hitler's ability to assert himself as effectively as he did with the Wehrmacht, but it also demonstrates to everyone attempting to deal critically with the historical problem of Hitler what sort of criteria are really relevant. Anyone who speaks of him as satanic or infernal is, in effect, making a theological statement. Whoever calls him a "demon" is ultimately reserving judgment about the nature of his acts. The difficulty is that language offers no negative equivalents to "hero" and "genius." Whoever is concerned that we may possibly be giving Hitler more than his due by seeking adequate terms for him misses the point, for only in this way can we hope to comprehend the seductive malevolence of the most devious and baleful man in German history.

Through suicide Hitler was able to elude formal judgment by his enemies, but not the judgment of history. There are many reasons to condemn him. They need not be recapitulated here. One of them, however, which has never before been given adequate consideration, is now irrefutably documented by the *War Diary of the High Command of the Wehrmacht:*

Hitler, who earlier than any other person in the world first sensed and then knew that the war was lost; who in 1944 actually stated before witnesses that it could no longer be won if the enemy succeeded in landing in the West, but then continued the war despite the successful landing; and who in view of the inexorably approaching defeat sought to exonerate himself of responsibility with pseudo-rational explanations of the outcome—this once-celebrated "Führer" who in 1934 had nominally become Supreme Commander of the German Armed Forces and after the reorganization of February 1938 had in fact assumed effective leadership, and had then gone on, step by step, to make himself military dictator, brought ineradicable guilt upon himself by prolonging the war.

**Excerpts from a 1945 Study
by Major Percy E. Schramm
on the Conflict in Leadership
Between Hitler and the
General Staff**

[The following pages are taken from a study I made as a prisoner of war in 1945 on the background of the Ardennes Offensive, or Battle of the Bulge, as the German counterattack in Belgium and Luxemburg in December 1944 was also known. I had been flown to Paris in order to prepare this monograph at the official U.S. operational history center then located in a chateau near Versailles. Several sources were available to me: my own records from the time of the battle and the period following it, now reprinted in the *War Diary;* the records of postwar interrogations of generals and General Staff officers who had participated in the operation; and further valuable information gleaned from personal conversations I was permitted to have with the chiefs of staff of the three armies involved: General Carl Wagener of the Fifth Armored *(Panzer)* Army, SS General Fritz Kraemer of the recently formed Sixth SS Armored Army, and Baron Rudolf-Christoph von Gersdorff of the Seventh Army. Later, while interned at Nuremberg as an expert witness for the defense at the International Military Tribunal, I arranged with General Alfred Jodl's defense counsel for the former Chief of Operations in the OKW to read the copy of this study I had been able to retain. The general read and returned it, again through his attorney, in April 1946, having endorsed it and added several marginal comments. The validity of the study was also confirmed verbally by the former Commanding General of the Fifth Armored Army, General Hasso von Manteuffel. Consequently the work from which the following pages are taken can be regarded as an objective, quasi-official memorandum prepared in my capacity as War Diarist of the Operations Staff of the High Command of the Wehrmacht. It is therefore left in the style in which it was originally written.[1]

[The following excerpts from my study on the background of the Ardennes Offensive begin in November 1944, after Field Marshal Gerd von Rundstedt and his immediate subordinate, the Commander-in-Chief of Army Group B, Field Marshal Walter Model, had received the general operational guidelines for the Ardennes Offensive and had protested that the goal of recapturing Antwerp— Hitler's proposed and ultimately ordered "big solution"—was far too ambitious an objective, and that the more limited goal—the "small solution"—of making a firm thrust to the Maas, which could be followed by subsequent advances as circumstances permitted, would in the long run be more successful.]

The conflict that becomes apparent in the reaction of the Commanders-in-Chief West and Army Group B to the operational guidelines established by the Führer and the OKW Operations Staff is far more important than the immediate issue under discussion. . . .To begin with, we might be inclined to say that this conflict lay in the contradiction between the opinions of professionals and those of a man who in every respect—and therefore also in military questions—was at best self-educated, no matter how good his individual ideas may have been. . . . [But in] General Jodl and his staff Hitler had a leadership organization readily at hand that could compensate for his own deficiencies so far as they were due to inadequate training.

---

[1]Schramm's involvement in the Battle of the Bulge began neither with this memorandum nor even with the historical record he kept for the *War Diary*. While the Ardennes Offensive was in its planning stage, he was charged with procuring from the Reich Archives—removed for safety from Berlin to Liegnitz—relevant staff studies and other material on matters such as the evaluation of terrain and the like, which had been prepared in connection with the Western campaign across the same region five years earlier.—ED.

The objection that the Chief of the Operations Staff and his officers had merely been Hitler's puppets, blindly carrying out his will, and that consequently the conflict between Führer Headquarters and Field Command was indeed only a disagreement between professionals and a self-educated dilettante, simply does not bear close examination. General Jodl not only had the chance to express his own thoughts and misgivings—and made continual use of it—but Adolf Hitler needed such a counterpoint, for his way of going about things was not to make important military decisions abruptly but rather to clarify them through long and often overly protracted discussions in a dialogue which might last for days.

It would be more accurate to think of the conflict as having arisen because of the High Command's distance from the front. Every staff runs this risk; it begins at the division level. The problem can be counteracted by regularly exchanging staff officers with frontline officers, . . . as well as by allowing the staff frequent trips to the front and conferences with officers and men who have had extensive combat experience.

All these methods were employed by the German High Command. But the concentration of all power in the hands of the Führer meant that for him to leave his headquarters for even two or three days might lead to the most serious difficulties. The same leadership problem applied to General Jodl. The expedient resorted to was that from time to time, particularly during major crises, General Staff officers from the OKW Operations Staff were sent to the front, and immediately on their return would submit oral and written reports of their experiences and impressions. The Führer also utilized award ceremonies and similar occasions as an opportunity to hear directly from officers and men about their experiences. Though many of them had relatively little to say or else tended, in view of their elation at the high recognition accorded them, to paint too rosy a picture, there were some who spoke, with utmost candor, of the difficulties and the cares of the front. . . .

Yet despite these and other efforts to counter the danger of alienation of the High Command from the front, the basic facts of the matter were unaltered. There remained an unbridgeable gap between those who experienced the reality of the war under fire and those whose knowledge was derived from hearsay and from reports and statistics. And this gap was further widened by the fact that the aerial situation over the Western Front and its rear echelons steadily deteriorated, so that countermeasures ordered by Führer Headquarters often presupposed conditions that no longer actually existed.

But this has not yet brought us to the decisive point. Let us suppose that Adolf Hitler himself, or at least General Jodl, could have gotten away for a time in order to study firsthand the war on the Western Front during the fall of 1944. Assume that they had been able to see, as clearly as the field commanders, that despite remarkable morale and an admirable record of successes—even in cases where they had been hastily thrown into action—the divisions on the Western Front, thinned out by heavy losses of dead and wounded, were no longer the same units that had once been able to win great victories. Let us assume also that it had been made clear that despite the statistically astounding logistical support record, there still remained grave deficiencies in equipment everywhere, with endless and insoluble difficulties in finding replacements, and that rail traffic conditions behind the front had become so hopelessly bad that at best a few trains might still move during the night or during rainy weather, while motorized traffic threatened to break down as well. If in each of these respects the picture had been perfectly clear, would the decision of the Supreme Commander have been any different? Would the Führer, in planning the Ardennes Offensive, then have decided for the "small solution" rather than the "big" one? ... The answer is clearly no—which brings us to the essential contradiction at the root of the irreconcilable strategic views of the Führer and the commanders in the West. Expressed in conceptual terms, the conflict is between the *General Staff* and a *revolutionary*.[2]

In the case of the former, we are dealing with an absolutely unique style of military judgment and decision-making. In the final analysis, it cannot be successful without inspiration, and to this extent the term "art of war" remains justified. In the course of time, however, the work of the professionals has more and more come to assume the

[2]In this context one should not misconstrue the expression "General Staff," for it represents a style of thinking that is common to higher military leadership everywhere (annotation from 1945).

character of a science.

The strength of the German General Staff, in which Field Marshals von Rundstedt and Model had been nurtured and with the style of which General von Manteuffel at least had a strong affinity, had consisted in going just as far methodically as it was possible to go in the craft of warfare, reducing the inevitable imponderables to a minimum. When the question of an offensive emerged, the General Staff would systematically explore all available options. . . . It would then attempt to reconstruct the thinking of the opponent and to consider how he would react, which in turn would make it possible to estimate the prospects of the operation. If the initial proposal turned out to be the best approach, it was time to test out on the map the various conceivable shifts in forces, together with as realistic as possible an evaluation of the condition reports of immediately available units as well as others that might be used. All this was followed by objective calculations in terms of kilometers, ground elevations, depths of streams and rivers, in tons and cubic meters of rail and motorized transportation capacity, and projection of the required effect of artillery and mortar fire and tactical air support. The results of these calculations were then considered, together with the predictable reaction by the enemy and the required additional forces to counter it, and all the positive and negative considerations finally balanced against each other. In sum, an operation involved countless factors, most of which could not be measured with absolute precision, but which, on the basis of long experience, could be more or less accurately estimated. There was no room for imagination and inspiration in these stages of staff work, and the faith and willpower of the leadership or of the troops were, in terms of this realistic appraisal, simply two more factors among others. The final task of such calculations was to reduce everything to a common denominator and reach the conclusion that with so many troops, so many supplies, and so much artillery and air support, it would in all probability be possible to go so far toward achieving the desired goal.

After this type of analysis had been made by the staffs of the Commanders-in-Chief West and Army Group B, and of the three armies involved, the conclusion they came to regarding the proposed Ardennes Offensive was that the area for the attack was correctly chosen, and the breakthrough would be possible. But the final objective of the attack could not be reached. With the available forces it would be possible to go only half the distance to Antwerp. Yet even to do this would make the offensive worthwhile. Once it had been successsful to this limited extent, it would be possible to re-evaluate the situation and—should the calculations suggest a positive outcome—try to go the rest of the way to the original goal.

Not only did Adolf Hitler reach his final decision in an entirely different manner, but he made his fundamental calculations on an entirely different basis. . . .[3]

[Hitler] harbored a perpetual suspicion of the facts and figures that were submitted to him.[4] By virtue of his extraordinary memory he was able to point out mistakes in them that any number of specialists had been unable to catch, and for this reason he was kept exhaustively informed of every detail. Thus one cannot say that he was not accurately informed. But it cannot be denied that he tended to take cognizance primarily of favorable information. It would be going too far to say that Hitler simply brushed aside uncongenial facts. It was more a matter of his chipping away at them, finding reasons why they could not be entirely true, or conceiving of countermeasures which he was sure would be able to transform them from negative to positive factors.

If the war had continued to go as well as it had in the beginning, of course, this side of Hitler's character would not have become so conspicuous. But ever since the tide began to run against him, the "realist" of yesterday became more and more like the bookkeeper whose accounts refused to balance. It was not that Hitler became an illusionist, for he still continued to stand on solid ground; he merely underestimated the power of the enemy—which he did not wish to acknowledge—and overestimated his own forces, which were no longer as strong as they had been.[5] Far removed from the troops, he failed especially to note the extent to which they were worn down by combat or to accept the fact that no degree of fa-

[3]Schramm excerpted the following three paragraphs of his study (here deleted) in the section of the first essay in this volume dealing with Hitler's military ability (see pp. 108–109 above).—ED.

[4]Beside this sentence General Alfred Jodl noted on the copy shown to him: "Very true. J."

[5]Noted at this point in the margin by General Jodl: "Then he is an illusionist after all."

naticism could compensate for what they had lost in physical energy and equipment.

Undoubtedly Hitler was able, by his methods, to get much more out of the German Wehrmacht than even the most sanguine optimist would have believed possible. But Hitler did not recognize its limits in his planning for the Ardennes Offensive. The course of the operation demonstrated that the field commanders had the better grasp of the situation.[6]

That there was no serious leadership crisis over the objectives of the Ardennes Offensive may be explained by the fact that the objective of Antwerp could, for the time being, be left hanging. It would in any case be necessary first to reach the Maas. If, in the event, it proved impossible for the Germans to secure a crossing over the Maas, the advocates of the "small solution" could expect that their point of view would automatically prevail. If it were possible to throw the enemy back beyond the Maas, and if one could by then see more clearly which sort of countermeasures might be expected from the enemy, then the question could be taken up again. At that point it would be possible to determine—rather than, as before, merely estimate—how many German forces would be available for the spearhead toward Antwerp and what forces the Americans and British presumably would have to oppose it.

Moreover, Field Marshal Model was personally inclined, somewhat like the Führer himself, to make the most impossible demands in order to achieve the greatest possible result. If he were opposed to Antwerp as an operational objective, he would still have been inclined to support it as a slogan.

What of those who advocated the "big solution"?

There can be no question but that Hitler supported the goal of Antwerp not only to urge on the generals and, through them, their troops, but that he actually believed it was possible to realize this goal. Whether General Jodl was convinced of this to the same extent, or whether he accepted the Führer's idea because he thought

---

[6]Underlined by General Jodl, who commented in the margin: "I would say this least of all in the case of the Ardennes Offensive. It was an act of desperation, like the breakout from a fortress threatened with starvation. J. 4/21"

a distant goal would keep the three armies on the track and deter them, in their advance, from dissipating their momentum by taking peripheral territory, is a question that he has not discussed even with his most intimate associates.[7] . . . If he did support the Führer's position, but with differences in emphasis, then more than anyone else he was obliged to maintain secrecy, in order to preserve the integrity of the High Command and prevent indecisiveness in the definition of objectives.

Führer Headquarters insisted, then, on the "big solution." . . . But the Führer reserved to himself another purpose for the offensive, if circumstances made it necessary. This explains why the High Command, as soon as it knew the offensive had been stopped short of the Maas, immediately switched to a plan that freed itself from both of the original alternatives. It ordered a series of limited thrusts in other sectors of the front that the enemy had been forced to leave exposed—first in northern Alsace, then on the Saar Front—the basic purpose being to use up the enemy's operational reserves and make it impossible for him to mount major new attacks.

In this respect the Führer and the field commanders were once more reconciled despite their basic differences in matters of principle. It also explains why the difference over strategic goals, which in the course of the final weeks before the Ardennes Offensive was repeatedly brought up by Field Marshal Model, with the support of Field Marshal von Rundstedt, did not lead to a graver split in the German leadership.

It would be interesting to know exactly how Army Group B had planned to use the battle in the Aachen area pocket as the point of departure for the "big solution"—but both of the men on whom this change in the projected goals of the offensive would have depended, Field Marshal Model and his Chief of Staff, General Krebs, are no longer alive.[8]

[7]General Jodl marked this paragraph in the margin, but made no explicit comment on it.

[8]Field Marshal Model committed suicide on April 21, 1945. For years it was assumed that General Krebs, who served as the last Chief of Staff of the German Army under Hitler, had fallen in the spring of 1945 in Berlin. The Russians have now reported that he committed suicide in Hitler's Berlin bunker.—ED.

Appendix II: Memorandum Dictated in 1946 by General Alfred Jodl on Hitler's Military Leadership

[General Alfred Jodl, former Chief of the Operations Staff of the High Command of the Wehrmacht, dictated this memoir, which he entitled "The Influence of Hitler on the Leadership of the War (Brief Reflections on Hitler as a Strategist)," to the wife of his defense counsel while he was a prisoner at Nuremberg—excepting the last two paragraphs. These he dictated later to his own wife, after he had been sentenced to death. The tone of the addendum, which his wife transcribed from shorthand, is understandable in view of the sense of indignation Jodl felt.[1]

[Anyone attempting to write the history of Alfred Jodl's life will find it difficult to penetrate the mask of the general who was condemned to death by the International Military Tribunal and executed by hanging on October 16, 1946. He felt constrained—if I understood him correctly—to wear this mask by virtue of the ethos he had grown to accept as an officer, and out of respect for the Chief of State whose failings he perceived far better than others, but whose positive gifts—as this brief memoir demonstrates—he still acknowledged even in the cell in which he awaited execution.

[1]Schramm refers to the fact that Jodl himself did not think his condemnation justified. Anyone who reads the transcript of the proceedings will agree that Jodl did not give the impression that he expected to be hanged in the end.—ED.

That Alfred Jodl, at the bottom of his heart, no longer believed in victory after the winter campaign of 1941–1942, and certainly not after Stalingrad the following winter, has already been mentioned. His tragedy was that he felt morally obligated, as a matter of official responsibility, not to divulge what he thought. Consequently, he moved sharply against anyone who arrived at the same conclusion. To General Walter Warlimont, his closest associate, he once said, in response to a skeptical remark, that Warlimont really belonged in a concentration camp.

[To grasp the full implications of Alfred Jodl's role is to perceive the frightful fate of those discerning General Staff officers who felt duty bound to be loyal to their Chief of State and Supreme Commander, who saw through and despised him as an autodidact but at the same time were fascinated by his "sixth sense," and in the end were condemned before the world as his accomplices.[2]

[2]Most revealing in this context is a note Jodl wrote on February 25, 1946, while imprisoned at Nuremberg, which was copied and graciously made available to me by his widow. In it he explains the motivation behind a speech which he delivered in autumn 1943 to an assembly of National Socialist party leaders in Munich. The drafts and documents he had assembled for this presentation, presented in evidence as Document L-172 at Nuremberg and reprinted in the *War Diary,* were not the final text of the speech, as Jodl himself pointed out to the court.

"I have the impression," he wrote, "that my speech of November 7, 1943, is causing the defense a great deal of concern.

"How it came about I have already explained.

"Not only I but dozens of officers have spoken before that circle—after my speech, for example, two other officers—because Hitler attached the greatest importance to mutual understanding between party leaders and officers.

"I also explained further that in Document L-172 the core [of the speech] dealing with the *purely* military presentation is lacking; only the trimmings are there. They had to express courage, confidence, faith, unity of will and action.

"In 1914–1918 I had experienced how front and homeland, soldier and worker, the leadership of the state and that of the people by the political parties had grown further and further apart in their thinking, until finally the state in the homeland collapsed and dragged the armed forces down in defeat and revolution as well. This experience remained so vivid that in the Second World War, I made it a guiding principle to do everything in my power to combat every division, every indication of breakdown—in short, all domestic conflicts insofar as they might affect the Wehrmacht. Each such manifestation at home would have provided fertile soil for effective enemy propaganda and

[Jodl's relationship with Hitler will be made clear by a passage that a General Staff officer, who was assigned to Führer Headquarters in 1945, wrote during the winter of 1945–1946 (before Jodl's death sentence was pronounced): "Jodl was not one of the people who crept before Hitler. He spoke his mind openly, bluntly, and often in very harsh terms. But what he said did not get through. The very first time I heard him briefing Hitler it was clear to me that Jodl did not have the slightest illusions about the real situation. He saw things objectively and clearly. He also gave the unmistakable impression, often in an almost cynical fashion that he made no effort to suppress, that so far as operational ability was concerned, he regarded himself superior to Hitler.[3] His stance in regard to Hitler was occasionally even pedantic. But he thereby also revealed clearly that he was convinced he was preaching to deaf ears. He did not allow himself to be put upon. He occasionally went so far as to put Hitler in the position of having to acknowledge that either he himself or else Jodl was an idiot. Hitler would not take him up on it. Everything Jodl said simply bounced off him with no visible effect. I was told that earlier Hitler had had a great deal of confidence in Jodl and consequently also in the Operations Staff of the OKW. But during

---

thereby weakened the striking force which could have been mobilized for war abroad. These dangers existed in Hitler's state exactly as in that of William II. Hitler could not shake off the entire burden of Germany's historical past. The place of the territorial princes had been taken by the *Gauleiter*. The racial and religious struggle had been unleashed by the party, and in place of opposition between parties, similar conflicts emerged within the functions of the party itself. Here there were more nationalistic or more socialistic directions. The antagonism between Wehrmacht and state leadership, which had not existed earlier, was a fact, and the controversies, jealousies, and power struggles between the individual administrative departments far exceeded the previously unavoidable level. Thus one has to understand that throughout the whole war I never voiced criticism except with a few confidants such as Scherff, Schmundt, and Hewel, and used every opportunity to work for understanding and unity. These were the prerequisites for the victory, to work for which was my sacred duty."

[3]In his diary for March 2, 1943, Goebbels wrote: "Göring very sharply condemns the Führer Headquarters. He is particularly disgusted with Jodl who, he tells me, has even gotten to the point of making up jokes about the Führer. That's all we need. The Führer puts too much trust in these people. . . ."—ED.

the battles in the Caucasus, Jodl had once visited Field Marshal List, who in Hitler's opinion had failed, and when he returned to Führer Headquarters he defended him against Hitler. Thereupon Hitler lost confidence in him and also broke off all personal contact with the entire OKW Operations Staff, with whose leaders he had often previously eaten. The only reason Jodl was not relieved at that time was that Hitler was concerned that any successor he could find would be even more 'unreliable.' "]

Among the many concepts more often used than understood is the word "strategy." Almost everyone knows it, almost everyone uses it, but many would have nothing to say if they were asked: "What is strategy, then?" People speak of it because they know or sense that the success or failure of strategy in war decides their fate also. Thus it concerns everyone directly, and everyone sees it much more clearly than he does the operational problems of battle. To judge or criticize the latter [i.e., tactics] is something people enjoy doing—even the officer corps, in fact, insofar as it does not belong to the General Staff. That is strange. Whether an attack should have been mounted sooner with weaker, or later with stronger forces, whether strength should have been concentrated on the right or the left wing, whether one should have broken through rather than encircled, or perhaps not even have attacked at all, whether the other fronts could have been weakened still further, whether one should have remained on the defensive, have ordered the troops to attack in order to pin down the enemy, or perhaps even have had them withdraw behind a sector of the battle front—these are all problems of military leadership, specifically operational ones, which even the carping critics tend to avoid. For in order merely to speak on these matters, one needs military maps, data concerning one's own and the enemy's strength, the condition of the troops, their equipment and armament, and their supply of munitions. But these are secrets that remain hidden in the files and charts of the General Staff, and even if they should later find their way into works on military history, they would never provoke a public controversy to the same extent as the strategic plans and problems of the war. The manner in which operations are conducted is regarded by everyone as a specialized scientific matter, no different than medical discussion of new methods of surgery.

The protective curtain of a clandestine science is drawn around tactics, with an impenetrably secret terrain surrounding it, so that no one will be able to find his bearings who in the course of a diligent life has not combined theory and practice in the auditorium and on maneuver, preparing himself to walk these tortuous paths. But in strategy everything appears simple and direct. Is it not obvious and self-evident to every layman that Hitler should not have attacked Russia, because Russia was stronger than we believed it to be, and because defeat was therefore inevitable? Has the frightful catastrophe that Germany suffered not provided irrefutable proof? In these terms, it does not seem difficult to describe the essence of strategy. But it is not so simple to analyze the basic elements and colors in this picture, which must be done in order to put together this seemingly uncomplicated and self-evident picture with its endlessly complex technological details.

Clausewitz could still define the concept of strategy very simply by saying that it is the teaching of the use of battles for the purposes of the war. The concept has remained, but what it comprehends has changed. Ever since war began to assume an ever more total character, that is, ever since it relentlessly drew the entire state, with all its functions, together with every citizen, regardless of occupation, sex, or age, into its orbit, the strategic leadership of war has developed into so universal a function that it has come to include every aspect of state leadership, thereby exceeding the limits of purely military responsibilities. Thus we see—in this war for the first time—how the concepts of "strategy" and "warlord," which once were identical, began to subdivide. No longer did we see any soldier who led the war as a whole, but only military operations. Roosevelt and Churchill, Hitler, Stalin, and Chiang Kai-shek were the strategists of this war, and—more or less heeding the advice of the soldiers standing at their side—they intervened as warlords only indirectly in the actual conduct of military operations. Only in Japan, which in this respect simply had not kept pace with the times, did the military machinery fight its way to political power and lead the country—though divided and without a strong political hand—in a war that was waged not as a means of politics, but rather with politics being made to serve as handmaiden of war. The reader should have a clear picture of this transformation before we go on to consider in greater detail Hitler's influence on the war, on the campaigns, and on the individual battles. Otherwise we cannot confront the question that has been posed again and again: How was it possible for the German military leaders and professionals to permit a layman and former corporal of the First World War to dictate to them the prescription for victory and defeat? Those who pose this question have not yet adequately understood what strategy in the modern sense is all about.

I believe it is necessary to define the concept in the following terms: Strategy is the supreme leadership activity in warfare. It comprehends foreign and domestic policy, military operations and economic mobilization, propaganda and popular leadership, and must harmonize these vital aspects of the war effort in terms of the purposes and the political goal of the war. Only when the concept of strategy is understood in such terms is it clear that no general but only a statesman can be a strategist, though this does not preclude the possibility that both functions may be united in one person, as was the case in China.

Hitler was a statesman. He was a dictator. He was Supreme Commander of the Wehrmacht and since 1941 Commander-in-Chief of the Army as well. He had unleashed the war, and it was up to him and no one else to lead it. He did in fact lead the war. It was Hitler who gave the order in the spring of 1939 to prepare military plans for the attack on Poland. No soldier could know whether the attack would take place, whether it would be provoked or unprovoked, a war of aggression or of defense; for even a politically defensive war could be waged by Germany—given its central position and the constant prospect of a two-front war—only as a military offensive. When the propaganda machine began to run and mobilization on the Polish border was ordered, all the leading soldiers were indeed quite clear about the operational questions confronting them, but the political, the strategic remained for them a veiled secret. Had Hitler himself not implied and even stated in his ad-

198 Hitler: The Man and the Military Leader

dresses that he confidently expected to reach a settlement with the West? Was the mobilization backed by a serious determination to attack Poland, or was it only a means of exerting pressure for negotiation, as had been the case in 1938 with Czechoslovakia? Was this hope not confirmed when, on August 26, 1939, the ordered attack was halted? The details of the struggle of the Great Powers to preserve the peace were unknown to the Commanders-in-Chief and their staffs, with the exception of Göring.

If there is anything that clearly demonstrates the revolutionary character of Hitler's method of leadership, it is that he did not concede to his military working staff, the OKW, and within it, the Operations Staff, the role of strategic adviser. All attempts I undertook in this direction failed. Hitler was willing to have a working staff that translated his decisions into orders which he would then issue as Supreme Commander of the Wehrmacht, but nothing more. The fact that even men like Frederick the Great would have their own thoughts and decisions tested and re-examined against the often contrary ideas of their generals made no difference to Hitler, who resented any form of counsel regarding the major decisions of the war. He did not care to hear any other points of view; if they were even hinted at he would break into short-tempered fits of enraged agitation. Remarkable—and, for soldiers, incomprehensible—conflicts developed out of Hitler's almost mystical conviction of his own infallibility as leader of the nation and of the war. To reflect individually on the dozen or more decisions that determined the course of the war would be psychologically and historically tempting, but that cannot be the purpose of this sketch. The man who succeeded in occupying Norway before the very eyes of the British Fleet with its maritime supremacy, and who with numerically inferior forces brought down the feared military power of France like a house of cards in a campaign of forty days, was no longer willing, after these successes, to listen to military advisers who had previously warned him against such overextensions of his military power. From that time on he required of them nothing more than the technical support necessary to implement his decisions, and the smooth functioning of the military organization to carry them out.

Quite apart from Hitler's arbitrarily dictatorial methods, there is the question of the position taken by senior military leaders regarding his individual decisions. These varied. Unanimous rejection, unanimous agreement, or divided counsel followed each other as in every war and under every regime. But it was always Hitler whose restless spirit would first cast its spotlight into the dark future long before the eyes of his military staff were able to perceive anything tangible or threatening in that darkness—with one single exception: the occupation of Norway. The danger that threatened our war effort if England had been able to secure bases in Norway and thereby block the sole reliable exit from the North Sea to the Atlantic was perceived first by the navy. But—as in the case of all ideas he himself had not conceived—Hitler was initially skeptical and hesitant, until in January 1940 he seized the initiative and ordered the most daring of solutions, once there could no longer be any doubt about the threatening intentions of England.

Let us leaf further, however, in the great memories which at some time in the future will form a book on Hitler's strategy. First we come upon the decision to attack in the West. The Commander-in-Chief of the Army [General Walther von Brauchitsch] did not want to do it. To remain on the defensive on the border and along the *Westwall,* letting the war go to sleep, was his desire, his contribution to peace, which he sought to cloak behind military reasons, particularly the inadequate preparation of the army for so gigantic a task. Not all leading soldiers shared this opinion and belief, but it was the prevailing opinion in the High Command of the Army. Hitler ordered the attack through Belgium and Luxemburg, later also through Holland. One has to use time, he said; it works for no one automatically, but only for him who makes good use of it. And he decided to attack in the course of the very same winter. The generals all objected; there was not a single one who did not warn against it. But it did them no good at all. Only the weather god was harder than Hitler, denying us the needed period of clear freezing weather. It was necessary to wait until the dry spring. May 10, 1940, was correctly chosen. Hitler staged his breakthrough via Maubeuge toward Abbeville. He had overruled the General Staff's thought of a broad encirclement [through Belgium, as in the Schlieffen Plan] by initially careful but then increasingly tenacious and unhesitating intervention in the operational leadership. Once more Hitler's will triumphed and his faith proved victorious.

First the [enemy] front collapsed; then Holland, Belgium, and France collapsed. The soldiers were confronted with a miracle. They were still amazed when Hitler gave the order to prepare for the invasion of England. Eight weeks earlier they would have regarded this order as the vagary of a madman. Now they applied themselves with faithful zeal to the work, careful and confident, exploring every dubious improvisation. But by September the British air force had not been subdued. Göring was skeptical; Raeder was cautious; in the Army High Command they were confident; Hitler wavered. He shared the army's belief that England could be beaten in a short time as soon as one was well established on the island. But whether the landing would succeed depended upon nautical imponderables which were strange to him. Perhaps this strategic decision was the only one in the course of the war in which Hitler let himself be counseled. The warnings of the Commander-in-Chief of the Navy together with an evaluation of the situation that I prepared for him decided the issue. The attempt to land in England was abandoned. Hitler turned toward the Mediterranean in order to strike at England there. But before doing so, he took a firm grip on the equipping of the army, which—all too slow, bureaucratic, and backward—had long been a thorn in his side. "The soldier should fight; that is his job. Everything else civilian specialists understand better." He created the Ministry for Weapons and Munitions under [Fritz] Todt, leaving only the building of airplanes and ships with the air force and the navy. From then on Hitler determined the monthly quota as well as the direction and scope of all production of weapons and munitions down to the last detail. All the Operations Staff [of the High Command of the Wehrmacht] had to do was to give him the exact figures: inventory, utilization, and production during the previous month. But beyond this, Hitler's astounding technical and tactical vision led him also to become the creator of modern weaponry for the army. It was due to him personally that the 75-mm anti-tank gun replaced the 37-mm and 50-mm guns in time, and that the short guns mounted on the tanks were replaced with the long 75-mm and 88-mm guns. The *Panther,* the *Tiger,* and the *Königstiger* [i.e., *Tiger II*] were developed as modern tanks at Hitler's own initiative.

But let us return to the chronological sequence of strategic decisions. There was a military breathing pause. Political considerations became paramount during the second half of 1940. Rumania requested German instructional and training troops. Reluctantly and carefully, but step by step, Bulgaria attached itself to the Axis. Only Spain showed a cold shoulder. To what extent the influence of Canaris on the Spanish generalissimo played a role in this is a question I will not go into.[4] Above all, it was bitter for Hitler to have to give up his plan to take Gibraltar with Spanish help or approval. This military intention of Hitler had the general sympathy of his military advisers, and even today I have no doubt that the attack on the mighty rock fortress, which we had meticulously thought through and prepared in detail, would have been successful.

But instead of being able to carry out this strategically correct plan, Hitler found himself constrained to hatch the cuckoo eggs that Italy had laid in the nest of our joint war effort. On his own initiative and despite the negative attitude of the Army High Command, Hitler had offered his friend Mussolini help in Africa. It was rejected with the explanation that tanks could not operate in the desert. But then in the last days of October 1940—in violation of all agreements not to disturb the peace of the Balkans—Mussolini attacked Greece. Hitler, who wanted to prevent this attack, arrived a few hours too late in Florence. He was enraged, but the god of war even more so. The latter had never been a friend of the Italians. And now he quickly changed sides. English tanks drove Graziani's beaten army back to the border of Cyrenaica, and instead of winning a quick victory over the Greeks, the Italians found themselves threatened with the loss of Albania and of the divisions which were holding on

[4]Jodl was absolutely correct in implying that Admiral Wilhelm Canaris, who had been head of German military intelligence, played a crucial role in Franco's successful effort to stay out of the Second World War; that is documented in this editor's monograph, *Hitler, Franco und Gibraltar* (Wiesbaden, 1962), pp. 84–87, 169–70.—ED.

there only with difficulty. Concern was now stronger than pride in Rome, and cries for help crossed over the Alps as far as the Reich Chancellery in Berlin. Hitler decided that in view of modern long-range aerial warfare we had to wage the war as far from the periphery of the Reich as possible. Therefore [Hitler ordered] help for Africa through Rommel and good mobile armored troops. He wanted no conflict with Greece, so he refused help in Albania. But for the spring of 1941 he ordered that an attack against Greece from Bulgaria be prepared in case this should become necessary after all, or even be forced on us by an English landing in Greece.

There was not much consultation before these decisions. They were unfortunately constrained—as much as Hitler's generals on purely military grounds resisted this commitment of forces to different theaters. For meanwhile the specter of a massive Russian concentration of forces on the eastern borders of Germany and Rumania had taken concrete form, and Hitler was weighing the thought of preventive war. The world has learned from the Nuremberg Trial of many voices that warned against this march [into Russia]. All agree that it was definitely Hitler's idea originally. Both [the fact that the idea originated with Hitler and that he was warned against it] are historical facts. The court judges according to good and evil, world history in terms of correct and false. I will not concern myself here with either of the two judgments, but rather only point out that the danger from the East was seen by all soldiers, and Hitler's concern was shared, more by some, less by others. Opinions differed whether the danger was really so acute and whether it might not have been possible to deal with it by political means. On that question it will be necessary to await a later judgment. Here we are interested only in the influence it had on Hitler's waging of the war, and of that the following can be said: the decision for the campaign against the USSR, Plan "Barbarossa," was his decision and his alone. He did, however, make the final decision only on April 1, 1941. For at this time an event occurred that effectively delayed the beginning of the attack against the almost completely assembled Soviet forces by four to five weeks. For Hitler it was like a beacon that revealed Stalin's intentions.

It was the military *coup* in Belgrade the night after Yugoslavia's accession to the Tripartite Pact.[5] Hitler was beside himself. He virtually dictated his decisions to the assembled Commanders-in-Chief and the Reich Foreign Minister. He tolerated no discussion of whether the political attitude of the Yugoslavian government should first be clarified diplomatically. So far as he was concerned, Yugoslavia was in league with Russia, prepared to strike us from behind when we marched into Greece, and was trying to establish contact with the English, who at the beginning of March had landed at Piraeus. And as a matter of fact, the Yugoslavian Army did mobilize on the borders. Beginning on April 6, it was overrun by German troops, even though these had very hastily concentrated, and within a few weeks it had reached the point of dissolution—[though these were] the same soldiers who then, only scantily clad, would for years wage a bitter guerrilla war under Tito's leadership, until they were developed into a new Communist army.

The attack on Russia began on June 22 [1941]. The two-front war had been unleashed. It could lead to success only if it were possible to win an annihilating victory over the enemy on one front. This failed by only a little, but that little sufficed, together with the catastrophe of the cold winter, to carry Hitler's train of victories, after having reached this culmination, over onto a declining track. When in 1942 he decided once more to commit all his forces in the attempt to break down the Russian colossus, he was not contradicted in principle by his military advisers; but there were many among them who would rather have seen the second major attack in the North, beginning with the capture of Leningrad, than in the direction of the Caspian Sea. The great apparent success of this campaign ended with the catastrophe on the Don and before Stalingrad. When toward the end of the year Rommel, defeated before the gates of Egypt, fell back on Tripoli as the Allies landed in French North Africa, it was clear not only to the responsible soldiers but to Hitler himself that the god of war had now turned from Germany and gone over to the other camp. With that, Hitler's activity as a strategist was essentially ended. From then on, he intervened more and more frequently in operational decisions, often down to matters

[5]The German-Italian-Japanese Pact was signed by Yugoslavia on March 25, 1941, followed by the coup on March 27.

of tactical detail, in order to impose with unbending will what he thought the generals simply refused to comprehend: that one had to stand or fall, that each voluntary step backwards was an evil in itself. Opinions differ as to whether he thereby hastened or delayed the end of the war. One thing only is certain: he could no longer come to a strategic decision. But perhaps there was no longer one to be reached.

He could not surrender. None of the opponents would consider negotiating since agreeing on unconditional surrender as their war-time goal. Therefore what was Hitler to do? He could only fight to the end or seek his own death. Throughout his whole life he had been a fighter, so he chose the first course. Heroism or insanity, opinion throughout the world will always differ on it. Could he not, in order to save his people unnecessary suffering, have come to an earlier end? As a matter of fact, this very thought did concern Hitler during the last days of his life. When he informed me on April 22 [1945] of his decision not to leave Berlin again but to die there, he added: "I should already have made this decision, the most important in my life, in November 1944, and should never have left the head-quarters in East Prussia."[6]

But his military advisers—today one often hears it said—should certainly have made it clear to him earlier that the war was lost. What a naive thought! Earlier than any other person in the world, Hitler sensed and knew that the war was lost. But can one give up a Reich and a people before they are lost? A man like Hitler could not do it. He should have fallen in battle rather than taking flight in death, it is said. He wanted to, and he would have done so if he had been physically able. As it was, he did not choose the easier death, but the more certain one. He acted as all heroes in history have acted and will always act.

He had himself buried in the ruins of his Reich and his hopes. May whoever wishes to condemn him for it do so—I cannot.

[Signed:] ALFRED JODL

[The foregoing reflections are complemented by the following pas-

---

[6]This sentence ends the original statement which Jodl dictated to his defense counsel's wife. The remaining two paragraphs were dictated to his own wife after he was convicted and sentenced to death, as explained in the introductory note.

sage in a letter Jodl sent to his wife. When she had written to him, after the interrogation at the Nuremberg Trial of Field Marshal Erhard Milch on March 8 and 11, 1946, concerning her own estimation of Hitler, he answered her that in many respects he agreed, although on one or another point he saw things somewhat differently, though for a number of reasons he did not care to go into it. He then went on as follows:]

When I read how Frank Thiess, breaking with historical tradition after fifteen hundred years, tries to reach a true picture of Justinian,[7] then I must think more than ever of the present and am reminded of how the history of that man who brought the whole world into flux was falsified during the course of his life, in part even by himself. And so I find myself thinking again and again whether it might not be my responsibility to set the historical record straight without the slightest regard to my personal defense. And I would do this except for two considerations. In the first place, that is not the primary purpose of the court, which can bring an end to any such attempt by application of the legal concept of "irrelevance." In the final analysis, the attempt would be futile, because the archives of the other side remain closed. In the second place, I ask myself: Do I then know this person at all, at whose side I led for so many years so thorny and self-abnegating an existence? Did he not play with my idealism, too, and only use it for purposes that he concealed in his innermost being? Who will boast of knowing another when that person has not opened to him the most hidden corners of his heart? Thus I do not even know today what *he* thought, knew, and wanted to do, but rather only what *I* thought and suspected about it. And if today a picture is unveiled in which one had once hoped to see a work of art, but one is confronted only with a diabolical distortion, then it is up to the historians of the future to rack their brains over the question of whether it was that way from the very beginning, or whether this picture had gradually transformed itself with the course of events. At times I often make the mistake of blaming [Hitler's] origins, only to remember how many peasants' sons have been given the name "the Great" by history. The ethical foundation is what counts.

[7]The reference is to novelist Frank Thiess's *Das Reich der Dämonen* (*The Empire of Demons*, 1941), with its very free treatment of Byzantine history.

Index

Aida (opera), 68
Allen, William Sheridan, 4n
Alt, Rudolf von, 64
Antiquity, 77. See also
  Architecture.
Anti-Semitism, 49–52; Jews
  accorded German nationality but
  not German citizenship, 57n.
  See also Hitler, Adolf, anti-
  Semitism of; National Socialism,
  family and racial policy of.
Anti-tank guns, 104–105, 200–201
Antonescu, Marshal Ion, 29
Anzio-Nettuno landing, 164
Architecture: of the Reich
  Chancellery, 59–60; of the
  Berghof, 60; Hitler's evaluation
  of classical, Gothic, baroque,
  and other styles, 62–63
Ardennes Offensive (Battle of the
  Bulge), 107, 136, 150, 156,
  171; planning of, 184–191
Armaments and War Production
  Ministry, 27n, 121n, 172;
  logistical crisis in 1944, 172n,
  173, 187. See also Weapons and
  Munitions Ministry (prede-
  cessor); Speer, Albert.

Art Nouveau, 64n
Atatürk, Kemal, 83
Atheism, 90
Atlantis (legendary lost
  continent), 77
Auschwitz, 95n
Austro-Prussian War, 80
Axmann, Arthur, 33

Bach, Johann Sebastian, 68
"Barbarossa," Operation, 202. See
  also Russia, German attack on.
Barlach, Ernst, 66
Battles. See Falaise Gap, Moscow,
  Stalingrad, Battles of; France,
  fall of; Lines of defense; Russia,
  German attack on.
"Bavarian Liberation Committee,"
  146
Becker, Dr. Carl Heinrich, 44
Beethoven, Ludwig van, 68
Bengal Lancers, The (film), 53
Berghof. See Führer Headquarters.
Berlin, 21–23, 81–82; Berlin
  Opera, 69
Bernhardi, General Friedrich
  von, 80
Bezymenski, Lev, 18n